The
Hikers Guide
to O'ahu

The
Hikers Guide to O'ahu

UPDATED AND EXPANDED

STUART M. BALL, JR.

A Latitude 20 Book
UNIVERSITY OF HAWAI'I PRESS
Honolulu

18 17 16 15 14 13   6 5 4 3 2 1

Library of Congress Cataloging-in-Publication Data
Ball, Stuart M., Jr., author.
  The hikers guide to Oʻahu / Stuart M. Ball, Jr.—Updated and expanded.
    pages cm
  "A latitude 20 book."
  Includes bibliographical references and index.
  ISBN 978-0-8248-3899-7 (pbk. : alk. paper)
  1. Hiking—Hawaii—Oahu—Guidebooks. 2. Oahu (Hawaii)—Guidebooks. I. Title.
  GV199.42.H32B35 2014
  796.5109969'3—dc23

                                    2013022781

Maps by Manoa Mapworks, Inc.

Designed by Mardee Melton
Printed by Sheridan Books, Inc.

※ CONTENTS ※

The Hikes

Color illustrations follow page 160

※ ACKNOWLEDGMENTS ※

Lynne Masuyama, my wife, joined me on many of the hikes in this book. She is an ideal hiking partner, providing support, guidance, and good company.

Mahalo to Fred Boll, Steve Brown, John Hall, and Richard McMahon for their advice and assistance. Thanks also to Richard Bailey, John Hoover, Kelvin Lu, Lynne Masuyama, Deborah Uchida, and Nathan Yuen for their great photographs. Finally, mahalo to Jane Eckelman of Manoa Mapworks, Inc., in Kailua for the detailed hike and section maps.

❈ INTRODUCTION ❈

Oʻahu is still truly a paradise for hikers. Despite the recent surge in trail use, most of the routes in this book remain relatively uncrowded. They will take you to lush valleys, cascading water-falls, windswept ridges, and remote seacoasts.

This guide includes fifty-two day hikes on the island of Oʻahu. Each hike has a section on highlights, directions to the trailhead, and a detailed description of the route. A narrative section covers points of interest and major hazards along the trail. As applicable, there are short notes about the plants, birds, geology, history, and legends of the area. Each hike also has its own topographic map keyed to the route description.

As you will see, this guidebook is very detailed. The information in it, however, is neither perfect nor up to date because of inadvertent errors and changing conditions. A landowner may revise his access policy. New housing construction may alter the approach to a trailhead. A winter storm may cause a landslide that blocks the route. Do not rely entirely on this book; use your own judgment and common sense as well.

Good luck and good hiking!

CHANGES IN THE UPDATED AND EXPANDED EDITION

Those of you who have used the second edition of my guide will notice some major changes in this updated and expanded edition. I have added ten new hikes: Kaluanui (Mariner's) Ridge, 'Ualaka'a, Ka'iwa Ridge, 'Āhuimanu, Mālaekahana Falls, Kahuku Shoreline, 'Ehukai, Mākua Rim, Pu'u o Hulu, and Ka'ena Point. I have also made major route changes in the Wahiawā Hills and Poamoho hikes.

Unfortunately, I had to delete eight good hikes. Ma'akua Gulch remains closed because of the 1999 lethal rockfall at nearby Kaliuwa'a (Sacred) Falls. The landowners/lessees shut off access to Kalena, Dupont, Kawainui, and 'Ōpae'ula because of unauthorized use by hikers. Pālehua-Palikea, Pu'u Kaua, and Kānehoa-Hāpapa are currently closed while the Hawai'i Division of Forestry and Wildlife develops access procedures for them.

For GPS users, I have added UTM coordinates to the route description for the midpoint or endpoint of each hike. The notes section includes expanded historical information from my new book, *Native Paths to Volunteer Trails: Hiking and Trail Building on O'ahu.*

Visit my Web site at http://home.roadrunner.com/~sball/ for updated route and access information.

❋ HIKING TIPS ❋

CLIMATE

O‘ahu has two seasons: summer (May to October) and winter (November to April). Summer is the warmer and drier season. Daytime temperatures at sea level are in the 80s, and nighttime temperatures are in the 70s. Trade winds from the northeast blow steadily to cool the islands. The trades, however, do produce cloud buildup over the mountains and some rain there.

Winter is the cooler and wetter season. Daytime temperatures at sea level are in the 70s and low 80s, and nighttime temperatures are in the 60s and low 70s. The winds are more variable in strength and direction, sometimes coming from the south or west. Southerly Kona winds produce mainland-type weather—clear skies or heavy cloud cover and rain.

CLOTHING

For short, easy hikes, wear the following:

- hiking boots, running or walking shoes (with tread)
- socks
- tabis (Japanese reef walkers) or other water footwear for gulch hikes
- lightweight pants or shorts, nylon, cotton, or cotton blend (no jeans)
- lightweight shirt, short or long sleeve, polyester, nylon, cotton, or cotton blend
- rain jacket, breathable fabric
- hat, broad brimmed

For long, difficult hikes, add these:

- additional upper layer, polyester or wool
- work gloves

EQUIPMENT

For short, easy hikes, bring the following:

- daypack
- 1 liter water
- food
- sunscreen
- cell phone (fully charged)

For long, difficult hikes, add these:

- extra water
- extra food
- first-aid kit
- space blanket
- flashlight and extra bulb and batteries
- whistle
- compass
- topographic map, hard copy or in-phone/GPS unit

PACK IT OUT

Most of the hikes in this book are trash free. Let's keep them that way. Pack out all your trash, including cigarette butts, gum wrappers, orange peels, and apple cores.

HEIAU

Heiau are early Hawaiian places of worship with stone or earth platforms. Do not disturb *heiau,* other ancient sites, or artifacts you may come upon while hiking. In addition, do not build new *ahu* (rock cairns) as they may confuse other hikers and local archaeologists.

INVASIVE PLANT SPECIES

Many of the trails on Oʻahu are overrun with invasive shrubs and trees, such as *Clidemia hirta* and fiddlewood. Their seeds are often spread by birds and, yes, hikers. Carefully clean the soles and sides of your boots after every outing.

EMERGENCIES

Don't have any! Seriously, come prepared with the right clothing and equipment. Bring along this book and follow the hike description closely. Start early, memorize key junctions, and constantly be aware of the route you are traveling. You can never be lost if you know where you came from. Above all, use your common sense and good judgment.

The mountains are a dangerous place for exhausted, disoriented, and/or injured hikers. If you do get into serious trouble, call the emergency number (911) on your cell phone, ask for Fire Rescue, and then settle down and wait. If the call is late in the day, you may have to spend the night out. You did bring your extra layer and space blanket, right?

Never rely entirely on a cell phone for emergencies or a GPS unit for route finding. Both can run out of power or become damaged. Phone reception may be poor or nonexistent in gulches and valleys. GPS results depend on the user and the quality of the unit and its maps.

It is still good practice to tell a relative or friend where you are hiking and when you will be out, especially if you are hiking alone. Make sure they know to call the emergency number and ask for Fire Rescue if you don't call or show up on time.

HAZARDS

There are hazards in hiking, as in any sport. Described below are the main hazards you should be aware of while hiking on Oʻahu. With the right clothing and equipment and good judgment on your part, you should be able to avoid or minimize these hazards and have an enjoyable outing.

Too Hot

Hiking on Oʻahu is usually a hot, sweaty experience. Drink plenty of water throughout the hike, as it is very easy to become dehydrated. Prolonged lack of water can lead to heat exhaustion and heatstroke.

The need for water on a hike varies from person to person. As a general rule, take one liter of water on the short, easy hikes. Take two or more liters on the long, difficult hikes. If you have to ration or borrow water, you didn't bring enough.

The sun on Oʻahu is very strong, even in winter. During midday wear a broad-brimmed hat and use lots of sunscreen.

Too Cold

Hiking on Oʻahu can sometimes be a wet, cold experience. A winter Kona storm with high winds and heavy rainfall can make you very cold very quickly. Insufficient or inappropriate clothing leads to chilling, which leads to hypothermia.

Always bring a rain jacket to protect you from wind and rain. Most of the time you won't even take it out of your pack, but bring it anyway! On the long ridge hikes, take an extra upper layer of polyester or wool that will keep you warm even when wet.

Leptospirosis

Leptospirosis is a bacterial disease found in freshwater ponds and streams contaminated with the urine of rats, mice, or mongooses. The bacteria can enter the body through the nose, mouth, eyes, or open cuts.

The incubation period is generally one to three weeks. Symptoms resemble those of the flu—fever, chills, sweating, head and muscle aches, weakness, diarrhea, and vomiting. If you show the symptoms during the incubation period, see your doctor immediately and mention that you have been exposed to stream water. If left untreated, the symptoms may persist for a few days to several weeks. In rare cases, the disease may become more severe and even lead to death.

You can take several precautions to prevent leptospirosis. First, never drink any stream water unless you have adequately boiled, filtered, or chemically treated it. None of the hikes in this book is so long that you cannot bring all the water you need with you. Second, on the stream hikes wear long pants to avoid getting cut and don't go swimming. That's harder for some people to do. Only you can decide how much risk you are willing to take.

High Streams

Oʻahu streams can rise suddenly during heavy rainstorms. Do not cross a fast-flowing stream if the water is much above your knees. Wait for the stream to go down. It is far better to be stranded for half a day than swept away.

Narrow Trail

Oʻahu is known for its knife-edge ridges and sheer cliffs. Trails in those areas tend to be very narrow with steep drop-offs on one or both sides. Oftentimes, the footing is over loose, rotten rock or slick mud.

If narrow sections make you feel overly uneasy, don't try them. There is no shame in turning back if you don't like what you see.

Rockfalls

Rockfalls occur sporadically in the O'ahu mountains. Most are small or take place away from the trail or when no one is around. Because of the steep slopes above, the narrow gulch hikes are particularly susceptible to rockfalls. As they occur with little or no warning, there is not much you can do about them. If caught in a rockfall, protect your head with your arms and pack and hope for the best.

Goat/Pig/Bird Hunters

On the hikes in the state forest reserves and parks you may meet goat, pig, or bird hunters. They are usually friendly, as are their dogs. They often use hiking routes to access hunting areas; however, the hunt usually takes place off trail. Stay away from areas where you hear dogs barking or shots being fired.

Hunting dogs are sometimes very aggressive toward other, unfamiliar dogs. Leave your pet dog at home when hiking in areas frequented by hunters.

Marijuana (Paka Lōlō) Growers

The danger from marijuana growers and their booby traps is much exaggerated. The growers do not plant their plots near recognized trails. All of the hikes in this book travel on established routes. Stay on the trail, and you should have no paka lōlō problems.

Hurricanes

Hurricane season on O'ahu is usually from June to December. Before starting a hike during that period, check the weather report to make sure no hurricanes are in the vicinity.

A Final Caution

The hazards just described are the main ones you may encounter, but the list is by no means all inclusive. Like life in general, hiking on O'ahu carries certain risks, and no hike is ever completely safe. *You have to decide how much risk you are willing to take.*

HIKE CATEGORIES

TYPE

There are four types of hikes on O'ahu: shoreline, foothill, valley, and ridge. Shoreline hikes follow the coastline. Foothill hikes cut across the topography. They cross a ridge, descend into a valley, and so on. They do this at lower elevations where the topography is relatively gentle. Foothill hikes are usually loop hikes.

Valley hikes follow a valley bottom upstream. Ridge hikes climb a ridge to the summit of a mountain or a mountain range. In both types, the route out is usually the same as the route in.

There are two types of trails on ridge hikes: graded and ungraded. An ungraded trail sticks to the crest of the ridge with all of its ups and downs. A graded trail is built into the side of the ridge just below its top. Although avoiding drastic elevation changes, a graded trail works into and out of every ravine along the flank of the ridge.

LENGTH

Length is the distance covered on the entire hike. If the hike is point to point, the length is one way. If the hike is out and back, the length is round-trip. If the hike is a loop, the length is the complete loop.

Length is measured on the U.S. Geological Survey topographic maps. The plotted distance is then increased by 10 to 20 percent and rounded to the nearest mile. The percentage increase attempts to account for trail meandering too small to be shown on the map.

None of the trails on Oʻahu has been measured precisely.
To convert the length to kilometers, multiply the miles by
1.609.

ELEVATION GAIN

Elevation gain includes only significant changes in altitude.
No attempt is made to account for all the small ups and downs
along the route. Measurements are taken from the U.S. Geological Survey topographic maps and then rounded to the
nearest 100 feet.

To convert the elevation gain to meters, multiply the feet
by 0.305.

DANGER

Danger rates the extent of two major hazards: narrow trail for
ridge and foothill hikes and flash flooding and rockfall for valley hikes. Those hazards have seriously injured or killed hikers in the past. For ridge and foothill hikes, the rating is based
on the length and difficulty of narrow trail sections over steep
slopes. For valley hikes, the rating is based on the frequency
and severity of rockfall and flash floods.

The categories are low, medium, and high. A rating of low
or medium does not imply that the hike is completely safe
from those hazards.

SUITABLE FOR

Use this index to determine which hikes best match your
ability. The categories are novice, intermediate, and expert.
Novices are beginning hikers. Experts are experienced hikers.
Intermediates are those in between.

Novice hikes generally follow a short, well graded, and marked trail with gradual elevation changes and few hazards. Expert hikes have a long, rough, sometimes obscure route with substantial elevation changes and multiple hazards. Most hikes fall between these two extremes. Some are even suitable for everyone because they start out easy and then get progressively harder the farther you go.

How difficult a hike seems to you depends on your hiking experience and physical fitness. An experienced, conditioned hiker will find the novice hikes easy and the expert hikes difficult. An out-of-shape beginner may well find some of the novice hikes challenging.

Use the index only as a rough guide. Read the route description and notes to get a better feel for the hike.

LOCATION

Location tells the general area of the hike. Given is the nearest town or subdivision. Also mentioned is the state park, state forest reserve, or mountain range where the hike is found.

TOPO MAP

Topo map refers to the U.S. Geological Survey quadrangle that shows the area of the hike. All maps referenced are in the 7.5-minute topographic series with a scale of 1:24,000 and a contour interval of 40 feet.

You can purchase topographic maps online from the Geological Survey at http://www.usgs.gov. Several commercial Web sites offer customized topo maps and map software for O'ahu. Topo maps are also available locally from Pacific Map Center at 94-529 Uke'e St., Unit 108, Waipahu; phone 677-6277.

ACCESS

There are two categories of access: Open and Conditional.

You may do Open hikes anytime without restriction.

You may do Conditional hikes subject to the terms required by the landowner. They usually include obtaining verbal or written permission. You may have to sign a liability waiver. In addition, there may be restrictions on the size and composition of the group and the time when you can do the hike. If you do not adhere to the landowner's conditions, you are trespassing.

The outdoor organizations mentioned in the appendix offer a good means of doing Conditional hikes. The organization gets the required permissions, saving you time and trouble. Check their schedules.

Visit my Web site at http://home.roadrunner.com/~sball/ for updated access information.

HIGHLIGHTS

The Highlights section briefly describes the hike and its major attractions.

TRAILHEAD DIRECTIONS

Trailhead Directions are detailed driving instructions from downtown Honolulu to the start of the hike. If you are at all familiar with Oʻahu, those directions should be sufficient to get you to the trailhead. If you are unfamiliar with the island, use Google Maps at http://maps.google.com, MapQuest at http://mapquest.com, or bring along a copy of *Bryan's Sectional Maps, The Oʻahu Mapbook,* or James A. Bier's *Oʻahu Reference Maps* to supplement the directions. The printed maps show the start of some of the hikes and can be purchased at local drugstores, bookstores, and tourist shops.

For some hikes the directions stop short of the actual trail-head. There are two reasons for suggesting that you do some extra road walking. First, in certain areas it is generally safer to park your car on a main road, rather than at the trailhead. Wherever you park, never leave valuables in your vehicle.

Second, the dirt roads leading to some of the trailheads are narrow, rough, and often muddy. The directions assume you have a two-wheel-drive car and that the road is dry. With a four-wheel-drive vehicle you may be able to get closer to the trailhead. On the other hand, if the road is wet, you may not even be able to drive as far as the directions recommend.

The directions also mention the bus route number and the stop nearest the trailhead. For route and schedule information, check the The Bus Web site at http://www.thebus.org or phone them at 848-5555.

ROUTE DESCRIPTION

This section provides a detailed description of the route that the hike follows. Noted are junctions, landmarks, and points of interest. Also mentioned are specific hazards, such as a rough, narrow trail section. Out and back hikes are described on the way in. Loop hikes and point-to-point hikes are described in the preferred direction.

Each hike has its own map. The solid line shows the route. The letters indicate important junctions or landmarks and are keyed to the route description. For example, map point A is always the point where you start the hike. The maps are reproductions of the U.S. Geological Survey quadrangles for the immediate area of the hike. As in the originals, the scale is 1:24,000, and the contour interval is 40 feet.

For GPS users, Universal Transverse Mercator (UTM) coordinates are provided for the turnaround or midpoint of each hike. They are based on the 1983 North American Datum (NAD83).

This section sometimes uses Hawaiian words to describe the route. They are listed below with their English definition.

makai	seaward; toward the ocean
mauka	inland; toward the mountains
pali	cliff
puʻu	hill or peak

I have also followed the common local practice of using place names as terms to indicate direction:

ʻEwa	westward from Honolulu
Koko Head	eastward from Honolulu

The word "contour" is sometimes used in the route description as a verb (that is, to contour). It means to hike roughly at the same elevation across a slope. Contouring generally occurs on trails that are cut into the flank of a ridge and work into and out of each side gulch.

Visit my Web site at http://home.roadrunner.com/~sball/ for updated route information.

NOTES

The Notes section provides additional information about the hike to make it safer and more enjoyable. Included are comments about trail conditions, major hazards, and the best time of day or year to take the hike. Also mentioned are scenic views, deep swimming holes, ripe fruit, and hungry mosquitoes. In addition, there are short notes about the plants and birds along the route and the geology, history, and legends of the area. At the end is a brief description of any alternatives to the basic route.

For hikers who enjoy botanizing and birding, I highly recommend two companion guide books: *A Hiker's Guide to Trailside Plants in Hawai'i* by John B. Hall and *Hawaii's Birds* by the Hawaii Audubon Society. For more trail history, read my new book, *Native Paths to Volunteer Trails: Hiking and Trail Building on O'ahu.*

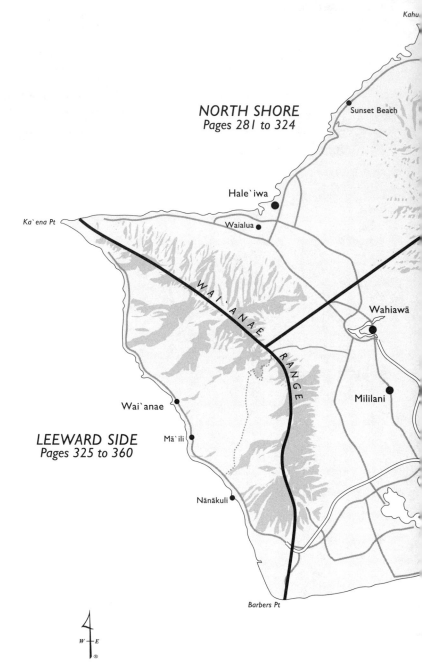

NORTH SHORE
Pages 281 to 324

Kahu

● Sunset Beach

Hale`iwa ●

Ka`ena Pt ——— Waialua ●

Wahiawā ●

W A I `A N A E

R A N G E

Wai`anae ●

Mililani ●

LEEWARD SIDE
Pages 325 to 360

Mā`ili ●

Nānākuli ●

Barbers Pt

W ——— E
N

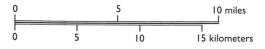

0	5	10 miles
0	5	10	15 kilometers

O`AHU

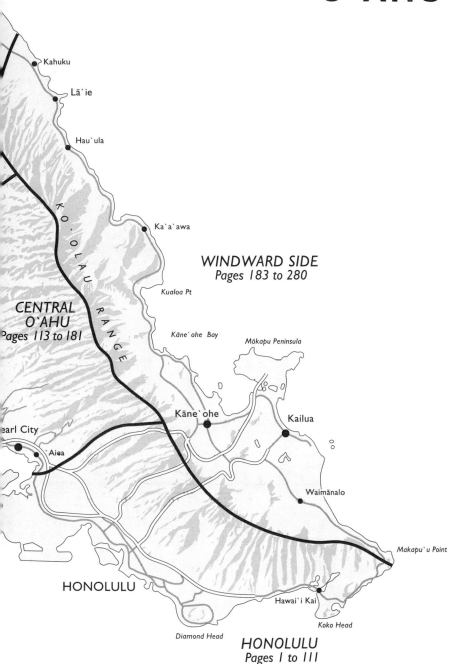

Kahuku

Lā`ie

Hau`ula

KO`OLAU RANGE

Ka`a`awa

WINDWARD SIDE
Pages 183 to 280

Kualoa Pt

CENTRAL O`AHU
Pages 113 to 181

Kāne`ohe Bay

Mōkapu Peninsula

Kāne`ohe

Kailua

earl City

Aiea

Waimānalo

Makapu`u Point

HONOLULU

Hawai`i Kai

Koko Head

Diamond Head

HONOLULU
Pages 1 to 111

HIKE SUMMARY

Hike	Location	Type	Length (miles)	Elev. Gain (feet)	Access	Suitable for Nov.	Int.	Exp.	Narrow Spots	Views	Swimming	Native Plants/ Birds
HONOLULU												
1. Koko Crater	Hawaiʻi Kai	Ridge	2	1,200	Open		x		x	x		
2. Kaluanui Ridge	Hawaiʻi Kai	Ridge	3	900	Private	x				x		
3. Kuliʻouʻou Ridge	Kuliʻouʻou	Ridge	5	1,800	Open	x	x			x		x
4. Kuliʻouʻou Valley	Kuliʻouʻou	Valley	2	300	Open	x						x
5. Hawaiʻiloa Ridge	Hawaiʻi Loa	Ridge	5	1,500	Cond.	x	x			x		x
6. Wiliwilinui	Waiʻalae Iki	Ridge	5	1,300	Open	x	x			x		x
7. Lanipō	Maunalani Heights	Ridge	7	2,000	Open		x			x		x
8. Mount Olympus	St. Louis Heights	Ridge	6	1,500	Open	x	x			x		x
9. Puʻu Pia	Mānoa	Foothill	2	500	Open	x				x		
10. Aihualama-ʻŌhiʻa	Mānoa	Foothill	8	1,700	Open	x				x		
11. ʻUalakaʻa	Makiki	Foothill	1	300	Open	x				x		
12. Makiki-Tantalus	Makiki	Foothill	8	1,500	Open	x	x			x		x
13. Nuʻuanu-Judd	Nuʻuanu	Foothill	5	1,000	Open	x	x			x	x	x
14. Kamanaiki	Kalihi	Ridge	5	1,400	Open	x	x			x		x
15. Bowman	Fort Shafter	Ridge	12	2,400	Open		x	x	x	x		x
16. Puʻu Keahi a Kahoe	Moanalua	Ridge	11	2,600	Open		x	x	x	x		x
17. Kamananui Valley	Moanalua	Valley	11	1,500	Open	x	x	x		x	x	x
CENTRAL OʻAHU												
18. ʻAiea Loop	ʻAiea	Foothill	5	900	Open	x	x			x		x
19. ʻAiea Ridge	ʻAiea	Ridge	11	1,800	Open	x	x	x		x		x
20. Kalauao	ʻAiea	Valley	4	700	Open	x	x	x			x	
21. Waimano Ridge	Pearl City	Ridge	15	1,700	Open		x	x		x		x
22. Waimano Valley	Pearl City	Valley	2	400	Open	x	x					
23. Waimano Pool	Pacific Palisades	Valley	3	700	Open	x	x				x	
24. Mānana	Pacific Palisades	Ridge	12	1,700	Open	x	x	x		x		x

#	Name	Area	Type	No.	Elevation	Status	1	2	3	4	5	6	7	8
25.	Schofield-Waikāne	Wahiawā	Ridge	14	1,200	Cond.	X					X	X	X
26.	Wahiawā Hills	Wahiawā	Foothill	4	1,300	Open	X					X	X	
27.	Poamoho	Helemano	Ridge	7	600	Cond.	X					X	X	X

WINDWARD SIDE

#	Name	Area	Type	No.	Elevation	Status	1	2	3	4	5	6	7	8
28.	Makapuʻu Point	Makapuʻu	Ridge	3	600	Open	X	X				X		
29.	Kaʻiwa Ridge	Lanikai	Ridge	2	600	Open	X	X				X		
30.	Olomana	Maunawili	Ridge	6	1,600	Open			X		X	X	X	
31.	Maunawili Falls	Maunawili	Valley	3	400	Open	X					X	X	X
32.	Maunawili	Maunawili	Foothill	9	600	Open	X	X				X	X	
33.	Likeke	Nuʻuanu Pali	Foothill	7	600	Open	X	X				X		
34.	ʻĀhuimanu	ʻĀhuimanu	Valley	1	200	Open						X		
35.	Puʻu Manamana	Kahana	Ridge	4	2,100	Open					X	X		X
36.	Kahana Valley	Kahana	Valley	6	400	Open	X	X			X	X	X	
37.	Puʻu Piei	Kahana	Ridge	3	1,700	Open	X	X			X	X		
38.	Hauʻula-Papali	Hauʻula	Foothill	7	1,500	Open	X	X				X		
39.	Koloa Gulch	Lāʻie	Valley	8	1,300	Cond.						X	X	
40.	Lāʻie	Lāʻie	Ridge	12	2,200	Cond.	X	X			X	X	X	
41.	Mālaekahana Falls	Lāʻie	Ridge	8	1,500	Cond.	X	X			X	X	X	X

NORTH SHORE

#	Name	Area	Type	No.	Elevation	Status	1	2	3	4	5	6	7	8
42.	Kahuku Shoreline	Kahuku	Shoreline	6	None	Open	X	X				X	X	
43.	ʻEhukai	Sunset Beach	Foothill	3	600	Open	X	X				X		
44.	Kaunala	Pūpūkea	Foothill	6	500	Cond.	X	X				X		
45.	Pūpūkea Summit	Pūpūkea	Ridge	9	900	Cond.	X	X				X		X
46.	Mākua Rim	Mokuleʻia	Ridge	11	2,350	Open	X	X		X		X		X
47.	Keālia	Mokuleʻia	Ridge	7	2,000	Open	X	X				X		

LEEWARD SIDE

#	Name	Area	Type	No.	Elevation	Status	1	2	3	4	5	6	7	8
48.	Puʻu o Hulu	Māʻili	Ridge	2	800	Open	X	X				X		
49.	Waiʻanae Kaʻala	Waiʻanae	Ridge	8	3,500	Open	X	X			X	X	X	
50.	Waiʻanae Kai	Waiʻanae	Foothill	6	2,200	Open	X					X		X
51.	Kuaokalā	Kaʻena	Foothill	6	1,200	Cond.	X	X				X		
52.	Kaʻena Point	Kaʻena	Shoreline	6	100	Open	X	X				X		X

HONOLULU

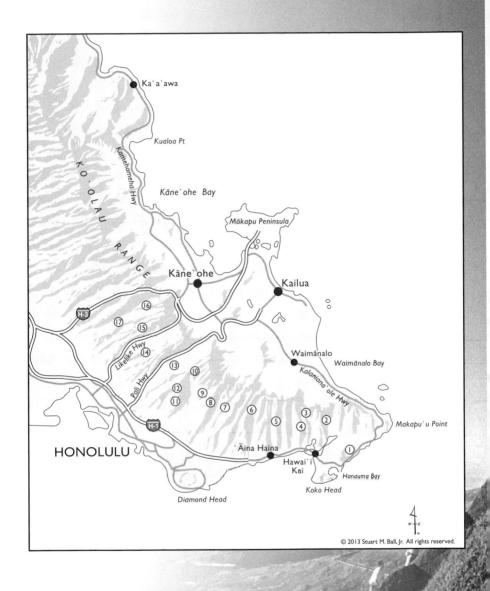

Ka`a`awa

Kualoa Pt

Kamehameha Hwy

KO`OLAU RANGE

Kāne`ohe Bay

Mōkapu Peninsula

Kāne`ohe

Kailua

H-3

⑯

⑰ ⑮

Likelike Hwy

⑭

Waimānalo

Waimānalo Bay

⑬

⑩

Kalaniana`ole Hwy

Pali Hwy

⑫

⑨

⑪ ⑧ ⑦

⑥

③

②

H-1

⑤ ④

Makapu`u Point

HONOLULU

`Āina Haina

Hawai`i Kai

①

Hanauma Bay

Koko Head

Diamond Head

Koko Crater

(KOHELEPELEPE)

TYPE:	Ungraded ridge
LENGTH:	2-mile round-trip
ELEVATION GAIN:	1,200 feet
DANGER:	Medium
SUITABLE FOR:	Intermediate
LOCATION:	Koko Head Regional Park near Hawai'i Kai
TOPO MAP:	Koko Head
ACCESS:	Open

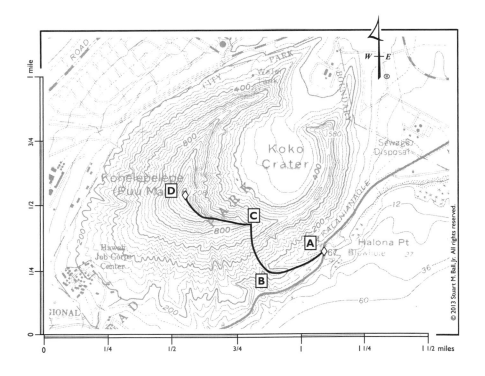

HIGHLIGHTS

This short, windy hike climbs a steep-sided volcanic cone. Along the way are a narrow rock arch and a chance to spot whales. At the top are the remains of an incline railway and a panoramic view of east Oʻahu.

TRAILHEAD DIRECTIONS

At Ward Ave. get on Lunalilo Fwy. (H-1) Koko Head bound (east).

As the freeway ends, continue straight on Kalanianaʻole Hwy. (Rte. 72).

The highway narrows to two lanes past Koko Marina Shopping Center in Hawaiʻi Kai.

Pass the entrance to Hanauma Bay Beach Park on the right.

Turn right at Hālona blowhole lookout and park in the large lot there (elevation 40 feet) (map point A).

BUS: Route 22 to Sandy Beach Park. Walk back 0.4 mile along Kalanianaʻole Hwy. to the blowhole parking lot.

ROUTE DESCRIPTION

From the parking lot, walk back along the right side of the highway toward Hanauma Bay.

As the guardrail ends, bear right and up onto a spur ridge composed of tuff.

Angle up a sloping ledge on the right side of the ridge.

Gain the ridgeline and climb gradually along it. Look for the low-lying native shrub ʻilima papa with its yellow-orange flowers.

The ridge curves to the right and levels off briefly (map point B).

Ascend very steeply across a natural arch. Use the foot-holds chiseled into the rock.

Continue steep climbing through scrub koa haole trees.

Reach a junction at the rim of Koko Crater (Kohelepelepe) (map point C). Turn left and up along the rim. Memorize that junction for the return trip.

Climb steeply to the top of a triangular rock formation.

Traverse a narrow, rocky section. Stay on top of the ridge and watch your footing.

Bear right around a large, balanced rock.

Negotiate another narrow stretch.

Jog left and then right through a band of gray rock.

The angle of ascent eases through scrub Christmas berry and koa haole. Be careful of barbed wire on the ground.

Pass two small concrete buildings on the right and some downed utility poles on the left. Watch for the native shrub 'a'ali'i.

Reach Pu'u Ma'i, the highest point on the crater rim (elevation 1,208 feet) (map point D) (UTM 04 0636275E, 2354264N). At the top are a partially collapsed metal viewing platform and the remains of an incline railway and a radar site.

NOTES

Koko Crater is the volcanic cone overlooking Hālona (peering place) blowhole and Sandy Beach. The exhilarating climb to its open summit is short and superb, but not for everyone because of several windy, narrow stretches. If the route looks too steep and scary, try the Makapu'u Point loop just down the road.

Take this hike during winter (November–April) when temperatures are cooler and the sun less intense. Migrating humpback whales are also on view then. Don't forget the two essentials for this hike—sunscreen and binoculars.

Most of the hike is a steep scramble over crumbly rock and loose dirt. The precipitous crossing of a natural arch is the most difficult part of the climb. Use the footholds chiseled into the rock. Don't let the wind catch you off balance in the narrow sections along the rim. Finally, tread gingerly if the rocks are wet and slippery from a sudden squall.

Koko Crater is a horseshoe-shaped double cone built by eruptions from two nearby vents. Much of the spewed ash landed downwind, forming a distinct summit on the southwest side of the crater. Over the years the ash hardened into tuff, the porous, stratified rock that you are walking on. Both Koko Crater and Diamond Head are remnants of the last volcanic activity on Oʻahu, known as the Honolulu Series.

On the spur ridge, look for the low-lying native shrub ʻilima papa. It has oblong, serrated leaves about 1 inch long. The yellow-orange flowers strung together have been used to make regal lei in both ancient and modern Hawaiʻi.

While on the crater rim, scan the ocean for humpback whales and the sky for tropic birds. The whales migrate from the North Pacific to the Hawaiian Islands, arriving in October and leaving in May. They congregate off the leeward coast of Maui and occupy themselves calving, nursing, breeding, and generally horsing around. The red-tailed tropic bird, or koaʻe ʻula, is white with a black eye patch and two central tail feathers elongated into streamers. Tropic birds feed by diving into the ocean for fish and squid. They nest in burrows or rock crevices on nearby Mānana Island.

Before reaching the top, watch for the native shrub ʻaʻaliʻi. It has shiny, narrow leaves and red seed capsules. Early Hawaiians used the leaves and capsules in making lei. When crushed or boiled, the capsules produced a red dye for decorating *kapa* (bark cloth).

At the summit is a 360-degree view of east Oʻahu. From the ocean clockwise are Hanauma (curved) Bay, Koko Head (Kuamoʻo Kāne), and the leeward coast to Diamond Head (Lēʻahi) and Waikīkī (spouting water). Completing the panorama are the Koʻolau (windward) Range ending at Makapuʻu (bulging eye) Point, Mānana (Rabbit) Island, and Sandy Beach. Across

Kaiwi (the bone) Channel is the neighbor island of Molokaʻi. On a clear day, you can also see the islands of Maui and Lānaʻi.

Clustered at the top are several abandoned concrete platforms and buildings, including the upper terminal of an incline railway. The site was a radar complex for long-range detection of aircraft during and after World War II. The railway provided comfortable transportation for soldiers manning the radars. An electric winch and a stout cable pulled a tram up the tracks. The cars featured angled seats that leveled out on the steep gradient below the summit. The railway tracks have recently become a popular and very crowded hiking route to the top.

The old Hawaiian name for Koko Crater is Kohelepelepe, or the inner lips of the vagina. According to a racy legend, the pig demigod Kamapuaʻa hotly pursued the fire goddess Pele on the Big Island. The goddess Kapo, Pele's sister, detached her *kohe* (vagina) and flung it to east Oʻahu to divert Kamapuaʻa. The trick apparently worked, as the pig demigod followed the so-called traveling vagina and left Pele alone. The vaginal imprint became the crater known as Kohelepelepe.

2

Kaluanui (Mariner's) Ridge

TYPE:	Ungraded ridge
LENGTH:	3-mile round-trip
ELEVATION GAIN:	900 feet
DANGER:	Low
SUITABLE FOR:	Novice
LOCATION:	Leeward Koʻolau Range above Hawaiʻi Kai
TOPO MAP:	Koko Head
ACCESS:	Route crosses private property; see the second paragraph of the Notes section

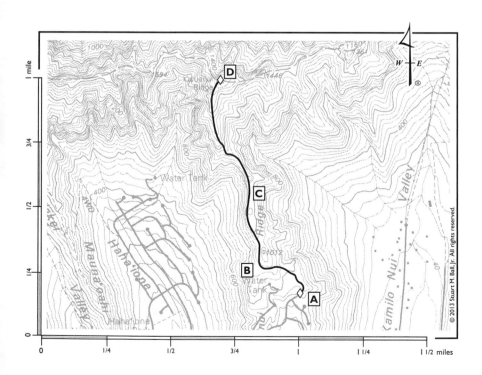

HIGHLIGHTS

This short, shady climb is a popular route to the summit of the Koʻolau Range. Along the way are some native dryland plants and spectacular leeward and windward views.

TRAILHEAD DIRECTIONS

At Ward Ave. get on Lunalilo Fwy. (H-1) Koko Head bound (east).

As the freeway ends, continue straight on Kalanianaʻole Hwy. (Rte. 72).

Drive by ʻAina Haina, Niu Valley Center, and Kuliʻouʻou.

Cross a bridge and enter Hawaiʻi Kai.

Turn left on Keāhole St. by Hawaiʻi Kai Towne Center.

At the fourth traffic light, Keāhole becomes Hawaiʻi Kai Dr.

At the next light continue straight, still on Hawaiʻi Kai Dr.

Immediately pass the Hawaiʻi Kai Post Office on the left and then turn left on Kaluanui Rd.

Ascend steadily through Mariner's Ridge subdivision to the road's end.

Park there on the street (elevation 660 feet) (map point A).

BUS: Route 1 on weekends or 1L on weekdays to Hawaiʻi Kai Dr. and Keāhole St. Walk 1.7 miles along Hawaiʻi Kai Dr. and up steep Kaluanui Rd. to the trailhead. Route 23 to Hawaiʻi Kai Dr. and Wailua Rd. Walk 1.5 miles to the trailhead.

ROUTE DESCRIPTION

Proceed up a rocky dirt road at the end of the pavement through a corridor of koa haole and Christmas berry trees.

Shortly, the road becomes a trail and climbs the open ridge on one switchback. To leeward are Koko Crater (Kohelepelepe) and Koko Head (Kuamoʻo Kāne). Covering the ground are native ʻūlei shrubs.

Gain the ridgeline just above a water tank and turn right up it (map point B).

At a flat eroded area the trail becomes a dirt road heading up the ridge. Ignore the abandoned dirt road that descends on the right.

Climb steadily on the left side of the ridge through groves of ironwoods. Look for native aʻaliʻi trees.

The road regains the ridgeline periodically and dips briefly twice (map point C). Watch for native ʻilima shrubs and a lone ʻiliahialoʻe (coastal sandalwood) on the left. From several viewpoints, you can see Hahaʻione Valley on the left and Kamilonui Valley on the right.

Resume steady climbing through shady ironwoods. The road follows the right side of the ridge for a stretch. Lauaʻe ferns line the sometimes deeply rutted road.

The route opens up and levels out briefly. To the left is the first view of the windward side.

Ascend moderately along the right side of ridge to the road's end and then turn left up a short trail.

Reach the Koʻolau summit at a rocky knob (elevation 1,560 feet) (map point D) (UTM 04 0634223E, 2357775N).

NOTES

This popular hike along Kaluanui (big pit) Ridge is short, mostly shady, and usually dry and breezy. The route follows a very scenic dirt road built in the 1960s when Henry J. Kaiser turned the wetlands area back of Maunalua Bay and around Kuapā fishpond into the residential community of Hawaiʻi Kai. As the road has seen better days, watch your footing, especially in the rutted sections, which can be slippery when damp. To avoid the crowds, start early or late, or hike during the week.

Note the No Trespassing sign at the trailhead indicating that the hike route crosses private property. Inclusion of this hike in this publication should not be taken as a recommendation to trespass.

Along the sunny switchback section is the sprawling native shrub 'ūlei. It has small, oblong leaves arranged in pairs; clusters of white, roselike flowers; and white fruit. Early Hawaiians ate the berries and used the tough wood for making digging sticks, fish spears, and *'ūkēkē* (the musical bow).

On the lower portion of the road, look for the native dryland shrubs 'a'ali'i and 'ilima. 'A'ali'i has shiny, narrow leaves and red seed capsules. Early Hawaiians used the leaves and capsules in making lei. When crushed or boiled, the capsules produced a red dye for decorating *kapa* (bark cloth). 'Ilima has oblong, serrated leaves, about 1 inch long. The yellow-orange flowers strung together have been used to make regal lei in both ancient and modern Hawai'i.

Watch also for a lone 'iliahialo'e, the native coastal sandalwood. It has oval, dull, gray-green leaves about 1 inch long. 'Iliahialo'e is partially parasitic, with outgrowths on its roots that steal nutrients from nearby plants. Early Hawaiians ground the fragrant heartwood into a powder to perfume their *kapa*. Beginning in the late 1700s, sandalwood was indiscriminately cut down and exported to China to make incense and furniture. The trade ended around 1840, when the forests were depleted of the tree.

While approaching the top, listen for the Japanese bush warbler (uguisu), a bird often heard but rarely seen. Its distinctive cry starts with a long whistle and then winds down in a series of notes. The bush warbler is olive brown on top with a white breast and a long tail.

The windward view from the summit knob is well worth the minimal effort required to get there. Below the sheer cliff are Waimānalo town and turquoise Waimānalo (potable water) Bay. Farther up the coast are lovely Kailua (two seas) and Kāne'ohe (bamboo husband) bays, separated by

Mōkapu (taboo district) Peninsula. On the left is flat-topped Puʻu o Kona (hill of leeward) along the summit ridge and triple-peaked Olomana (forked hill) in the distance. On a clear day, the islands of Molokaʻi, Lānaʻi, and Maui are visible above the summit ridge to the right.

3

Kuli'ou'ou Ridge

TYPE:	Ungraded ridge
LENGTH:	5-mile round-trip
ELEVATION GAIN:	1,800 feet
DANGER:	Low
SUITABLE FOR:	Novice, Intermediate
LOCATION:	Kuli'ou'ou Forest Reserve above Kuli'ou'ou
TOPO MAP:	Koko Head
ACCESS:	Open

HIGHLIGHTS

This popular hike climbs a dry, shady ridge to the top of the Ko'olau Range. Along the way are some native plants and a stately forest of Cook pines. From the summit lookout are superb views of the windward coast.

TRAILHEAD DIRECTIONS

At Ward Ave. get on Lunalilo Fwy. (H-1) Koko Head bound (east).

As the freeway ends, continue straight on Kalaniana'ole Hwy. (Rte. 72).

Drive by 'Āina Haina and Niu Valley Center on the left.

Pass Holy Trinity Catholic School and Church on the right.

Turn left on Kuli'ou'ou Rd. and head into Kuli'ou'ou Valley.

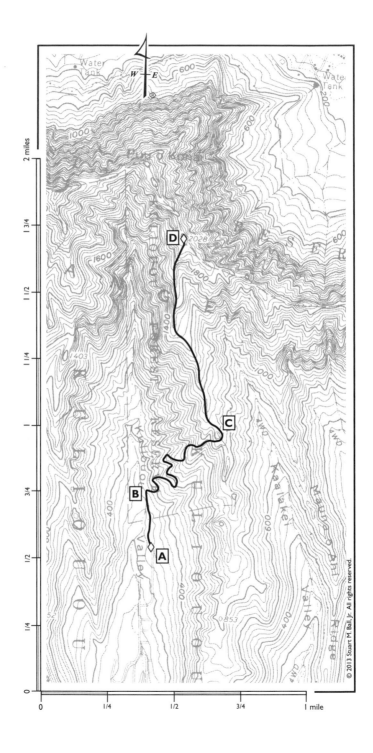

At the stop sign turn left and then right, still on Kuliʻouʻou Rd.

Pass Kuliʻouʻou Neighborhood Park on the right. The park has restrooms and drinking water.

At the Dead End sign, turn right on Kālaʻau Pl.

Park on the street just before it ends at a turnaround circle (elevation 260 feet) (map point A).

BUS: Route 1 on weekends or route 1L on weekdays to Kalanianaʻole Hwy. and Kuliʻouʻou Rd. Walk 1.3 miles along Kuliʻouʻou Rd. and Kālaʻau Pl. to the trailhead.

ROUTE DESCRIPTION

At the back of the circle go around a yellow gate and take the one-lane, paved road on your left leading down to Kuliʻouʻou Stream.

Before crossing the stream, bear right on a grassy road by the second utility pole.

Register at the hunter/hiker check-in mailbox on the left.

The road narrows and becomes the Kuliʻouʻou Valley Trail. Cross a small gully.

Contour above the intermittent stream through an introduced forest of Christmas berry, koa haole, and guava. Look for the low-lying native shrub ūlei in the open sections.

Reach a signed junction by some small boulders and a patch of lauaʻe ferns (map point B). Turn sharp right and up on the Kuliʻouʻou Ridge Trail. (The valley trail continues straight.) Just after the junction watch for noni, a small tree with large, shiny green leaves and warty fruits.

Climb gradually up the side of the valley through groves of Formosa koa and logwood on long switchbacks. Look and listen for the red-billed leiothrix.

After the first switchback are good views of Kuliʻouʻou Valley.

After the eighth one, the trail enters a grove of ironwood trees.

After the tenth one, ascend straight up a side ridge briefly.

Bear right off the side ridge and continue climbing via two short switchbacks.

Just before the top, work up a gully lined with ironwoods.

Reach the ridgeline (map point C) and turn left up the ridge. Memorize that junction for the return trip.

Climb steadily up the ridge on its right side.

After regaining the ridgeline, wind through a stand of large Cook pines.

Skirt to the right of an eroded spot.

Shortly afterward, pass two covered picnic tables on the right.

The trail climbs steeply and then levels off briefly in a lovely area lined with stately pines.

Ascend steadily along the left side of the broad ridge through Cook pines and ironwoods.

After passing a bench on the left, break out into the open. To the left you can see the sheer walls of Kuliʻouʻou Valley. Along the route are the native trees ʻōhiʻa and lama.

The ridge narrows, and the trail becomes rough and eroded in spots. The steep sections have plastic steps. Look to the left for an unusual view of the backside of Diamond Head (Lēʻahi). To the right are Koko Crater (Kohelepelepe) and Koko Head (Kuamoʻo Kāne) overlooking Hawaiʻi Kai and Maunalua Bay.

Climb steeply on the plastic staircase.

Reach the Koʻolau summit at an eroded hill and an End of Trail sign (elevation 2,028 feet) (map point D) (UTM 04 0632430E, 2358156N).

NOTES

Kuliʻouʻou Ridge is a popular route to the summit of the Koʻolau Range. The hike is reasonably short, mostly shady, and usually mud free. Novices can climb the graded switchbacks to the picnic tables. More experienced hikers can head for the summit lookout with its superb view of the windward coast.

Before you start the hike, a few cautions are in order. Look out for mountain bikers and trail runners on the switchback section. Beyond the picnic tables, the trail becomes steep and eroded in spots. Watch your footing, especially on the descent. In the worst areas, plastic steps have been installed to slow the erosion and stabilize the trail.

On the switchbacks, look and listen for the red-billed leiothrix, a songbird introduced from China in 1918. The leiothrix is olive green above with an orange-yellow throat and underside. It is frequently seen on the ground, foraging for insects, fruits, and seeds.

The switchbacks pass through a section reforested in 1934–1935 by the Civilian Conservation Corps (CCC). CCC crews planted hundreds of Formosa koa and thousands of logwood trees along the slopes of Kuli'ou'ou Valley to reduce water runoff and thus erosion. The workers undoubtedly built a rudimentary trail network to access the planting areas, but volunteers and the staff of Na Ala Hele, the state trail program, constructed the current alignment in 1991–1992.

In 1935, CCC crews also planted the groves of tall Cook pines along the ridge near the picnic tables. Named after Captain James Cook, the pines are native to New Caledonia's Isle of Pines in the South Pacific, between Fiji and Australia. They are columnar in shape and have overlapping, scalelike leaves about ¼ inch long, rather than true needles.

Beyond the pines, the trail climbs through a more open native forest of 'ōhi'a and lama trees. 'Ōhi'a has oval leaves and clusters of delicate red flowers. Early Hawaiians used the flowers in lei and the wood in outrigger canoes. The hard, durable wood was also carved into god images for *heiau* (religious sites).

Lama has oblong, pointed leaves that are dark green and leathery. Its fruits are green, then yellow, and finally bright red when fully ripe. Lama was sacred to Laka, goddess of the hula. Early Hawaiians used the hard, light-colored wood in temple construction and in hula performances.

Along the open ridge, listen for the Japanese bush warbler (uguisu), a bird often heard but rarely seen. Its distinctive cry starts with a long whistle and then winds down in a series of notes. The bush warbler is olive brown on top with a white breast and a long tail.

After the steep final climb, relax on the summit and take in the magnificent view. In front of you is the broad sweep of Waimānalo (potable water) Bay. To the right the sheer summit ridge ends at Makapuʻu (bulging eye) Point. Offshore is Mānana Island, a seabird sanctuary. Along the coast to the left is Kailua (two seas) Bay, stretching to Mōkapu (taboo district) Peninsula. Puʻu o Kona (hill of leeward) is the flat-topped peak on the summit ridge to the left.

Kuliʻouʻou means sounding knee, referring to the sound made by the *pūniu* (knee drum). Early Hawaiians made the drum out of a coconut shell. They cut off the top portion and covered it with the stretched skin of kala, the surgeonfish. The *pūniu* was tied to the right thigh of the player, just above the knee.

The Kuliʻouʻou Valley hike also starts from the same trailhead. That short, pleasant walk makes an attractive alternative for beginning hikers.

4

Kuliʻouʻou Valley

TYPE:	Valley
LENGTH:	2-mile round-trip
ELEVATION GAIN:	300 feet
DANGER:	Low
SUITABLE FOR:	Novice
LOCATION:	Kuliʻouʻou Forest Reserve above Kuliʻouʻou
TOPO MAP:	Koko Head
ACCESS:	Open

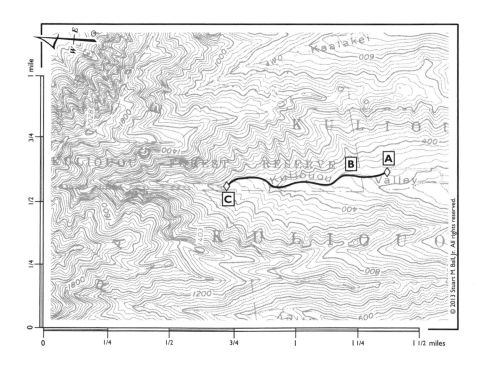

HIGHLIGHTS

This short, uncrowded hike explores a lovely leeward valley. The stream there is usually dry, so the walk is a quiet one, the stillness broken only by the sigh of the wind and the song of the white-rumped shama and the native ʻelepaio.

TRAILHEAD DIRECTIONS

At Ward Ave. get on Lunalilo Fwy. (H-1) Koko Head bound (east).

As the freeway ends, continue straight on Kalanianaʻole Hwy. (Rte. 72).

Drive by ʻĀina Haina and Niu Valley Center on the left.

Pass Holy Trinity Catholic School and Church on the right.

Turn left on Kuliʻouʻou Rd. and head into Kuliʻouʻou Valley.

At the stop sign turn left and then right, still on Kuliʻouʻou Rd.

Pass Kuliʻouʻou Neighborhood Park on the right. The park has restrooms and drinking water.

At the Dead End sign, turn right on Kālaʻau Pl.

Park on the street just before it ends at a turnaround circle (elevation 260 feet) (map point A).

BUS: Route 1 on weekends or 1L on weekdays to Kalanianaʻole Hwy. and Kuliʻouʻou Rd. Walk 1.3 miles along Kuliʻouʻou Rd. and Kālaʻau Pl. to the trailhead.

ROUTE DESCRIPTION

At the back of the circle, go around a yellow gate and take the one-lane, paved road on the left leading down to Kuliʻouʻou Stream.

Before crossing the stream, bear right on a grassy road by the second utility pole.

Register at the hunter/hiker check-in mailbox on the left.

The road narrows and becomes the Kuliʻouʻou Valley Trail. Cross a small gully.

Contour above the intermittent stream through an introduced forest of Christmas berry, koa haole, and guava. Look for the low-lying native shrub ūlei in the open sections.

Reach a signed junction by some small boulders and a patch of lauaʻe ferns (map point B). Continue straight on the valley trail. (On the right, the Kuliʻouʻou Ridge Trail switchbacks up the side of the valley.)

Cross several more side gullies. Look for kukui and noni trees there.

The improved trail descends briefly to Kuliʻouʻou Stream and ends there.

Climb steadily under arching Christmas berry and guava on a rocky, narrow route.

Pass a small waterfall chute on the left.

Reach a second waterfall chute with a small pool, which is usually dry (elevation 520 feet) (map point C) (UTM 04 0632128E, 2357411N).

NOTES

Kuliʻouʻou Valley is the perfect hike for beginners. The walk is short and shady on a well-groomed and graded path. Most hikers take the nearby ridge trail, leaving the valley uncrowded and peaceful. Unfortunately, the route does have some mosquitoes despite the usually dry conditions. If you want to see the stream running, take this hike on the day after a heavy rainstorm in winter.

Kuliʻouʻou means sounding knee, referring to the sound made by the *pūniu* (knee drum). Early Hawaiians made the drum out of a coconut shell. They cut off the top portion and covered it with the stretched skin of kala, the surgeonfish. The *pūniu* was tied to the right thigh of the player, just above the knee.

On the trail, look for the sprawling native shrub ʻūlei in the sunny sections. It has small, oblong leaves arranged in pairs; clusters of white, roselike flowers; and white fruit. Early Hawaiians ate the berries and used the tough wood for making digging sticks, fish spears, and *ʻūkēkē* (the musical bow).

In the forest, look and listen for the white-rumped shama. It is black on top with a chestnut-colored breast and a long black and white tail. The shama has a variety of beautiful songs and often mimics other birds. A native of Malaysia, the shama has become widespread in introduced forests such as this one.

Lining the gullies are kukui trees. Their large, pale green leaves resemble those of the maple, with several distinct lobes. Early Polynesian voyagers introduced kukui into Hawaiʻi. They used the wood to make gunwales and seats for their outrigger canoes. The flowers and sap became medicines to treat a variety of ailments. Early Hawaiians strung the nuts together to make *lei hua* (seed or nut garlands). The oily kernels became house candles and torches for night spearfishing.

Watch for the ʻelepaio, a small native bird. It is brown on top and white underneath with a black throat and a dark tail, usually cocked. The bird roams the forest understory, catching insects on the fly or on vegetation. ʻElepaio are very curious, which is why you can sometimes see them.

Although the route description ends at the second waterfall, farther exploration upstream is possible. The path, however, quickly becomes rough and ill defined. Eventually it disappears altogether as the valley walls close in. Walk in the streambed until a high waterfall blocks the way.

The Kuliʻouʻou Ridge hike starts from the same trailhead. That popular climb offers an appealing route to the Koʻolau (windward) summit for intermediate hikers.

5

Hawai'iloa Ridge

TYPE:	Ungraded ridge
LENGTH:	5-mile round-trip
ELEVATION GAIN:	1,500 feet
DANGER:	Low
SUITABLE FOR:	Novice, Intermediate
LOCATION:	Honolulu Watershed Forest Reserve above Hawai'i Loa
TOPO MAP:	Koko Head
ACCESS:	Conditional; must be a Hawai'i resident; show a state ID and sign a liability waiver at the subdivision security station.

HIGHLIGHTS

This popular hike mostly rambles along a gently rolling ridge. Near the end, however, is a stiff climb to the scenic Ko'olau summit. Along the way are intriguing native dryland and rain forest plants.

TRAILHEAD DIRECTIONS

At Ward Ave. get on Lunalilo Fwy. (H-1) Koko Head bound (east).

As the freeway ends, continue straight on Kalaniana'ole Hwy. (Rte. 72).

Pass 'Āina Haina Public Library on the left.

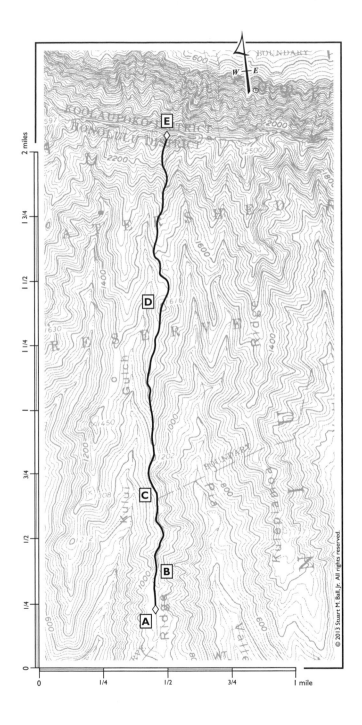

By Kawaiku'i Beach Park, turn left on Pu'u 'Ikena Dr. To make the left turn, bear right around a small circle and then cross Kalaniana'ole at the traffic light.

Stop at the security station and check in.

Ascend steadily through Hawai'i Loa Ridge subdivision.

At the stop sign continue straight on a road lined with iron-wood trees.

The road ends at a small recreation area used by residents.

Park in the small lot on the right just past a water tank (elevation 1,100 feet) (map point A).

BUS: Route 1 on weekends or route 1L on weekdays to Kalaniana'ole Hwy. and Pu'u 'Ikena Dr. Walk 1.8 miles up Pu'u 'Ikena Dr. to the trailhead.

ROUTE DESCRIPTION

Take the gravel path at the far end of the parking lot.

By a chain and a trailhead marker, bear left off the path onto the Hawai'iloa Ridge Trail.

Break out into the open on the wide, windswept ridge. Look for the native shrubs 'ūlei and pūkiawe among the Christmas berry and yellow strawberry guava trees (waiawī).

Cross a rocky, eroded section (map point B). To the right are views of Koko Crater (Kohelepelepe) and Koko Head (Kuamo'o Kāne).

Walk through three stands of ironwood trees.

Traverse a relatively level section of the ridge (map point C). Ignore a side trail on the right. Look for the native lama tree and 'akoko and 'ilima shrubs.

Ascend gradually through a long stretch of guava. The trail briefly follows several wires from an old fence line. Look for the 'elepaio, a small native bird.

Cross another relatively level section and then descend gradually. Don't trample the moss, which often lines the trail.

After passing a downed koa trunk, resume the ascent through a dark guava forest.

Bear left around the top of a distinct, moss-covered knob and descend its backside on two switchbacks (map point D).

Keep to the right side of the ridge through native koa and ʻōhiʻa trees. On the left are several ʻiliahi (sandalwood) trees.

As the ridge flattens, work left again through uluhe fern. Look for native hala pepe trees on the right.

By several large guava trees, jog right and then left up an eroded slope to regain the distinct crest of the ridge.

Ascend steadily along the open ridge, sometimes on plastic planks, sometimes on a deeply rutted trail. Ropes may provide some assistance in the nonplanked sections. Look for native kōpiko trees and ʻākia shrubs.

Climb a long staircase of plastic steps up an eroded, steep slope. On the left above the last step is a lone lapalapa tree with its fluttering leaves.

Ascend a second steep staircase. Listen for the Japanese bush warbler.

Reach the Koʻolau summit at a small knob (elevation 2,520 feet) (map point E) (UTM 04 0630499E, 2358554N). On the right are several native pūʻahanui (kanawao) shrubs.

NOTES

This popular hike comes in two parts. The first is an enjoyable walk on a gently rolling ridge. The second is a steep, slippery climb to the Koʻolau summit. Many hikers do the first part and then turn around at the moss-covered knob. The scramble to the top, however, is well worth the effort for the marvelous views and native plants en route.

The small parking lot at the trailhead has only ten spaces. On sunny weekends and holidays, start early to be sure of getting a spot. The security guard refuses entry to hikers once the limit of ten vehicles has been reached.

Although ungraded, the route in the lower portion is mostly dry and wide. Look out for small guava stumps in the path. In the upper portion, the trail is eroded and slippery in spots. Test all ropes before using them. The very steep stretches have recycled plastic steps to stabilize the treadway and make the going easier. Nevertheless, watch your footing constantly, especially on the return.

Along the initial section are the native shrubs 'ūlei and pūkiawe. Sprawling 'ūlei has small, oblong leaves arranged in pairs; clusters of white, roselike flowers; and white fruit. Early Hawaiians ate the berries and used the tough wood for making digging sticks, fish spears, and *'ūkēkē* (the musical bow). Pūkiawe has tiny, rigid leaves and small white, pink, or red berries.

Before entering the guava tree tunnel, look for the native shrub 'akoko. It has rounded, oblong leaves arranged in pairs. The branches are dark brown and jointed with white rings. Early Hawaiians used the milky sap mixed with charcoal to stain their outrigger canoe hulls.

For much of the hike, the trail is lined with yellow strawberry guava trees (waiawī). They have glossy, light green leaves and smooth brown bark. Unfortunately, their yellow fruit has a tart, bitter taste. Cattle, grazing in the adjacent valleys, probably spread the guava to the ridgetop.

In the stands of guava, watch for the 'elepaio, a small native bird. It is brown on top and white underneath with a black throat and a dark tail, usually cocked. The bird roams the forest understory catching insects on the fly or on vegetation. 'Elepaio are very curious, which is why you can sometimes see them.

Before the final climb look for hala pepe, a tall, slender native tree. The narrow leaves hang in bunches from the branch tips. The tree produces clusters of yellowish blossoms and then red berries. Early Hawaiians used the flowers in making lei.

While climbing to the summit, take a breather and look leeward. From left to right you can see Koko Crater (Kohelepelepe), Koko Head (Kuamo'o Kāne), Diamond Head (Lē'ahi), and Waikīkī (spouting water). In the distance is the Waiʻanae (mullet water) Range.

Want another excuse to take a break? Look for kōpiko, a native member of the coffee family. It has leathery, oblong leaves with a light green midrib. Turn the leaf over to see a row of tiny holes (*piko* or navel) on either side of the midrib. The kōpiko produces clusters of little white flowers and fleshy, orange fruits.

Just below the summit, listen for the Japanese bush warbler (uguisu), a bird often heard but rarely seen. Its distinctive cry starts with a long whistle and then winds down in a series of notes. The bush warbler is olive brown on top with a white breast and a long tail.

At the top you can see the windward coast from Kualoa (long back) Point to Waimānalo (potable water). The triple-peaked mountain just to the left is Olomana (forked hill), with Mōkapu (taboo district) Point behind. Along the summit ridge to the left is Kōnāhuanui (large fat testicles), the highest peak in the Koʻolau (windward) Range. To the right along the ridge is flat-topped Puʻu o Kona (hill of leeward).

After taking in the expansive view, look for the native shrub pūʻahanui (kanawao), a relative of hydrangea. It has large, serrated, deeply creased leaves and clusters of delicate pink flowers. Early Hawaiians used the plants for medicinal purposes.

For a more challenging outing, combine the Hawaiʻiloa Ridge and Wiliwilinui hikes. Go up Hawaiʻiloa, turn left along the Koʻolau summit ridge, and then go down Wiliwilinui. The summit section is for experienced hikers only because the trail is narrow, overgrown, and sometimes socked in.

6

Wiliwilinui

TYPE:	Ungraded ridge
LENGTH:	5-mile round-trip
ELEVATION GAIN:	1,300 feet
DANGER:	Low
SUITABLE FOR:	Novice, Intermediate
LOCATION:	Honolulu Watershed Forest Reserve above Wai'alae Iki
TOPO MAP:	Koko Head
ACCESS:	Open

HIGHLIGHTS

This short, popular hike follows a dirt road and then a steep trail to the Ko'olau summit. Along the route is an assortment of native forest plants. At the top are spectacular views of both sides of the island.

TRAILHEAD DIRECTIONS

At Ward Ave. get on Lunalilo Fwy. (H-1) Koko Head bound (east).

As the freeway ends, continue straight on Kalaniana'ole Hwy. (Rte. 72).

Just past Kalani High School at the third traffic light, turn left on Laukahi St.

Drive up through Wai'alae Iki subdivision.

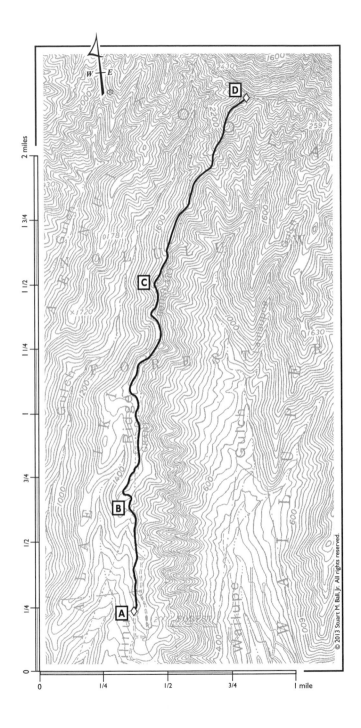

Stop at the guard station for Waiʻalae Iki V and get a parking permit.

At the road's end, turn left on Okoʻa St.

The road narrows after going through a small circle.

Before the paved road ends, park in the small lot reserved for hikers on the left (elevation 1,180 feet) (map point A). If all eight spaces are taken, continue along Okoʻa St. to a gravel overflow lot on the left.

BUS: Route 1 on weekends or route 1L on weekdays to Kalanianaʻole Hwy. and Laukahi St. Walk 2.5 miles up Laukahi and Okoʻa St. to the trailhead. Route 235 goes partway up Laukahi St. but runs only on weekday mornings and afternoons.

ROUTE DESCRIPTION

Proceed up Okoʻa St., which soon narrows to one lane.

Pass the overflow lot and go around a locked yellow gate.

The paved road ends at a water tank.

Continue straight on a dirt road, which climbs Wiliwilinui Ridge. The road is lined with yellow strawberry guava (waiawī) and ironwood trees.

A utility line comes in on the right and parallels the ridge all the way to the summit (map point B). To the right is a good view of Koko Crater (Kohelepelepe) and Koko Head (Kuamoʻo Kāne).

Pass a series of Cook pines along the ridgeline.

Contour left around a large knob on the ridge.

Go around two more knobs with native koa trees on top.

The road ends at a vehicle turnaround with a bench and a bike rack (map point C).

Pick up the Wiliwilinui Trail on the left.

Climb steadily on plastic steps through koa to a group of utility poles.

Stroll through a pleasant, level section. Watch for native 'ōhi'a and kōpiko trees and look for 'amakihi, a yellowish green native bird.

Ascend to a second group of utility poles on a small knob.

After a short level stretch, begin the final climb to the summit through uluhe ferns. The initial steep section has a staircase made of recycled plastic planks.

Pass a lone loulu palm on the left.

The trail becomes a series of plastic steps alternating with deeply rutted sections. Ropes may provide assistance over the steeper spots. Watch your footing constantly, especially if the ground is slick. Look and listen for the Japanese bush warbler.

The angle of ascent decreases past a green utility relay station.

Reach the Ko'olau summit at a small knob (elevation 2,480 feet) (map point D) (UTM 04 0629324E, 2358950N).

NOTES

With its road, utility lines, and relay station, this hike is hardly a wilderness experience. Nevertheless, the short length and magnificent views make Wiliwilinui (large wiliwili tree) a popular outing. The route combines a pleasant road walk with a steep ridge climb. Built by Hawaiian Electric Company in the late 1940s, the road is wide and well graded, although slick and muddy in spots. Keep your eye out for mountain bikers. On the trail section, watch your footing, especially on several steep, deeply rutted sections near the top. Novices should go as far as they feel comfortable.

Much of the dirt road is lined with strawberry guava trees (waiawī). They have glossy, light green leaves and smooth brown bark. Unfortunately their yellow fruit has a tart, bitter taste. Cattle, grazing in the adjacent valleys, probably spread the guava to the ridgetop.

Along the ridgetop are tall Cook pines planted by Territorial

Forestry in 1927. Named after Captain James Cook, the pines are native to New Caledonia's Isle of Pines in the South Pacific, between Fiji and Australia. They are columnar in shape and have overlapping, scalelike leaves about ¼ inch long, rather than true needles.

Near the road's end, native koa and 'ōhi'a trees begin to replace the guava and other introduced species. Koa has sickle-shaped foliage and pale yellow flower clusters. Early Hawaiians made surfboards and outrigger canoe hulls out of the beautiful red-brown wood. Today it is made into fine furniture. 'Ōhi'a has oval leaves and clusters of delicate red flowers. Early Hawaiians used the flowers in lei and the wood in outrigger canoes. The hard, durable wood was also carved into god images for *heiau* (religious sites).

Along the trail look for kōpiko, a native member of the coffee family. It has leathery, oblong leaves with a light green midrib. Turn the leaf over to see a row of tiny holes (*piko* or navel) on either side of the midrib. The kōpiko produces clusters of little white flowers and fleshy, orange fruits.

Before the final climb, listen for the Japanese bush warbler (uguisu), a bird often heard but rarely seen. Its distinctive cry starts with a long whistle and then winds down in a series of notes. The bush warbler is olive brown on top with a white breast and a long tail. More readily seen is the 'amakihi, the most common native forest bird on O'ahu. It is yellowish green with a slightly curved gray bill and feeds on nectar, fruits, and insects.

From the summit are superb views of both sides of the island. In front is the windward coast from Kualoa (long back) Point to Waimānalo (potable water). The triple-peaked mountain dead ahead is Olomana (forked hill), with Mōkapu (taboo district) Point behind. Along the summit ridge to the left is Kōnāhuanui (large fat testicles), the highest peak in the Ko'olau (windward) Range. To leeward are Koko Head (Kuamo'o Kāne), Diamond Head (Lē'ahi), and Waikīkī (spouting water). In the distance is the Wai'anae (mullet water) Range.

At the top look down and left for a small group of native loulu palms clinging to the cliff. They have rigid, fan-shaped fronds in a cluster at the top of a ringed trunk. Early Hawaiians used the fronds for thatch and plaited the blades of young fronds into fans and baskets. On the way down look for a lone loulu on the right after the relay station.

For a more challenging outing, combine the Wiliwilinui and Lanipō hikes. Go up Wiliwilinui, turn left along the Koʻolau summit ridge, and then go down Lanipō. You can also turn right along the summit ridge and go down Hawaiʻiloa Ridge. The summit connectors are for experienced hikers only as the trail is narrow, overgrown, and sometimes socked in.

7

Lanipō

(MAU'UMAE RIDGE)

TYPE:	Ungraded ridge
LENGTH:	7-mile round-trip
ELEVATION GAIN:	2,000 feet
DANGER:	Low
SUITABLE FOR:	Intermediate
LOCATION:	Honolulu Watershed Reserve above Maunalani Heights
TOPO MAP:	Honolulu, Koko Head
ACCESS:	Open

HIGHLIGHTS

This early Hawaiian route follows the crest of Mau'umae Ridge to the Ko'olau summit. Along the up-and-down trail are a rich variety of native plants and a hidden volcanic crater. From the summit lookout is a splendid view of much of the windward coast.

TRAILHEAD DIRECTIONS

At Ward Ave. get on Lunalilo Fwy. (H-1) Koko Head bound (east).

Take the Koko Head Ave. exit (26A) in Kaimukī.

At the top of the off-ramp, turn left on Koko Head Ave.

Cross Wai'alae Ave.

At the first stop sign turn left, still on Koko Head Ave.

At the next stop sign turn right on Sierra Dr.

Switchback up the ridge to Maunalani Heights.

Pass Maunalani Community Park on the right and Maunalani Nursing Center on the left. The park has restrooms and drinking water.

At the end of Sierra Dr. by a stop sign and the last bus stop, bear right and up on Maunalani Circle.

The road swings left in a broad arc.

On the right look for a chain-link fence enclosing a Board of Water Supply tank.

Park on the street next to the fence (elevation 1,040 feet) (map point A).

BUS: Route 14 to the end of Sierra Dr. Walk 0.2 mile up Maunalani Circle to the trailhead.

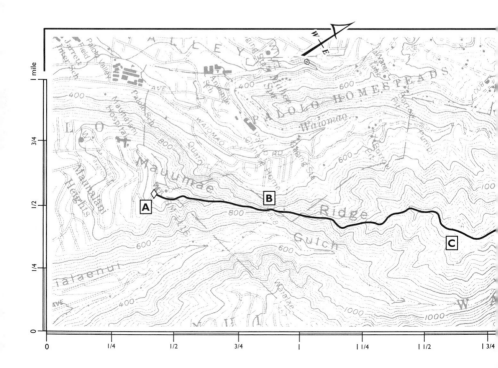

ROUTE DESCRIPTION

Walk back down the road to a signed junction at the corner of the fence. Turn left on the Mauʻumae Ridge Trail, which follows a narrow right-of-way between two chain-link fences. The passageway is directly across from the garage of 4970 Maunalani Circle.

At the end of the fences, keep left through a small grove of ironwood trees.

Reach the crest of Mauʻumae Ridge and bear right along it.

Descend moderately along the mostly open ridge, which has a short rocky section. Along the trail are Formosa koa trees and the native dryland shrubs ʻūlei, ʻaʻaliʻi, and ʻilima.

Pass a utility pole on the left (map point B). Ignore a side trail leading down into Pālolo Valley on the left.

Begin a long climb interspersed with two dips. On the left is a memorial bench. To the right is Waiʻalae Nui Gulch.

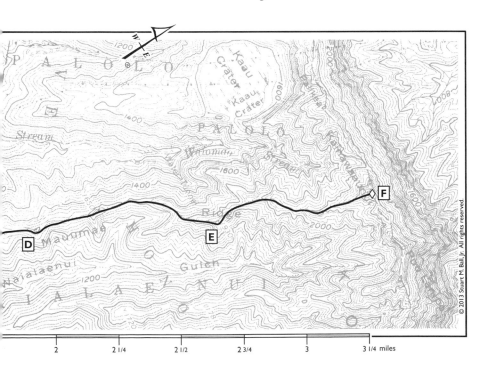

After the second dip, ascend steeply through native koa trees. The ridge is massive and well forested.

The trail levels out briefly through ironwood and native alahe'e trees.

Climb steeply again on a badly eroded trail. Avoid the worst part by taking a bypass trail on the right.

Stroll through a lovely stretch of native koa and 'iliahi (sandalwood) trees.

Ascend a flat grassy knob with a 360-degree view (map point C). Look behind you for an unusual view of the backside of Diamond Head (Lē'ahi). Along the coast to the left is Maunalua Bay and Koko Head.

The vegetation gradually changes from dryland to rain forest. Native 'ōhi'a trees form a loose canopy, and uluhe ferns cover the ground. Look for two native birds: the red 'apapane and the yellowish green 'amakihi.

Climb a second, shady knob topped by three Cook pines (map point D).

Traverse a long, relatively gentle section underneath magnificent koa, 'iliahi, and 'ōhi'a trees. Look for native kōpiko trees and maile and naupaka kuahiwi shrubs in the understory. The trail drops below the ridgeline several times.

As the trail resumes serious climbing, reach a small, grassy lookout by a koa skeleton. Across Pālolo Valley is Ka'au Crater, nestled below the Ko'olau summit ridge. A waterfall cascades from the lip of the crater.

The ridge narrows, and the vegetation thins.

After a stiff ascent, reach a flat, open knob with a view of the final climb (map point E).

Descend off the knob, passing a spindly Cook pine on the right.

Ascend steeply on a rutted trail past kōpiko and other native shrubs to a broad hump.

Descend the backside of the hump and then begin the final climb to the summit along the open, windswept ridge.

As the top nears, the trail steepens and becomes severely eroded.

Reach the Ko'olau summit at a peak called Kainawa'auika (elevation 2,520 feet) (map point F) (UTM 04 0628289E, 2359394N). To the right is a lone 'ōhi'a āhihi tree with its fluttering leaves.

NOTES

Lanipō is the classic O'ahu ridge hike. It offers a challenging climb, breathtaking windward views, and a surprising variety of native plants. As a bonus, you get to see a little known volcanic crater and a lovely waterfall.

The hike follows Mau'umae (wilted grass) Ridge, an early Hawaiian route once used by bird catchers, maile collectors, and sandalwood cutters. In 1910, the Kaimuki Land Company began to develop Palolo Hill (now Maunalani Heights), a tract on the lower part of the ridge. The following year the company partnered with the Hawaiian Trail and Mountain Club to reopen the ridge route above the subdivision to the Ko'olau summit. Club stalwarts rode the Kaimukī streetcar line to its end along Wai'alae Road and then climbed up Wilhelmina Rise to reach the current trailhead.

Start early to avoid the hot sun in the open lower section of the trail. Watch your footing constantly because the ungraded route is often rough, sometimes muddy, and occasionally narrow. The middle section of the trail may be overgrown with grass and scratchy uluhe ferns. The cool and wet upper section is slippery and deeply rutted in spots. Test any ropes you find before using them.

Some hikers are put off by the initial rocky descent, which, of course, must be climbed on the way back in the hot afternoon. Don't be discouraged! The native plants and the spectacular views farther in are well worth the extra effort.

On the lower part of the trail, look for the native dryland shrubs ʻaʻaliʻi and ʻilima. ʻAʻaliʻi has shiny, narrow leaves and red seed capsules. Early Hawaiians used the leaves and capsules in making lei. When crushed or boiled, the capsules produced a red dye for decorating *kapa* (bark cloth). ʻIlima has oblong, serrated leaves about 1 inch long. The yellow-orange flowers strung together have been used to make regal lei in both ancient and modern Hawaiʻi.

In the dry section of the trail, koa is the most common native tree. It has sickle-shaped foliage and pale yellow flower clusters. Early Hawaiians made surfboards and outrigger canoe hulls out of the beautiful red-brown wood. Today it is made into fine furniture.

Less common along the route is ʻiliahi, the native sandalwood tree. Its small leaves are dull green and appear wilted. ʻIliahi is partially parasitic, with outgrowths on its roots that steal nutrients from nearby plants. Early Hawaiians ground the fragrant heartwood into a powder to perfume their *kapa*. Beginning in the late 1700s, sandalwood was indiscriminately cut down and exported to China to make incense and furniture. The trade ended around 1840 when the forests were depleted of ʻiliahi.

In the wetter middle section of the trail, native ʻōhiʻa gradually replaces koa as the dominant tree. ʻŌhiʻa has oval leaves and clusters of delicate red flowers. Early Hawaiians used the flowers in lei and the wood in outrigger canoes. The hard, durable wood was also carved into god images for *heiau* (religious sites).

Underneath the ʻōhiʻa, look for kōpiko, a native member of the coffee family. It has leathery, oblong leaves with a light green midrib. Turn the leaf over to see a row of tiny holes (*piko* or navel) on either side of the midrib. The kōpiko produces clusters of little white flowers and fleshy, orange fruits.

In the forest canopy, watch for the ʻamakihi, the most common native forest bird on Oʻahu. It is yellowish green with a slightly curved gray bill and feeds on nectar, fruits, and insects.

If the ʻōhiʻa are in bloom, you may glimpse the scarce ʻapapane. It has a red breast and head, black wings and tail, and a slightly curved black bill. In flight, the ʻapapane makes a whirring sound as it darts from tree to tree searching for insects and nectar.

From the grassy lookout you can see Kaʻau (forty), a circular crater on the left at the base of the Koʻolau summit ridge. The crater was probably formed by steam explosions, as rising molten rock encountered groundwater. Both Kaʻau and Diamond Head Craters are remnants of the last volcanic activity on Oʻahu known as the Honolulu Series.

According to Hawaiian legend, the demigod and trickster Māui wanted to join all the islands together. From Kaʻena (the heat) Point he threw a great hook toward Kauaʻi, hoping to snare the island. Initially the hook held fast, and Māui gave a mighty tug on the line. A huge boulder, known as Pōhaku o Kauaʻi, dropped at his feet. The hook sailed over his head and fell in Pālolo Valley, forming Kaʻau Crater. The crater may have been named after Kaʻauhelemoa, a supernatural chicken that lived in the valley.

From the summit lookout on Kainawaʻauika (also known as Kainawaʻanui) are some impressive windward views. In front is Olomana (forked hill) with its three peaks. On the right is a portion of Waimānalo (potable water) Bay. Farther along the coast are Kailua (two seas) and Kāneʻohe (bamboo husband) bays, separated by Mōkapu (taboo district) Peninsula. To the left along the sheer Koʻolau (windward) summit ridge are Mount Olympus (Awāwaloa) and twin-peaked Kōnāhuanui (large fat testicles).

To reach the actual peak of Lanipō (dense), turn right along the Koʻolau summit ridge to the second knob. For a more challenging outing, continue past Lanipō and go down the Wiliwilinui Trail. The summit section is for experienced hikers only because it is steep, narrow, overgrown, and sometimes socked in.

8

Mount Olympus
(AWĀWALOA)

TYPE:	Ungraded ridge
LENGTH:	6-mile round-trip
ELEVATION GAIN:	1,500 feet
DANGER:	Low
SUITABLE FOR:	Novice, Intermediate
LOCATION:	Honolulu Watershed Reserve above St. Louis Heights
TOPO MAP:	Honolulu
ACCESS:	Open

HIGHLIGHTS

In back of Mānoa Valley is the massive peak of Olympus. The hike to its broad summit follows often misty and windy Waʻahila Ridge. Along the way are impressive views and a variety of native plants.

TRAILHEAD DIRECTIONS

At Ward Ave. get on Lunalilo Fwy. (H-1) Koko Head bound (east).

Take the King St. exit (25A).

At the first traffic light, turn left underneath the freeway onto Waiʻalae Ave.

At the third traffic light, turn left on St. Louis Dr.

Switchback up St. Louis Heights.

A block before St. Louis Dr. ends, turn right on Peter St.

Turn left on Ruth Pl. at the bus turnaround circle.

Enter Waʻahila Ridge State Recreation Area.

Park in the lot at the road's end (elevation 1,080 feet) (map point A). The recreation area has restrooms uphill to the right.

BUS: Route 14 to Peter St. and Ruth Pl. Walk 0.4 mile along Ruth Pl. and through the recreation area to the trailhead.

ROUTE DESCRIPTION

Take the paved driveway at the back of the parking lot.

Almost immediately, cross another paved driveway and continue straight on the wide Waʻahila Ridge Trail through tall Cook pines.

Pass a water tank on the left.

Climb steadily through ironwood and strawberry guava trees.

After the trail levels off, turn left and down to bypass a utility line tower.

Descend steeply through ironwoods and then cross an open, windswept saddle. Mānoa Valley is on the left and Pālolo Valley on the right.

Climb over three small but rough humps on Waʻahila Ridge. Among the Christmas berry and silk oak trees is the native tree alaheʻe with its shiny leaves.

At a fork, keep right to bypass a large knob with utility poles on top (map point B).

Climb gradually through thick strawberry guava, passing several banyan trees on your left.

The trail opens up under a lovely canopy of native ʻōhiʻa and koa trees. Introduced fiddlewood encroaches in the understory.

Reach a grassy lookout where a side ridge comes in on the right. *Makai* (seaward) are Diamond Head (Lēʻahi), Waikīkī, and downtown Honolulu.

Reach a signed junction by an End of Improved Trail sign (map point C). Bear right and up on a narrow trail along the main ridge. (To the left, the wide Kolowalu Trail heads down a side ridge into Mānoa Valley.)

After a relatively level stretch, climb steeply to a knoll. On top are kī (ti) plants and native ʻōhiʻa ʻāhihi trees. Look for the ʻamakihi, a yellowish green native bird.

Almost immediately, descend steeply to the right to bypass a rock face on the ridgeline. Watch for purple Philippine ground orchids.

Ascend to a second knoll with good views of the back of Mānoa Valley (map point D). Across the valley are the wooded volcanic cinder cones of Round Top and Tantalus (Puʻu Ōhiʻa). Along the Koʻolau summit are the peaks of Kōnāhuanui and Olympus.

The ridge levels, and the strawberry guava finally gives way to native forest. Watch for kōpiko trees along the trail.

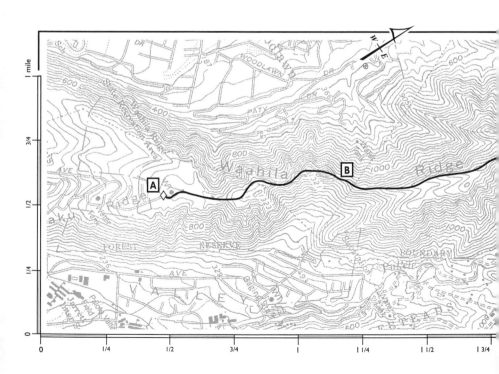

Ascend steadily on the now open ridge to a prominent knob below the summit. Look for a lone loulu palm there.

Cross a short, level section and then climb steeply, at times on a deeply eroded trail. On the left and right are overgrown remnants of the historic Castle-Olympus Trail.

Reach the Koʻolau summit ridge and turn right along it (map point E).

Go over a small hump and pass a cleared overlook.

Climb briefly to reach the lush, broad summit of Mount Olympus (Awāwaloa) (elevation 2,486 feet) (map point F) (UTM 04 0626786E, 2359803N).

NOTES

Mount Olympus is the imposing peak along the Koʻolau summit on the east side of Mānoa (vast) Valley. Early Hawaiians

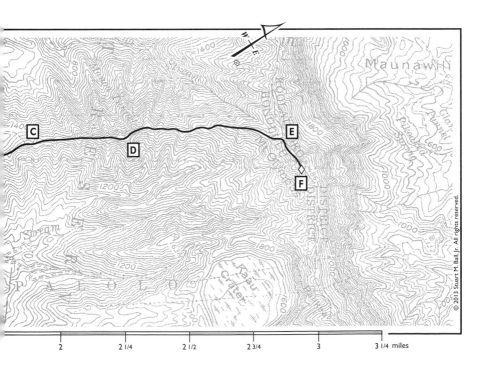

called the mountain Awāwaloa (long valley). Perhaps because of its commanding presence, students at Punahou, a nearby private school, renamed the peak in the early 1840s after the mythical home of the Greek gods. Although the effort required to reach the top is hardly Olympian, the climb does provide a challenge for intermediate hikers. The exciting finish along the open, windswept summit ridge is particularly memorable.

The route as far as the grassy lookout is a popular novice hike. Although ungraded, the trail is wide and well trodden for the most part. Take care on the rooty and rocky spots, especially if you are new to hiking. Beyond the Kolowalu (eight creeping) junction the trail becomes rough, narrow, and sometimes muddy. It may be overgrown with scratchy uluhe ferns and *Clidemia* shrubs. Watch your footing at all times.

The hike starts in a grove of tall Cook pines planted in 1931–1932 for reforestation. They have overlapping, scalelike leaves about ¼ inch long, rather than true needles. Named after Captain James Cook, they are native to New Caledonia's Isle of Pines in the South Pacific, between Fiji and Australia.

Past the pines, the trail is lined with strawberry guava trees (waiawī ʻulaʻula). They have glossy, dark green leaves and smooth brown bark. Their dark red fruit is delicious, with a taste reminiscent of strawberries. The guavas usually ripen in August and September. Pickings may be slim along the trail, however, because of its popularity. The strawberry guava is a native of Brazil but was introduced to Hawaiʻi from England in the 1800s.

In the forest understory, look and listen for the white-rumped shama. It is black on top with a chestnut-colored breast and a long black and white tail. The shama has a variety of beautiful songs and often mimics other birds. A native of Malaysia, the shama has become widespread in introduced forests such as this one.

Past the windswept saddle are a few native alaheʻe trees. Their oblong leaves are shiny and dark green. Alaheʻe has fragrant white flowers that grow in clusters at the branch tips.

Early Hawaiians fashioned the hard wood into farming tools and hooks and spears for fishing.

After the Kolowalu junction, watch for the 'amakihi, the most common native forest bird on O'ahu. It is yellowish green with a slightly curved gray bill and feeds on nectar, fruits, and insects. If the native 'ōhi'a trees are in bloom, you may also catch a glimpse of an 'apapane in the forest canopy. It has a red breast and head, black wings and tail, and a slightly curved black bill. In flight, the 'apapane makes a whirring sound as it darts from tree to tree searching for nectar and insects.

At the top of the knoll past the Kolowalu junction, look for native 'ōhi'a 'āhihi trees found only on O'ahu. They have narrow, pointed leaves with red stems and midribs. Their delicate red flowers grow in clusters and are similar to those of the more common 'ōhi'a. Queen Lili'uokalani mentioned the 'āhihi lehua (blossom) in her haunting love song, "Aloha 'Oe."

When the strawberry guava finally ends, watch for kōpiko, a native member of the coffee family. It has leathery, oblong leaves with a light green midrib. Turn the leaf over to see a row of tiny holes (*piko* or navel) on either side of the midrib. The kōpiko produces clusters of little white flowers and fleshy, orange fruits.

Before reaching the summit ridge, look right and down for a view of Ka'au Crater. The abandoned Castle-Olympus Trail built in 1910 by the Hawaiian Trail and Mountain Club switchbacks across the hike route several times on its way down to the crater. In the other direction, the obscure route contours around the back of Mānoa Valley all the way to the Nu'uanu overlook.

After the steep climb, enjoy the remarkable views from the overlooks along the Ko'olau summit. Over 2,000 feet down lies the windward side of the island. Along the coast are Kailua (two seas) and Waimānalo (potable water) bays, framed by Mōkapu (taboo district) and Makapu'u (bulging eye) points. Slightly to the right is triple-peaked Olomana (forked hill). To the left along the sheer, fluted flanks of the summit ridge is Kōnāhuanui (large fat testicles), the highest peak in the Koʻolau (windward) Range. For a better view of Kaʻau (forty) Crater, walk to the far side of the broad summit of Olympus.

At the true summit is a lush thicket of native vegetation. Look for hāpuʻu tree ferns with delicate, sweeping fronds. Their trunks consist of roots tightly woven around a small central stem. The brown fiber covering the young fronds of hāpuʻu is called *pulu*. Also in evidence are ʻōlapa trees with their fluttering leaves.

For a shorter but tougher approach to Mount Olympus, take the Kolowalu (eight creeping) Trail. It starts in Mānoa (vast) Valley and climbs to the junction with the Waʻahila Ridge Trail. See the Puʻu Pia (arrowroot hill) hike for driving instructions to the trailhead.

Pu'u Pia

TYPE:	Foothill
LENGTH:	2-mile round-trip
ELEVATION GAIN:	500 feet
DANGER:	Low
SUITABLE FOR:	Novice
LOCATION:	Honolulu Watershed Forest Reserve above Mānoa
TOPO MAP:	Honolulu
ACCESS:	Open

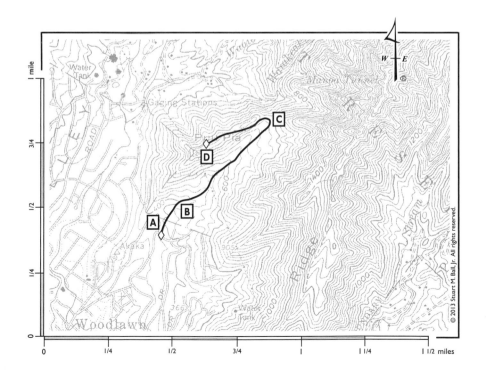

HIGHLIGHTS

This short, delightful walk climbs Pu'u Pia, a rounded hill toward the back of Mānoa Valley. From the bench at the top are scenic views of the valley and the surrounding ridges and peaks.

TRAILHEAD DIRECTIONS

Get on S. King St. Koko Head bound (east).

Turn left on Punahou St.

Pass Punahou School on the right and enter Mānoa Valley.

The road splits and narrows to two lanes. Take the right fork onto E. Mānoa Rd.

Pass Mānoa Market Place on the right.

Toward the back of the valley the road splits again. Take the right fork, still on E. Mānoa Rd.

At the road's end, turn left on Alani Dr.

Park on Alani Dr. just before its intersection with Woodlawn Dr. (elevation 370 feet) (map point A).

BUS: Route 6 to Alani Dr. and Woodlawn Dr.

ROUTE DESCRIPTION

Continue along Alani Dr. on foot. The paved one-lane road soon turns to dirt after passing the last house.

Climb over a wire across the road.

Parallel an intermittent stream on your left.

Reach a signed junction in a clearing with a lone, vine-covered paraserianthes (albizia) tree and a covered picnic table (map point B). Keep left on the road, which is the Pu'u Pia Trail. (The path to the right is the Kolowalu Trail, which ascends to Wa'ahila Ridge.)

Climb gradually along the side of a wide gulch through rose apple, paperbark, and other introduced trees. Watch for purple Philippine ground orchids and look for the white-rumped shama.

Cross an intermittent side stream on a plank bridge.

Swing left around the back of the gulch through tall eucalyptus trees (map point C). Ignore side trails to the left and right.

Ascend gradually along the left side of Pu'u Pia under native koa trees.

Gain the ridgeline and bear left up it through strawberry guava trees.

Reach the top of Pu'u Pia at a grassy clearing with a bench (elevation 880 feet) (map point D) (UTM 04 0624906E, 2358699N). A makeshift trail continues briefly along the ridge to two utility poles and the base of a survey marker. Along the way, look for the native shrub naupaka kuahiwi.

NOTES

Pu'u Pia (arrowroot hill) is another good hike for beginners. The climbing is gradual and the trail is short and well groomed, although muddy and rooty at times. The views of Mānoa (vast) Valley are well worth the minimal effort required to get to the top.

Pia or arrowroot is a perennial herb introduced to Hawai'i by early Polynesian voyagers. Its large, lobed leaves resemble those of a papaya. Pia produces a tall flower stalk and an underground tuber similar to a potato. Early Hawaiians used powdered starch from the tuber as a thickening for *haupia* (coconut pudding).

On the trail, look and listen for the white-rumped shama. It is black on top with a chestnut-colored breast and a long black-and-white tail. The shama has a variety of beautiful songs and often mimics other birds. A native of Malaysia, the shama has become widespread in introduced forests such as this one.

Along the Pu'u Pia ridge are native naupaka kuahiwi shrubs and koa trees. Naupaka kuahiwi has light green, toothed leaves and white half-flowers. Koa has sickle-shaped foliage and pale yellow flower clusters. Early Hawaiians made surfboards and outrigger canoe hulls out of the beautiful red-brown wood. Today it is made into fine furniture.

From the summit bench is a 360-degree view around Mānoa Valley. Facing the ocean, you can see the University of Hawai'i and Waikīkī (spouting water). On the left, Wa'ahila (Mānoa rain) Ridge climbs to Mount Olympus (Awāwaloa) on the Ko'olau (windward) summit ridge. On the ridge to the right are the wooded volcanic cinder cones of Round Top ('Ualaka'a) and Tantalus (Pu'u 'Ōhi'a). At the back of the valley is Kōnāhuanui (large fat testicles), the highest peak in the Ko'olau Range.

For a more difficult ridge hike, take the Kolowalu (eight creeping) Trail. It branches off the Pu'u Pia Trail at the shelter and ascends steeply to Wa'ahila Ridge. From there you can climb Mount Olympus or follow the ridge *makai* (seaward) to Wa'ahila State Recreation Area.

10

ʻAihualama-ʻŌhiʻa
(VIA MĀNOA FALLS)

TYPE:	Foothill
LENGTH:	8-mile round-trip
ELEVATION GAIN:	1,700 feet
DANGER:	Low
SUITABLE FOR:	Novice, Intermediate
LOCATION:	Honolulu Watershed Reserve above Mānoa
TOPO MAP:	Honolulu
ACCESS:	Open, for groups up to twelve persons. For larger groups, obtain a permit for Mānoa Falls Trail from State Division of Forestry and Wildlife, Room 325, 1151 Punchbowl St., Honolulu (phone 587-0166).

HIGHLIGHTS

This hike climbs to the top of Tantalus (Puʻu ʻŌhiʻa) from Mānoa Valley. Along the way is lovely Mānoa Falls. On Tantalus are some panoramic views and a surprising variety of native plants.

TRAILHEAD DIRECTIONS

Get on S. King St. Koko Head bound (east).
Turn left on Punahou St.
Pass Punahou School on the right and enter Mānoa Valley.
The road splits and narrows to two lanes. Take the left fork onto Mānoa Rd.

At the stop sign, proceed straight across the intersection on a much wider Mānoa Rd.

Pass Mānoa Elementary School on the right.

Park on Mānoa Rd. just before it narrows at the intersection with Waʻakaua St. (elevation 280 feet) (map point A).

BUS: Route 5 to Mānoa Rd. and Kumuone St. Walk 0.5 mile to the start of the hike.

ROUTE DESCRIPTION

Continue along Mānoa Rd. on foot.

Walk underneath a pedestrian overpass leading to Treetops Restaurant in Paradise Park.

Follow the main road as it curves left and then right around the lower parking lot. Hiker parking is available there for a fee.

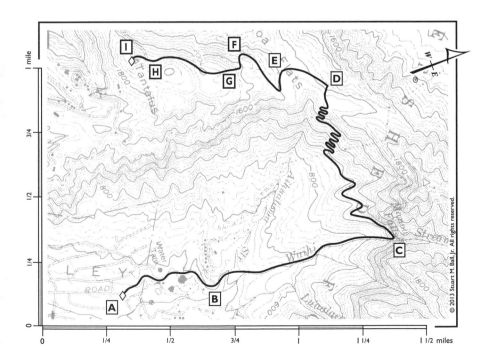

As the paved road turns left to Harold L. Lyon Arboretum, proceed straight on a gravel road through a chain-link gate (map point B).

Pass compost toilets on the left.

At the road's end, cross 'Aihualama Stream on a bridge.

Swing left and up on the Mānoa Falls Trail and then descend briefly to ford a small side stream. Look and listen for the white-rumped shama.

Angle across a flat, damp section toward Waihī Stream. The trail is graveled and lined with plastic planks. Stay on the defined path to minimize trampling and erosion.

Ascend gradually along the stream. On the left is a hau tree tangle. Above are introduced paraserianthes (albizia) trees with their whitish bark and layered branches. The path is paved with rocks in several spots.

Climb more steeply as the valley narrows. The trail is often rooty, muddy, and rocky.

Go through a bamboo grove on raised plastic steps.

Just before the falls, reach a signed junction with the 'Aihualama Trail in a grove of mountain apple trees. For now, continue a short distance to a rock platform to view lovely Mānoa (Waihī) Falls (map point C).

Backtrack to the signed junction. Turn right and up on the 'Aihualama Trail. The path is narrow and rocky at first but soon widens.

Work in and out of three gulches through bamboo groves and past huge banyan trees. Look for yellow ginger and red heliconia along the way. Ignore side trails heading up the gulches.

Climb the side of Mānoa Valley on fourteen switchbacks (count 'em, but don't cut 'em). Kī (ti) plants line the trail. After the eighth switchback are two concrete posts. Between nine and thirteen, a dense stand of cinnamon trees blots out much of the light.

At the top of the ridge, enter a bamboo forest and turn right on a muddy, rooty trail.

Reach a signed junction with the Pauoa Flats Trail (map

point D). Turn left on it. (To the right the flats trail leads to Nu'uanu Valley overlook.) Memorize that junction for the return trip.

Begin crossing Pauoa Flats on a very rooty trail.

Reach another signed junction. Continue straight on the flats trail. (To the right, the Nu'uanu Trail leads down to the Judd Trail and Nu'uanu Valley.)

The trail forks after the Nu'uanu junction. Keep left, still on the flats trail.

Reach a signed junction (map point E). Continue straight on the flats trail. (To the right, the Kalāwahine Trail connects with the Mānoa Cliff Trail and Tantalus Dr.)

Begin climbing the flank of Tantalus.

Swing left and then switchback right. The trail is lined with fragrant white and yellow ginger and colorful kāhili ginger.

By some native 'ōhi'a trees, reach a signed junction with a posted trail map (map point F). Bear left onto the Mānoa Cliff Trail and immediately enter a native forest restoration area through a gate in a fence. (To the right, the cliff trail leads back to the Kalāwahine Trail.) On the left just beyond the gate is a native kōpiko tree, identified by marker no. 19.

Contour around the side of Tantalus.

Reach another signed junction (map point G). Turn sharp right and up on the Pu'u 'Ōhi'a Trail. (The cliff trail continues straight, to Round Top Dr.) Just before and after that junction are several native white hibiscus trees, known as koki'o ke'oke'o.

Ascend gradually through 'ōhi'a and koa trees and then bamboo. On the right you can see Nu'uanu Pali between the peaks of Lanihuli and Kōnāhuanui.

Go around to the right of a Hawaiian Telephone installation.

Turn right on a one-lane paved road.

The road dips and then climbs gradually.

Reach an intersection (map point H). Take the road on the left heading up Tantalus. (The road on the right leads down to Tantalus Dr. The Pu'u 'Ōhi'a Trail continues on the left, descending steeply to Tantalus Dr.)

The road ends at a second Hawaiian Telephone installation with a tower.

Take the path by a short utility pole.

Reach the summit of Tantalus (Pu'u 'Ōhi'a) (elevation 2,013 feet) (map point I) (UTM 04 0622903E, 2359424N). The concrete base of a triangulation station provides a good viewing platform. Look for native 'ōhi'a 'āhihi trees *mauka* (inland) of the summit.

NOTES

The 'Aihualama hike combines a pleasant walk in Mānoa (vast) Valley with a steady climb to the top of Tantalus (Pu'u 'Ōhi'a). The short stroll to the falls at the back of the valley is popular with tourists and locals alike, especially on weekends. Few people go beyond the falls because of the long ascent to the ridgetop. Around Tantalus you may see other hikers, as there are several other approaches to the summit.

This hike uses five of the eighteen different trails in the Honolulu *mauka* trail system. Because of the many trails in the area, the route has numerous junctions, which come fast and furiously. Fortunately, all are signed, and most are obvious. Memorize the key junctions for the return trip.

The trails making up this hike are generally well graded, although muddy and rooty in spots. Because of the heavy traffic, the wet and eroded sections of the Mānoa Falls Trail have been improved with gravel, plastic steps, and wooden walkways. The upgraded trail allows you to keep just ahead of the hungry mosquitoes along the stream. The 'Aihualama (eat lama fruit) Trail climbs out of the valley on long, lazy switchbacks to connect with the Pauoa Flats Trail and the route to the Tantalus summit.

The 'Aihualama area has a long and colorful past. The first scene of the grisly Hawaiian legend of Kahalaopuna takes place along 'Aihualama Stream. In 1895, royalist rebels fleeing government forces used an old Hawaiian trail along the stream as an escape route after a skirmish at the back of Mānoa Valley. The royalists had tried to overthrow the recently founded Republic of Hawai'i and return Queen Lili'uokalani to the throne.

In 1919, the Hawaiian Sugar Planters Association (HSPA) established a small station, later known as Lyon Arboretum, in the 'Aihualama area to carry out reforestation projects. For easier access to the *mauka* (inland) section, HSPA crews built a trail that switchbacked up the steep slope to Pauoa Flats. In 1978, volunteers under the direction of the Sierra Club, Hawai'i Chapter, restored the deteriorated arboretum switchbacks and built a new contour route connecting them with the Mānoa Falls Trail.

The falls trail passes several groves of tangled hau trees with large, heart-shaped leaves. Their flowers are bright yellow with a dark red center and resemble those of a hibiscus. Early Hawaiians used the wood for kites and canoe outriggers, the bark for sandals, and the sap as a laxative.

Along the way look and listen for the white-rumped shama. It is black on top with a chestnut-colored breast and a long black-and-white tail. The shama has a variety of beautiful songs and often mimics other birds. A native of Malaysia, the shama has become widespread in introduced forests such as this one.

Mānoa Falls makes a refreshing rest stop or a good turn-around point for novice hikers. Early Hawaiians aptly named the falls Waihī (trickling water). Stay on the viewing platform to lower the risk of being hit by rock falling from the cliffs. If it's late July, you may get some delicious mountain apples ('ōhi'a 'ai) from the grove in front of the falls.

Lining the middle switchbacks of the 'Aihualama Trail are kī (ti) plants. They have shiny leaves, 1–2 feet long that are arranged spirally in a cluster at the tip of a slender stem. Early Polynesian voyagers introduced ti to Hawai'i. They used the leaves for house thatch, skirts, sandals, and raincoats. Food to be cooked in the *imu* (underground oven) was first wrapped in ti leaves. A popular sport with the commoners was *ho'ohe'e kī*, or ti-leaf sledding. The sap from ti plants stained canoes and surfboards.

Near the junction of the Mānoa Cliff and Pu'u 'Ōhi'a Trails, look for the native hibiscus, koki'o ke'oke'o. It is a small tree with dark green, oval leaves. Its large flowers have white petals and pink to red stamens.

To the left of the Hawaiian Telephone access road is a small volcanic crater, mostly hidden by vegetation. An explosive eruption from that crater formed a cinder cone downwind, the summit of Tantalus. Lava from that eruption flowed across the flats and down into upper Pauoa Valley. Both Tantalus and Diamond Head Craters are remnants of the last volcanic activity on O'ahu, called the Honolulu Series.

From the top of Tantalus is a 360-degree view. To leeward you can see Diamond Head (Lē'ahi), Waikīkī (spouting water), Pearl Harbor (Pu'uloa), and, in the distance, the Wai'anae (mullet water) Range. *Mauka* (inland) is Tantalus Crater, and beyond is the Ko'olau (windward) summit. From left to right along the ridge is Pu'u Keahi a Kahoe (hill of Kahoe's fire), Lanihuli (turning royal chief), Nu'uanu Pali (cool height cliff), Kōnāhuanui (large fat testicles), and Olympus (Awāwaloa).

Mauka of the Tantalus summit are several native 'ōhi'a 'āhihi trees, found only on O'ahu. They have narrow, pointed leaves with red stems and midribs. Their delicate red flowers grow in clusters and are similar to those of the more common 'ōhi'a. Queen Lili'uokalani mentioned the 'āhihi lehua (blossom) in her haunting love song, "Aloha 'Oe."

For a shorter hike from the same trailhead, turn right on the Pauoa Flats Trail to the Nu'uanu Valley overlook. For an exciting traverse, combine the 'Aihualama-'Ōhi'a and Nu'uanu-Judd hikes. Go up 'Aihualama to the valley overlook and then down Nu'uanu-Judd. Leave a car at each trailhead or take the bus.

11

'Ualaka'a

TYPE:	Foothill
LENGTH:	1-mile loop
ELEVATION GAIN:	300 feet
DANGER:	Low
SUITABLE FOR:	Novice
LOCATION:	Honolulu Watershed Reserve above Makiki
TOPO MAP:	Honolulu
ACCESS:	Open

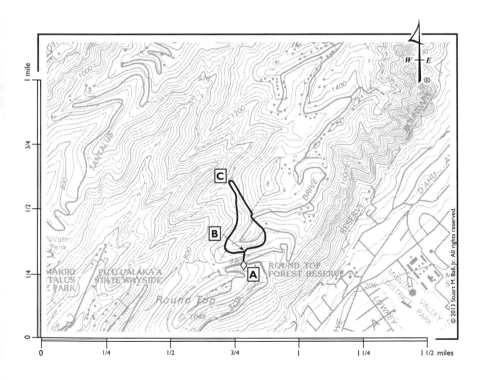

HIGHLIGHTS

This short loop winds through the forest between two volcanic cones. Along the way are banyan tree arches and a lookout over Diamond Head.

TRAILHEAD DIRECTIONS

Get on S. King St. Koko Head bound (east).

Turn left on Ke'eaumoku St.

After going over the freeway, turn right on Wilder Ave.

Take the first left on Makiki St.

After crossing Nehoa St. at the first traffic light, the road forks. Keep right on Round Top Drive.

Ascend gradually around Round Top.

As the road switchbacks right, turn left into Pu'u 'Ualaka'a State Park.

As the entrance road swings left, park in an open area on the right (elevation 940 feet) (map point A). Don't block the nearby private driveway. If the area is full, continue up the paved road to the park and leave your car there. Walk back down the road to the trailhead.

BUS: None within reasonable walking distance of the trailhead.

ROUTE DESCRIPTION

Take the 'Ualaka'a Trail to the right of the parking area.

Climb the hillside on two switchbacks.

Reach a signed junction (map point B). Continue straight on the 'Ualaka'a Trail. (To the left is the return portion of the loop.)

Ascend gradually through tangled hau trees. Look and listen for the white-rumped shama.

Cross Round Top Drive by a small parking area with a concrete trash can.

Continue the gradual climb on one switchback.

Reach a second junction. Keep right toward nearby Round Top Dr. (To the left, a short trail leads to a lookout over lower Mānoa Valley, Waikīkī, and Diamond Head [Lē'ahi].)

Turn right on Round Top Dr. Watch for cars, as this is the most dangerous part of the hike!

Shortly afterward, turn left off the paved road onto the signed Makiki Valley Trail.

Go under a banyan tree arch.

Descend gradually along the flank of Sugarloaf (Pu'u Kākea), a volcanic cone. Notice the black cinders embedded in the slope on the right.

Reach a signed junction by a banyan tree. Continue straight on the Makiki Valley Trail. (On the right, the Moleka Trail climbs to Round Top Dr. and the Mānoa Cliff Trail.)

Reach a signed four-way junction by a bench and a posted trail map (map point C) (UTM 04 0622418E, 2358140N). Turn sharp left onto the 'Ualaka'a Trail. (Slightly left is the Maunalaha Trail, which descends steeply to the Hawai'i Nature Center. To the right, the Makiki Valley Trail continues to Tantalus Dr.)

Contour along the slope past huge banyan trees.

Another banyan tree arch spans the trail.

Cross a double row of Cook pines. Look for macadamia nut trees nearby.

Reach the familiar junction completing the loop (map point B). Turn sharp right and retrace your steps back to the parking area (map point A).

NOTES

'Ualaka'a makes a great family outing. The uncrowded loop is short and shady with minimal elevation change. After the hike, enjoy a picnic at nearby Pu'u 'Ualaka'a State Park.

The two trails making up the loop are wide and graded but have a few rooty and slippery sections. Territorial Forestry constructed the Makiki Valley Trail in 1915 to access the forest reserve from the Tantalus and Round Top roads. Volunteer crews under the direction of the Sierra Club, Hawai'i Chapter, built the 'Ualaka'a Trail during the summer of 1980.

The 'Ualaka'a Trail gets it name from nearby Pu'u 'Ualaka'a (Round Top), a volcanic cone. Several stories exist about the derivation of 'Ualaka'a, which means rolling sweet potato. According to one, King Kamehameha had the hill above Mānoa (vast) Valley planted in sweet potato. When harvested, the potatoes obligingly rolled downslope to be gathered in the valley. Another story involves a rat biting the stem of a potato, which then rolled downhill.

The route initially passes several groves of tangled hau trees with large, heart-shaped leaves. Their flowers are bright yellow with a dark red center and resemble those of a hibiscus. Early Hawaiians used the wood for kites and canoe outriggers, the bark for sandals, and the sap as a laxative.

In the forest, look and listen for the white-rumped shama. It is black on top with a chestnut-colored breast and a long black and white tail. The shama has a variety of beautiful songs and often mimics other birds. A native of Malaysia, the shama has become widespread in introduced forests such as this one.

While contouring around Sugarloaf (Pu'u Kākea), notice the black cinder embedded in the slope to the right. Pu'u Kākea is a cinder cone formed by an eruption during the last volcanic activity on O'ahu, known as the Honolulu Series.

Just after the second banyan tree arch, the route crosses a double row of tall Cook pines, perhaps originally planted as windbreak. The trees are columnar in shape and have overlapping, scalelike leaves about ¼ inch long, rather than true needles. Named after Captain James Cook, the pines are native to New Caledonia's Isle of Pines in the South Pacific, between Fiji and Australia.

12

Makiki-Tantalus

TYPE:	Foothill
LENGTH:	8-mile loop
ELEVATION GAIN:	1,500 feet
DANGER:	Low
SUITABLE FOR:	Novice, Intermediate
LOCATION:	Honolulu Watershed Reserve above Makiki
TOPO MAP:	Honolulu
ACCESS:	Open

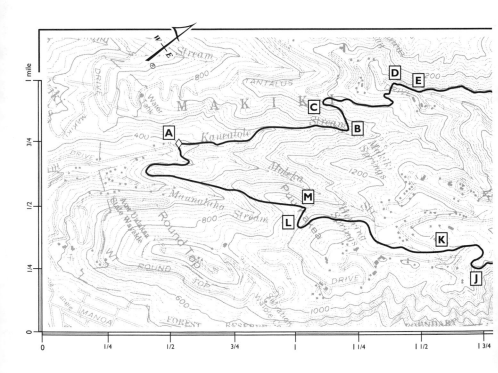

HIGHLIGHTS

This elongated loop hike circles Tantalus (Puʻu ʻŌhiʻa) peak. Along the roundabout route are multiple trail junctions and a surprising variety of native forest plants. From scenic overlooks are views of three valleys and the Koʻolau Range.

TRAILHEAD DIRECTIONS

Get on S. King St. Koko Head bound (east).
  Turn left on Keʻeaumoku St.
  After going over the freeway, turn right on Wilder Ave.
  Take the first left on Makiki St.
  After crossing Nehoa St. at the first traffic light, bear left on Makiki Heights Dr.

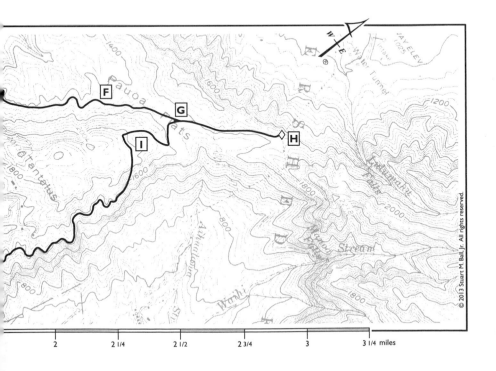

As the road switchbacks to the left, continue straight on an unnamed paved road.

Enter Makiki Forest Recreation Area.

Park in the gravel lot on the left just before a green gate (elevation 360 feet) (map point A).

BUS: Route 4 to Wilder Ave. and Makiki St. Walk 1.0 mile up Makiki St. and Makiki Heights Dr. to the recreation area.

ROUTE DESCRIPTION

Continue along the paved road on foot or take the Makiki Arboretum Trail, which parallels the road.

After passing Hawai'i Nature Center on the right, reach a signed junction. Turn right into a driveway leading to the Kānealole and Maunalaha Trails.

Pass restrooms, a boot cleaning station, and a drinking fountain.

Cross Kānealole Stream on a bridge and turn left upstream on a gravel path. Nearby is a bulletin board with trail information.

Pass several *lo'i* (*kalo* or taro terraces) on the left.

Reach another signed junction by a bench and several Cook pines. Keep left on the Kānealole Trail. (To the right is the Maunalaha Trail, which is the return portion of the loop.)

After crossing a small bridge, pass native and Polynesian introduced plants identified with labels. The trail is graveled and lined with plastic rails.

Cross Kānealole Stream on a second bridge and turn right upstream. (To the left is the Forestry and Wildlife District Office and Baseyard.) Watch for the white-rumped shama.

Ascend gradually next to Kānealole Stream, following a partially buried water pipe.

Pass a stand of bamboo and then tangled hau groves on the right.

Under a kukui tree, reach a signed junction at the end of the Kānealole Trail (map point B). Turn left and up on the Makiki Valley Trail. (To the right, the valley trail crosses the stream and contours to Round Top Dr.)

Climb steadily up a ridge on two switchbacks past huge mango trees.

At the third switchback, reach a signed junction (map point C). Turn sharp right and up on the Nahuina Trail. (The valley trail continues straight, through a large fallen trunk, and eventually reaches Tantalus Dr.)

Contour along the side of the ridge, crossing several gullies.

Climb gradually on four long switchbacks. Kī (ti) plants line the trail, and a native koa tree arches overhead just before the fourth switchback.

At the ridgetop, reach a signed junction at the end of Nahuina Trail (map point D). Turn right on paved Tantalus Dr. Just down the road on the right is a good view of Diamond Head and Waikīkī.

At the end of the stone wall on the left, reach another signed junction (map point E). Bear left off the road onto the Kalāwahine Trail. (The one-lane paved road just to the right of the trail leads up to the top of Tantalus.)

Begin to contour along the flank of Tantalus (Puʻu ʻŌhiʻa), working into and out of numerous gulches. Look and listen for the white-rumped shama in the introduced forest.

Pass a wooden bench on the right and go through native snail habitat marked with signs. Delicate maidenhair ferns cling to the cliff, which is composed of cinder from an eruption of Tantalus.

Farther along is a grove of coffee trees with their shiny leaves.

Reach a signed junction (map point F). Keep left on the Kalāwahine Trail. (The Mānoa Cliff Trail curves right and contours around Tantalus.)

After a brief descent, the path climbs gradually to Pauoa Flats.

In the flats, reach a signed junction at the end of the Kalāwahine Trail (map point G). Turn left on the Pauoa Flats Trail. (The flats trail to the right is the return portion of the loop.)

Almost immediately, reach another signed junction. Continue straight on the flats trail. (To the left, the Nuʻuanu Trail heads down into Nuʻuanu Valley and connects with the Judd Trail.)

In a bamboo grove, reach a third signed junction. Continue straight on the flats trail. (To the right, the ʻAihualama Trail leads down to Mānoa Falls.)

Walk through dark cinnamon trees on a muddy trail.

Reach windy Nuʻuanu Valley overlook (elevation 1,640 feet) (map point H) (UTM 04 0623787E, 2360851N) and a memorial bench. Nearby are some native ʻōhiʻa ʻāhihi trees, their leaves fluttering in the wind.

Retrace your steps past the ʻAihualama and Nuʻuanu junctions to the junction with the Kalāwahine trail (map point G). Now continue straight on the flats trail.

Begin climbing the flank of Tantalus.

Swing left and then switchback right. The trail is lined with fragrant white and yellow ginger and colorful kāhili ginger.

By some native ʻōhiʻa trees, reach a signed junction with a posted trail map (map point I). Bear left onto the Mānoa Cliff Trail and immediately enter a native forest restoration area through a gate in a fence. (To the right, the cliff trail leads back to the Kalāwahine Trail.) On the left, just beyond the gate, is a native kōpiko tree, identified by marker no. 19. On the right, look for a native *Clermontia kakeana* tree with its purple and white tubular flowers.

Reach another signed junction. Continue straight on the cliff trail. (To the right, the Puʻu ʻŌhiʻa Trail leads to the top of Tantalus.)

Leave the restoration area through another gate.

Begin contouring around Tantalus (Puʻu ʻŌhiʻa), working into and out of several small gulches. Underfoot is cinder from the Tantalus eruption. Watch for native māmaki trees and the native white hibiscus, kokiʻo keʻokeʻo.

On the left, pass a viewpoint with a bench and more ʻōhiʻa āhihi trees. At the back of Mānoa Valley you can see two waterfalls. Across the valley along the summit ridge is Mount Olympus (Awāwaloa).

On the right in a grove of bamboo, pass the remains of Mānoa Cliff Bamboo Rest Bench, built in 1987.

The Mānoa Cliff Trail ends at a signed switchback. Turn right and up on the connector trail to Round Top Dr. (map point J).

Ascend briefly to cross a broad ridge through strawberry guava.

Descend into a small gulch and bear left down it. The trail widens and is lined with plastic planks.

Cross paved Round Top Dr. to reach a signed junction at a small parking lot (map point K). Continue straight and down on the Moleka Trail.

Descend gradually through bamboo, paralleling Moleka Stream but well above it. Underfoot are cinders from the eruption of Sugarloaf (Puʻu Kākea).

Climb briefly on two switchbacks up the side of Puʻu Kākea on a narrow trail.

By a banyan tree, reach a signed junction at the end of the Moleka Trail (map point L). Turn right on the wide Makiki Valley Trail. (To the left, the valley trail contours back to Round Top Dr.)

By a posted trail map and a bench, reach a signed junction with the ʻUalakaʻa and Maunalaha trails (map point M). Take the latter by bearing slightly left and down. (The ʻUalakaʻa Trail requires a sharp left and leads to Round Top Dr. To the right, the valley trail contours to Tantalus Dr.)

Descend steeply through eucalyptus, first on the left side of the ridge past trailing asparagus fern and then on its top. The eroded trail is rocky and rooty.

Bear right off the ridgeline by several Cook pines.

Descend the slope on two switchbacks following a line of pines.

At the familiar junction with the bench, turn left and retrace your steps back to the parking lot (map point A).

NOTES

Makiki-Tantalus is a grand sightseeing tour on Oʻahu's best-developed trail network. The hike uses eight of the eighteen different trails in the Honolulu *mauka* trail system. Because of the many trails in the area, the route has numerous junctions, which come fast and furiously. Fortunately, all are signed, and most are obvious. Follow the narrative closely to stay on course.

Maintained by Na Ala Hele, the state trail program, the loop route is generally wide and well graded, although muddy and rooty in spots. On the return, watch your step on the narrow sections of the Moleka Trail. Take your time descending the rocky, rooty Maunalaha (flat mountain) Trail.

The trails making up this hike have a long and varied history. The Kānealole Trail was originally a dirt road laid out in 1906 to facilitate construction of a water main from springs along Kānealole Stream to a reservoir in Makiki. The Kalāwahine (formerly Castle-Olympus) and Mānoa Cliff trails were projects of the fledgling Hawaiian Trail and Mountain Club in 1910–1911. Both were widened and regraded by the Honolulu Unit of the Civilian Conservation Corps in 1935. Territorial Forestry constructed the Makiki Valley Trail and improved the Maunalaha Trail in 1915 to provide easier access for reforestation crews. The Moleka and Nahuina are the newest trails, built by volunteers under the direction of the Sierra Club, Hawaiʻi Chapter, in 1979.

The Mānoa (vast) Cliff Trail also has a long history as a nature trail. In 1936, Territorial Forester Charles S. Judd erected wooden, hand-painted signs identifying forty native shrubs and trees along the route. Since then the signs have been renewed periodically, and the current ones are keyed to an inexpensive pamphlet, *Mānoa Cliff Trail Plant Guide,* available from the Hawaiʻi Nature Center office at the start of the hike.

On the Kānealole Trail, look and listen for the white-rumped shama. It is black on top with a chestnut-colored breast and a long black and white tail. The shama has a variety of beautiful songs and often mimics other birds. A native of Malaysia, the shama has become widespread in introduced forests such as this one.

While contouring around Tantalus (Puʻu ʻŌhiʻa) on the Kalāwahine (day of women) Trail, notice the black cinder underfoot and embedded in the cliff to the right. Tantalus is a cinder cone formed by an eruption from a nearby crater. Both Tantalus and Sugarloaf (Puʻu Kākea) are remnants of the last volcanic activity on Oʻahu, known as the Honolulu Series.

The Kalāwahine Trail passes through native snail habitat. Look carefully for them on both sides of the leaves of nearby shrubs and trees. Do not disturb the snails or allow them to fall to the ground. Years ago, many valleys on Oʻahu had their own species of snail. Now most are gone because of shell collecting, habitat loss, and predation from introduced snails and rats.

From the windy overlook at the end of the Pauoa Flats Trail, you can look down into Nuʻuanu (cool height) Valley with its reservoir. The massive peak across the valley is Lanihuli (turning royal chief). The saddle to the right of Lanihuli is Nuʻuanu Pali (cliff). You can see the windward coast through the gap in the Koʻolau (windward) summit ridge. To the right of the Pali is mist-shrouded Kōnāhuanui (large fat testicles) (elevation 3,105 feet), the highest point in the Koʻolau Range.

Near the overlook are several native ʻōhiʻa ʻāhihi trees found only on Oʻahu. They have narrow, pointed leaves with red stems and midribs. Their delicate red flowers grow in clusters and are similar to those of the more common ʻōhiʻa. Queen Liliʻuokalani mentioned the ʻāhihi lehua (blossom) in her haunting love song, "Aloha ʻOe."

On the return leg of the loop, the Mānoa Cliff Trail passes through a fenced native forest restoration area, perhaps the most sublime section of the entire hike. Within the enclosure, a small group of dedicated volunteers has weeded much of the introduced vegetation, allowing the native species to thrive. Look especially for *Clermontia kakeana,* a small native tree with spindle-shaped leaves clustered at the branch ends and lovely purple and white tubular flowers.

Just past the entrance gate, watch for kōpiko, a native member of the coffee family. It has leathery, oblong leaves with a light green midrib. Turn the leaf over to see a row of tiny holes (*piko* or navel) on either side of the midrib. The kōpiko produces clusters of little white flowers and fleshy, orange fruits.

Other native trees in the restoration area and along the cliff trail are the native hibiscus, kokiʻo keʻokeʻo, and the māmaki. The hibiscus has dark green, oval leaves and large white flowers with pink to red stamens. The showy flowers frequently fall right on the trail. Māmaki has leathery, light green leaves with toothed margins and prominent veins. Along the stems are the white, fleshy fruits. Early Hawaiians used the bark and sap in making *kapa* (bark cloth). They also steeped the leaves to prepare a tea as a tonic.

There are several variations to the route as described. You can, of course, do the hike in the opposite direction if you don't mind reading the narrative in reverse. For a shorter loop, turn right on the Mānoa Cliff Trail to eliminate the extension to the Nuʻuanu Valley overlook. For a mini loop, turn right on the Makiki Valley Trail and then right again on the Maunalaha Trail.

Other hikes in the Makiki-Tantalus area are ʻAihualama-ʻŌhiʻa, ʻUalakaʻa, and Nuʻuanu-Judd.

13

Nu'uanu-Judd

TYPE:	Foothill
LENGTH:	5-mile round-trip
ELEVATION GAIN:	1,000 feet
DANGER:	Low
SUITABLE FOR:	Novice, Intermediate
LOCATION:	Honolulu Watershed Reserve above Nu'uanu
TOPO MAP:	Honolulu
ACCESS:	Open

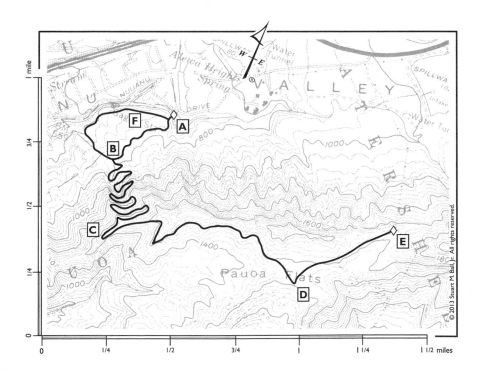

HIGHLIGHTS

This hike combines a valley loop with a ridge climb. At the end is a windy overlook of Nu'uanu Valley and Pali. On the return is lovely Jackass Ginger pool.

TRAILHEAD DIRECTIONS

At Punchbowl St. get on Pali Hwy. (Rte. 61 north) heading up Nu'uanu Valley.

Pass Queen Emma Summer Palace on the right.

Bear right on Nu'uanu Pali Dr.

As the road forks, keep right, still on Nu'uanu Pali Dr.

Cross a side stream on a stone bridge.

Pass Polihiwa Pl. and then several houses on the left.

On the right, look for several low concrete barriers just after a guardrail and before a small bridge spanning a reservoir spillway.

Park off the road before or after the bridge (elevation 720 feet) (map point A).

If you are uneasy about parking at the isolated trailhead, turn right on Kimo Dr. just before Nu'uanu Pali Dr. forks. Cross Nu'uanu Stream on a bridge and park on the street. Walk back across the bridge, turn right on Nu'uanu Pali Dr., and follow the rest of the driving instructions to the trailhead.

BUS: Route 4 to Nu'uanu Pali Dr. and Kimo Dr. Walk 0.7 mile along Nu'uanu Pali Dr. to the trailhead.

ROUTE DESCRIPTION

Go around the barriers and walk across a flat clearing formerly used as a parking lot.

Descend to Nu'uanu Stream through ironwood trees on the signed Judd Trail.

Cross the stream immediately upon reaching it. (Do not take the trail heading downstream along the near bank.)

On the far bank, reach a signed junction in a bamboo grove. Continue straight on the wide trail heading away from the stream. (The trail on the right along the stream is the return leg of the Judd loop.)

Swing right and contour into and out of several small gullies through eucalyptus and Cook pines. Ignore side trails heading upslope or down to the stream.

Enter the Charles S. Judd Memorial Grove of Cook pines.

As the trail descends, bear left into a shallow gully and cross it.

Almost immediately, reach a signed junction (map point B). Turn left and up on the Nu'uanu trail through Cook pines and cinnamon trees. (The Judd loop continues straight downhill and is the route on the return.)

Ascend gradually up the side of Nu'uanu Valley on sixteen switchbacks (count 'em, but don't cut 'em). After the eleventh, leave the Cook pines behind. After the thirteenth, pass a rock cliff dripping with water. After the fifteenth, angle up a short but slippery rock face. Along the trail are kī (ti) plants.

Walk under a banyan tree and reach the top of a ridge (map point C). Turn left along it.

Climb steadily on a wide, grassy trail under native koa and 'ōhi'a trees. On the right across Pauoa Valley is Tantalus (Pu'u 'Ōhi'a), a wooded volcanic cone. On the left are views of Nu'uanu Valley, Honolulu, and, in the distance, the Wai'anae Range. In the canopy, look for two native birds: the yellowish green 'amakihi and the red 'apapane.

At a small clearing by a bench, bear right off the ridgeline.

Contour along the right side of the ridge. Look for bamboo orchids on the high side of the trail.

Cross a side ridge by two large 'ōhi'a trees.

Descend gradually toward Pauoa Flats. The trail widens and becomes rooty as it enters the flats.

Reach a signed junction at the end of the Nu'uanu Trail (map point D). Turn left on the Pauoa Flats Trail. (To the right, the flats trail connects with the Mānoa Cliff Trail.)

In a bamboo grove, reach another signed junction. Keep left on the flats trail. (To the right, the 'Aihualama Trail leads down to Mānoa Falls.)

Walk through dark cinnamon trees on a muddy trail.

Reach windy Nu'uanu Valley overlook and a memorial bench (elevation 1,640 feet) (map point E) (UTM 04 0623787E, 2360851N). Nearby are several native 'ōhi'a 'āhihi trees.

Retrace your steps along the Pauoa Flats and Nu'uanu Trails.

At the junction with the Judd Trail, turn left to complete the loop (map point B).

Descend the ridge in a series of gentle switchbacks. Ignore a side trail on the left.

After emerging from the Cook pines, swing right and cross two gullies with tangled hau groves.

Contour well above Nu'uanu Stream along the edge of the pine grove.

Pass a small rusted stake on the left and almost immediately reach an obscure junction. Turn left on a makeshift trail descending to Jackass Ginger (Kahuailanawai) pool (map point F). (The Judd Trail continues to contour above the stream.)

After a cooling swim, climb back up from the pool and turn left on the main trail heading upstream.

Contour above the stream briefly and then descend to walk alongside it.

Pass a large banyan tree on the far bank and go through a bamboo grove.

Reach the initial junction and stream crossing.

Turn left, recross Nu'uanu Stream, and climb the far bank to the main road (map point A).

NOTES

Most people just take the short Judd loop, go for a swim in Jackass Ginger pool, and call it a day. If you have a little more ambition and stamina, try the less popular Nu'uanu extension up the side of the valley. The views from the ridgetop and the overlook are well worth the climb.

The loop trail gradually developed from routes used by early Hawaiians and planting crews of the Civilian Conservation Corps. Unemployed workers hired by the Territory of Hawai'i completely rebuilt the Judd loop in 1954. Volunteers under the direction of the Sierra Club, Hawai'i Chapter, constructed the contour portion of the Nu'uanu Trail in 1983. The switchback section was completed in 1991 by private and Forestry labor.

Both trails making up this hike are generally well graded although muddy and rooty in spots. The sixteen switchbacks of the Nu'uanu Trail are mostly long and lazy but may contain loose rock underfoot. Numerous side trails can make the Judd loop difficult to follow, especially on the return along the stream. If you lose the official trail, keep heading upstream until you reach the initial crossing by the bamboo grove. Watch your step crossing the stream and watch your backside for marauding mosquitoes.

On the initial section of the Judd loop is a large grove of Cook pines. They have overlapping, scalelike leaves about ¼ inch long, rather than true needles. Named after Captain James Cook, the pines are native to New Caledonia's Isle of Pines in the South Pacific, between Fiji and Australia. The grove and the loop trail are named after Charles S. Judd, the territorial forester during the 1930s when the pines were planted.

On top of the ridge, look back into lower Nu'uanu Valley, the site of a pivotal battle in Hawaiian history. In 1795 Kamehameha, chief of the Big Island, invaded O'ahu, landing a large force at Wai'alae and Waikīkī. Opposing him was an army entrenched below Pūowaina (Punchbowl) under the direction of Kalanikūpule, the son of Kahekili, a Maui chief who had earlier occupied O'ahu. The invaders attacked and overran the fortified positions, forcing the O'ahu warriors to retreat up Nu'uanu Valley. A pivotal holding action took place at Pū'iwa (startled) near the present Judd St., where the defenders were protected by a long rock wall. The battle was hotly contested until the invaders brought up a field cannon and trained sharpshooters. The fire from the cannon shattered rocks in the wall, and the sharpshooters killed a key commander. The startled O'ahu warriors broke ranks and retreated up the valley, closely pursued by the attackers. Gradually the retreat turned into a rout. Some defenders escaped up the sides of the valley. Most, including Kalanikūpule, made a last stand at Nu'uanu Pali and were killed or driven over the cliff there. With the victory, Kamehameha extended his control over all the Hawaiian Islands except Kaua'i.

Along the ridgetop, watch for the 'amakihi, the most common native forest bird on O'ahu. It is yellowish green with a slightly curved gray bill and feeds on nectar, fruits, and insects. If the native 'ōhi'a trees are in bloom, you may also catch a glimpse of an 'apapane in the forest canopy. It has a red breast and head, black wings and tail, and a slightly curved black bill. In flight, the 'apapane makes a whirring sound as it darts from tree to tree searching for nectar and insects.

From the windy viewpoint at the end you can look down into Nu'uanu (cool height) Valley with its reservoir. The massive peak across the valley is Lanihuli (turning royal chief). The saddle to the right of Lanihuli is Nu'uanu Pali (cliff). You can see the windward coast through the gap in the Ko'olau (windward) summit ridge. To the right of the Pali is mist-shrouded Kōnāhuanui (large fat testicles) (elevation 3,105 feet), the highest point in the Ko'olau Range.

Near the overlook are 'ōhi'a 'āhihi trees found only on O'ahu. They have narrow, pointed leaves with red stems and midribs. Their delicate red flowers grow in clusters and are similar to those of the more common 'ōhi'a. Queen Lili'uokalani mentioned the 'āhihi lehua (blossom) in her haunting love song, "Aloha 'Oe."

On the way back, stop for a swim at lovely Jackass Ginger pool. Its original name may have been Kahuailanawai (tranquil water), as the stream tumbles over rapids into a deep, placid swimming hole. In the early 1900s, local youths renamed the pool after a nearby donkey and the surrounding yellow ginger.

For an exciting traverse, combine the Nu'uanu-Judd and 'Aihualama hikes. Go up Nu'uanu to the valley overlook and then down 'Aihualama past Mānoa (vast) Falls. Leave a car at each trailhead or take the bus.

14

Kamanaiki

TYPE:	Ungraded ridge
LENGTH:	5-mile round-trip
ELEVATION GAIN:	1,400 feet
DANGER:	Low
SUITABLE FOR:	Novice, Intermediate
LOCATION:	Honolulu Watershed Forest Reserve above Kalihi
TOPO MAP:	Honolulu
ACCESS:	Open

HIGHLIGHTS

This hike climbs partway up the ridge on the right side of Kalihi Valley. From lookouts en route and at the end are scenic views of the valley and the Koʻolau summit ridge. Along the way is a surprising variety of native plants.

TRAILHEAD DIRECTIONS

At Punchbowl St. get on Lunalilo Fwy. (H-1) heading ʻEwa (west).

Take Likelike Hwy. (exit 20A, Rte. 63 north) up Kalihi Valley.

At the sixth traffic light, turn right on Nalaniʻeha St. by the pedestrian overpass.

Cross Kalihi Stream on a bridge.

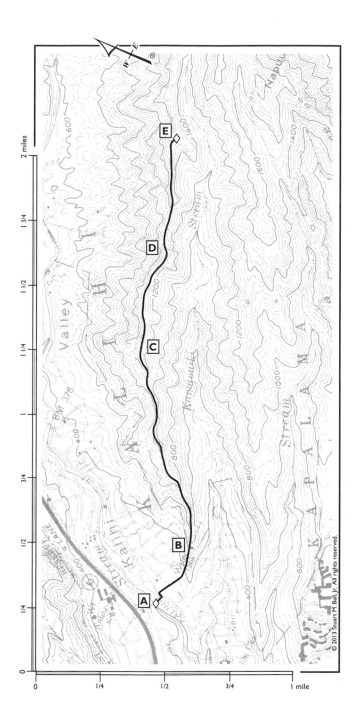

Park on the street near the intersection with Kalihi St. (elevation 240 feet) (map point A).

BUS: Route 7 to Kalihi St. and Nalaniʻeha St.

ROUTE DESCRIPTION

At the end of Nalaniʻeha St., turn left on Kalihi St. by the Kalihi Uka pumping station.

Almost immediately, turn right on Manaiki Pl.

Take the concrete stairway at the road's end. The stairway starts just to the left of a utility pole and house no. 1801.

Climb steeply up the stairs to the ridgeline.

Bear left on a trail heading up the ridge through an ironwood grove. Lining the route are small kolomona trees with bright yellow flowers.

Ascend two more flights of stairs to a water tank (map point B).

Keep the tank on the left and continue up the ridge under ironwoods.

Break out into the open briefly through scattered Formosa koa trees and then climb steeply over a hill.

Ascend through a stand of tall Sydney blue gum to a second prominent hill along the ridge.

Emerge from the introduced forest into a grassy area dotted with native koa and ʻōhiʻa trees.

Reach a small, eroded knob with good views up and down Kalihi Valley (map point C).

Traverse a narrow windswept section with Christmas berry trees.

Reach a second, less distinct knob by several rose apple trees.

Continue along the ridge past a small ironwood grove to another viewpoint (map point D). Look for maile, a native twining shrub.

Traverse another windswept section on a sometimes narrow trail. Among the 'ōhi'a and strawberry guava trees is the native herb ko'oko'olau.

Climb steadily to a flat-topped hill covered with guava. A cable or rope may provide some assistance on the steepest section. On the far side of the hill are several 'iliahi (sandalwood) trees.

Ascend gradually through strawberry guava and scratchy uluhe ferns. Look for the native shrub naupaka kuahiwi.

Pass a tall ironwood tree on the left.

Shortly afterward, reach a grassy clearing on top of a broad hill (elevation 1,560 feet) (map point E) (UTM 04 0620925E, 2362414N). On the right, an obscure trail leads down a side ridge to Kamanaiki Stream. On the left are commanding views of the back of Kalihi Valley and the Ko'olau summit.

NOTES

This hike climbs partway up the ridge between Kalihi (the edge) and Kamanaiki (the small branch) valleys. The route provides a good introduction to the pleasures and pitfalls of ungraded ridge hiking on O'ahu—superb views and intriguing native plants but also steep climbs and narrow sections. The only real negative is the noise from vehicles on Likelike Hwy. below.

The route up the ridge is straightforward and easy to follow. The ungraded trail, however, has several stiff climbs and a few narrow spots. Some sections may be overgrown with introduced shrubs, such as ōwī (Jamaica vervain) and lantana, and bristly native uluhe ferns. Watch your step, as the vegetation can hide steep drop-offs. Novices should hike as far as feels comfortable and then turn around.

The hike initially ascends through introduced forest. Easily recognized is Sydney blue gum, which has smooth bark with blue-gray patches and very narrow, pointed leaves.

The tree is a member of the eucalyptus family and a native of
Queensland, Australia. Workers from the Civilian Conservation Corps probably planted the grove to reforest the ridge in
1934.

As the introduced forest gives way to native koa and 'ōhi'a
trees, look for the 'amakihi, the most common native forest
bird on O'ahu. It is yellowish green with a slightly curved gray
bill and feeds on nectar, fruits, and insects.

After the first viewpoint, watch for two native shrubs,
maile and ko'oko'olau. Maile has shiny, pointed leaves, tangled
branches, and fruit resembling a small olive. The fragrant leaves
and bark have been used to make distinctive open-ended lei
in both ancient and modern Hawai'i. Ko'oko'olau is an herb
related to the daisy and sunflower families. It has pointed, serrated leaves and flower heads with yellow petals. Early Hawaiians steeped the leaves to make a tea used as a tonic.

Just past the flat-topped hill are a few native 'iliahi (sandalwood) trees. Their small leaves are dull green and appear
wilted. 'Iliahi is partially parasitic, with outgrowths on its
roots that steal nutrients from nearby plants. Early Hawaiians
ground the fragrant heartwood into a powder to perfume their
kapa (bark cloth). Beginning in the late 1700s, sandalwood
was indiscriminately cut down and exported to China to make
incense and furniture. The trade ended around 1840 when the
forests were depleted of 'iliahi.

In the final stretch is the native shrub naupaka kuahiwi.
It has light green, toothed leaves and white half-flowers.
The unusual appearance of the flowers has given rise to several unhappy legends. According to one, a Hawaiian maiden
believed her lover unfaithful. In anger she tore all the naupaka
flowers in half. She then asked him to find a whole flower to
prove his love. He was, of course, unsuccessful and died of a
broken heart.

From the viewpoints along the ridge you can look down
into two valleys: Kamanaiki on the right and Kalihi on the left.

Mauka the Koʻolau (windward) summit ridge rises abruptly in the back of Kalihi Valley. Along the top are the peaks of Puʻu Kahuauli (dark site hill) on the left and massive Lanihuli (turning royal chief) in front. To leeward you can see west Honolulu and the ʻEwa (crooked) Plain.

15

Bowman

TYPE:	Ungraded ridge
LENGTH:	12-mile round-trip
ELEVATION GAIN:	2,400 feet
DANGER:	Medium
SUITABLE FOR:	Intermediate, Expert
LOCATION:	Honolulu Watershed Forest Reserve above Fort Shafter
TOPO MAP:	Honolulu, Kāneʻohe
ACCESS:	Open

HIGHLIGHTS

This very strenuous hike climbs to the Koʻolau summit from Kalihi Valley. Along the sometimes narrow ridge are incredible views and interesting native plants. Near the top is a hair-raising scramble up the flank of a volcanic cone.

TRAILHEAD DIRECTIONS

At Punchbowl St. get on Lunalilo Fwy. (H-1) heading ʻEwa (west).

Take Likelike Hwy. (exit 20A, Rte. 63 north) up Kalihi Valley.

At the sixth traffic light and by the pedestrian overpass, turn left on Nalaniʻeha St.

At its end, turn left on Kula Kōlea Dr.

At the next intersection, turn right on Naʻai St.

Park on the street near its end (elevation 320 feet) (map point A).

BUS: Route 7 to Kalihi St. and Nalani'eha St. Walk 0.5 mile along Nalani'eha St. to Likelike Hwy. and the trailhead.

ROUTE DESCRIPTION

Continue along Na'ai St. on foot.

At its end by Kalihi Elementary School, turn left on Hālina St.

Just before the road ends at a water tank, turn right into the school playing field and head for the basketball court.

Just before reaching the black and white backboard, turn left up a rock ledge on a makeshift trail (map point B).

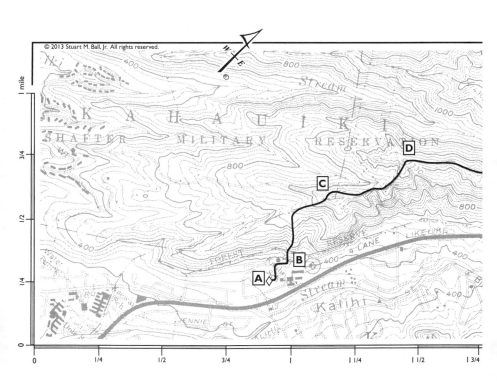

Pass a low retaining wall on the left.

Ascend straight up toward a utility pole.

At the pole, bear left and contour briefly.

Resume steep climbing, first through an open grassy area and then through mixed ironwood and Christmas berry trees. The native shrub ʻūlei carpets the ground in the sunny sections, and lauʻae ferns cover the shady areas.

The trail levels off somewhat through an ironwood grove.

Cross an open grassy area.

The trail ends at a junction with a dirt road. Turn right on the road and memorize the junction for the return trip.

Climb steeply on the road, following some utility lines.

At the crest of the ridge, reach a junction with Radar Hill Rd. (map point C). Bear slightly right and downhill on it. (To the left, the road is partly paved and leads down to Fort Shafter.)

The dirt road skirts a hump in the ridge, dips, and then climbs steeply to the left.

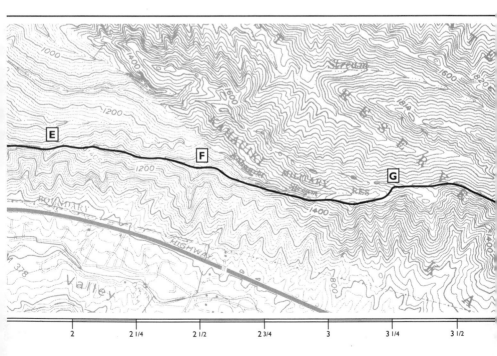

At the ridgetop, reach a junction (map point D). Turn right on the Bowman Trail. (The road swings left and down past a wooden utility pole.)

Almost immediately, pass a small concrete building on your right.

Pass United States Military Reservation (USMR) marker no. 22 on the left.

Keep left while descending briefly through an ironwood grove.

Enter a long stretch of guava (waiawī) trees. Moss lines the trail.

At the top of a hill, reach an opening that provides a view of the entire ridge to be climbed. On the right is the base of USMR marker no. 21.

Descend briefly and cross a level section through mixed introduced forest.

Climb briefly to a knob with two rocks on top (map point E).

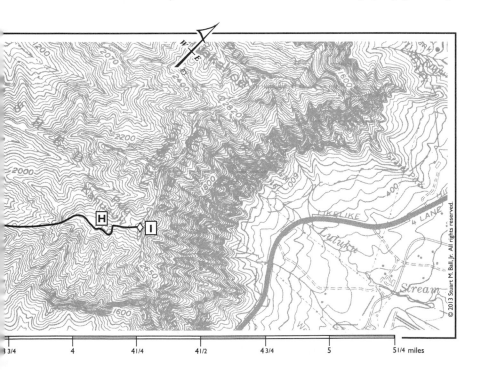

3 3/4   4   4 1/4   4 1/2   4 3/4   5   5 1/4 miles

Pass two large banyan trees on the left.

Walk under a lovely canopy of native lama trees between two small humps in the ridge.

Enter the native rain forest, dominated by koa and 'ōhi'a trees. In the understory are naupaka kuahiwi shrubs and uluhe ferns.

Cross a level section through uluhe.

Ascend gradually to a hill with a banyan tree on the left. Marker no. 20 is on the right (map point F). There are good views up Kalihi Valley toward the Ko'olau summit.

Come abreast of the last house in Kalihi Valley.

Traverse a series of short, steep ascents and descents.

Cross a narrow but level section, inching to the right of a rock face.

Ascend steeply, perhaps with the aid of a cable.

Shortly afterward, pass marker no. 18 on your left in an ironwood grove.

Climb gradually to marker no. 17 at the top of a hill.

Walk through a relatively level section lined with native hāpu'u tree ferns and 'ie'ie. Overhead arch huge koa trees.

Reach the head of Kahauiki Valley. Keep right and up along the ridge.

Descend briefly and then climb steeply through uluhe.

Reach the junction of the two ridges forming the head of Kahauiki Valley (map point G). Bear right to continue to the Ko'olau summit.

Begin climbing gradually toward Pu'u Kahuauli. Along the summit ridge to the right are the peaks of Lanihuli and Kōnāhuanui. Look for the native trees kōpiko and 'ōhi'a with yellow blossoms.

After a steep ascent, reach a junction under a spreading koa tree. Continue straight along the main ridge on the grassy trail. (The faint trail on the prominent side ridge to the right leads down to Likelike Hwy.)

Bear right to contour around a distinctive hump in the ridge.

Once past the hump, turn sharp left up the ridge.

Climb the steep side of Kamanaiki cone, perhaps with the assistance of a cable.

Bear left across the precipitous face of the cone on a narrow, slippery trail (map point H).

Switchback once and resume steep climbing. Cables may be provided for the worst sections.

The ridge broadens and the angle of ascent eases. Take in the panoramic leeward view. You can see the top of Diamond Head (Lēʻahi), downtown Honolulu, and Pearl Harbor (Puʻuloa). In the distance is the Waiʻanae Range.

The muddy trail winds through stunted ʻōhiʻa trees. Watch for the native shrub pūʻahanui (kanawao) with its creased and toothed leaves.

Climb a small, grassy gully with exposed rock on the right.

At the end of the gully, turn right along the ridge.

Bear left, following the ridge. Look for the native tree ʻōlapa with its fluttering leaves.

Reach the Koʻolau summit at Puʻu Kahuauli (elevation 2,740 feet) (map point I) (UTM 04 0621935E, 2365244N).

NOTES

Bowman is the most difficult of the ungraded ridge trails in the Koʻolau (windward) Range. The hike starts with a stiff climb, follows a narrow up-and-down ridge, and culminates in the spectacular ascent of the Kamanaiki cone. The only detraction is the noise from vehicles on Likelike Highway below.

The trail dates from World War I, when the U.S. Army mobilized the Hawaiʻi National Guard. A guard regiment, renamed the First Hawaiian Infantry, was stationed at Fort Shafter in 1918. The next year the soldiers opened up a ridge route *mauka* (inland) of the fort to the Koʻolau summit for training and recreational purposes. The trail was named after guard member and post commandant Lieutenant Colonel Donald S. Bowman.

Start early to avoid the hot sun on the initial climb to the Bowman Trail. Walk gingerly through the narrow, crumbly sections along the ridge. Overgrowing vegetation may mask some dangerous spots. On the final climb, test all cables before using them. Turn around if you don't feel comfortable with the exposure.

On the Bowman Trail past the guavas (waiawī), look for the lama tree, a remnant of the native dryland forest. Lama has oblong, pointed leaves that are dark green and leathery. Its fruits are green, then yellow, and finally bright red when fully ripe. Lama was sacred to Laka, goddess of the hula. Early Hawaiians used the hard, light colored wood in temple construction and in hula performances.

Farther along the ridge begins the native rain forest, dominated by koa and ʻōhiʻa trees. Koa has sickle-shaped foliage and pale yellow flower clusters. Early Hawaiians made surfboards and outrigger canoe hulls out of the beautiful red-brown wood. Today it is made into fine furniture. ʻŌhiʻa has oval leaves and clusters of delicate red flowers. Early Hawaiians used the flowers in lei and the wood in outrigger canoes. The hard, durable wood was also carved into god images for *heiau* (religious sites).

In the forest canopy, watch for the ʻamakihi, the most common native forest bird on Oʻahu. It is yellowish green with a slightly curved gray bill and feeds on nectar, fruits, and insects. If the ʻōhiʻa are in bloom, you may glimpse the scarce ʻapapane. It has a red breast and head, black wings and tail, and a slightly curved black bill. In flight, the ʻapapane makes a whirring sound as it darts from tree to tree searching for insects and nectar.

Before the final climb, look for kōpiko, a native member of the coffee family. It has leathery, oblong leaves with a light green midrib. Turn the leaf over to see a row of tiny holes (*piko* or navel) on either side of the midrib. The kōpiko produces clusters of little white flowers and fleshy, orange fruits.

The steep, sometimes cabled section climbs Kamanaiki cone, a remnant of the last volcanic activity on Oʻahu, known as the Honolulu Series. During the eruption, lava poured from the cinder cone down both sides of the ridge into Kalihi and Manaiki Valleys.

After climbing the cone, calm down by looking for the native shrub pūʻahanui (kanawao), a relative of hydrangea. It has large, serrated, deeply creased leaves and clusters of delicate pink flowers. Early Hawaiians used the plants for medicinal purposes.

Near the summit is the native tree ʻōlapa. Its leaves are opposite and oblong, and flutter in the slightest wind. In a special hula stance named after the tree, dancers mimic the exquisite movements of the leaves. Early Hawaiians used the bark, leaves, and purple fruit to make a blue-black dye to decorate their *kapa* (bark cloth).

The view from the top is world class or no class, depending on the weather. On a clear day, you can see the windward coast from Kāneʻohe (bamboo husband) Bay to Makapuʻu (bulging eye) Point. Over 2,000 feet below are Hoʻomaluhia Botanical Garden, with its lake, and Kāneʻohe town. The mist-shrouded peak along the summit to the left is Puʻu Keahi a Kahoe (hill of Kahoe's fire). To the right, across Kalihi (the edge) Valley, is massive Lanihuli (turning royal chief). In the distance on the right is triple-peaked Olomana (forked hill).

For a more challenging outing, combine the Bowman and Puʻu Keahi a Kahoe hikes. From Bowman, turn left along the Koʻolau summit ridge and then descend either side of the Keahi a Kahoe loop. The summit connector is for experienced hikers only, as it is narrow, overgrown, and frequently socked in.

Alternate access to Bowman is available through Fort Shafter on Radar Hill Rd. However, you must get written permission from the army. See the Schofield-Waikāne hike for their address.

16

Pu'u Keahi
a Kahoe

TYPE:	Ungraded ridge
LENGTH:	11-mile loop
ELEVATION GAIN:	2,600 feet
DANGER:	High
SUITABLE FOR:	Intermediate, Expert
LOCATION:	Honolulu Watershed Forest Reserve above Moanalua
TOPO MAP:	Kāne'ohe
ACCESS:	Open

HIGHLIGHTS

Pu'u Keahi a Kahoe is the mist-shrouded peak in back of Kamananui (Moanalua) Valley. This challenging climb to its summit features narrow, windswept ridges and sheer cliffs. Along the loop are lofty lookouts and a rich variety of native trees and shrubs.

TRAILHEAD DIRECTIONS

At Punchbowl St. get on Lunalilo Fwy. (H-1) heading 'Ewa (west).

Near Middle St. keep left on Moanalua Fwy. (H-201) to 'Aiea. Take the exit marked Moanalua Valley–Red Hill.

From the off-ramp, turn right on Ala Aolani St. heading into Moanalua Valley.

The road ends at Moanalua Valley Park. The park has restrooms and drinking water.

Park on the street just before the park entrance (elevation 240 feet) (map point A).

BUS: Route 16 to Ala Aolani and Ala Lani Streets on weekday mornings and afternoons only. Walk 0.4 mile along Ala Aolani St. to the park.

ROUTE DESCRIPTION

Enter Moanalua Valley Park and proceed along Kamananui Valley Road, the one-lane dirt/gravel track at the back of the parking lot.

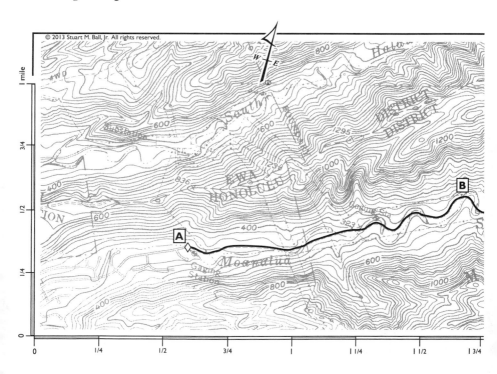

Walk around a locked green gate.

On your left by a huge monkeypod tree, pass a muddy driveway leading to the Douglas Damon house site (marker no. 3 and sign).

Cross Kamananui Stream seven times on stone bridges. Look and listen for the white-rumped shama in the introduced forest.

On the right under a mango tree at the seventh crossing is Pōhakukaluahine, a large boulder covered with petroglyphs (map point B) (marker no. 10 and sign).

Around the bend from the petroglyph rock and before the next stream crossing, reach a junction (marker no. 11). Continue straight on the dirt road. (To the right, a short loop trail leads up to the May Damon house site.)

Ford the stream four times. Along the stream are kukui trees and tangled groves of hau.

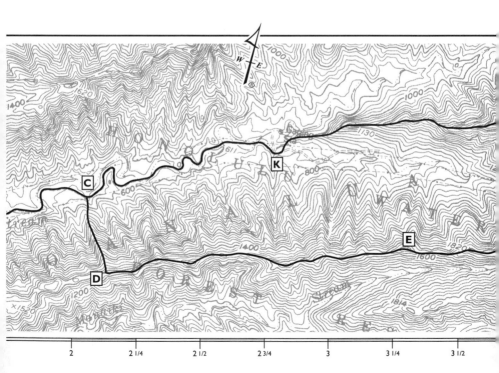

The road gradually climbs, passing a more open, grassy area on the right.

As the road levels off by a low, eroded embankment, reach a junction just past marker no. 12 (map point C). Turn right onto a trail through yellow strawberry guava (waiwī lena) and native koa trees.

Shortly afterward, bear right through grass and uluhe ferns.

Turn left into a guava grove.

Bear right and up beside a large patch of uluhe.

Angle left across the patch and begin ascending steadily up a side ridge.

The ridge becomes rocky, rooty, and better defined. Look for native lama and alahe'e trees among the guava.

Just past a huge native 'iliahi (sandalwood) tree, bear right off the ridge to bypass another rock face.

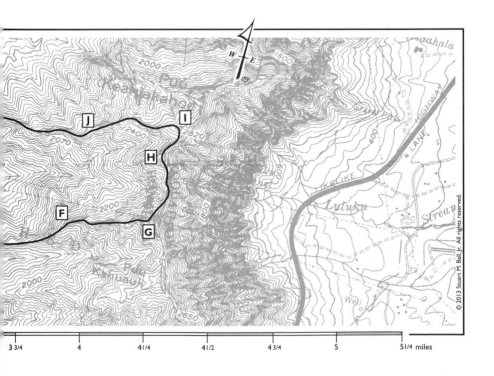

Scramble back left to the narrow ridgeline and continue the steep climbing through guava.

At the ridgetop, reach a junction with the Tripler (Kauakaulani) Ridge Trail (map point D). Turn left on it. (To the right, the trail heads down the main ridge to a U.S. Army housing area above Tripler Medical Center.)

Traverse a relatively gentle, moss-lined section through strawberry guava.

Climb gradually over a series of small humps in the ridge. The guava reluctantly gives way to a native forest of koa and ʻōhiʻa trees. In the understory are the native shrubs pūkiawe and naupaka kuahiwi and the native lily ʻukuʻuki. Watch for the native birds ʻamakihi and ʻapapane.

Crawl under a huge downed koa.

Cross a short grassy section above a small landslide, now growing over.

Climb steadily to a large knob (map point E). On its backside is a small, grassy clearing with a good view of the remaining route up Tripler Ridge, across the summit, and down Keanaakamanō, the middle ridge. Listen for the Japanese bush warbler.

Descend steeply on an eroded trail and then ascend gradually to a second large knob with a view of a large landslide *mauka* (inland). Gnarled koa trunks and branches span the trail.

Descend briefly and resume climbing past the landslide on the left. Look for native maile shrubs and kōpiko and ʻōhiʻa ʻāhihi trees along the trail.

Reach the top of a broad knob and a junction marked by a downed koa tree. Continue straight on the main ridge. (To the left, a steep trail leads down a side ridge to the end of Kamananui Road.)

Negotiate a particularly steep, narrow section.

Reach a junction just before a small flat clearing marked by a metal pipe (map point F). Continue straight along the main ridge. (To the left, an old Hawaiian Electric access route, known informally as the power-line trail, descends into Kamananui Valley.)

As the vegetation hunkers down, climb steeply to a false summit.

Cross a short level stretch and then ascend gradually over several small humps. Along the trail are native kūkaemoa (alani) and pūʻahanui (kanawao) shrubs.

Reach the Koʻolau summit at a flat, grassy knob (elevation 2,760 feet) (map point G) (UTM 04 0621771E, 2365589N).

Turn left along the summit, passing a power-line tower.

Descend steeply on the narrow ridge. Look for native lapa-lapa trees.

Cross a level section marked by several metal posts.

Reach a junction where the posts diverge. Keep left and up, following the red posts. Native ʻōhelo shrubs with their red berries cling to the cliff.

Pass a lone metal rod on the left.

Bear left around the embankment on the far side of another power-line tower. Native loulu palms loom out of the mist.

Climb steeply past a Hawaiian Electric microwave antenna with a fiberglass cover.

Reach the top of Kahoʻomoeʻihikapulani peak (map point H) and descend its backside, still on the summit ridge.

Traverse a relatively level but extremely narrow and rough section. Watch for the native shrub ohe naupaka with its yellow, tube-shaped flowers.

Ascend very steeply on grass, keeping to the edge of the ridge.

Reach the flat summit of Maunakapu (elevation 2,820 feet) (map point I) (UTM 04 0621815E, 2366190N) with its benchmark.

There the trail splits. Take the left fork heading down Keanaakamanō, the middle ridge of Kamananui Valley. (The right fork continues a short distance along the summit ridge to the top of Puʻu Keahi a Kahoe and the Haʻikū Stairs.)

The ridge narrows and is severely windswept.

The ridge widens briefly (map point J). Keep to the left to avoid going down a side ridge.

Descend steeply, bear right, and then descend very steeply.

The ridge alternately widens and contracts. Watch out for narrow spots hidden by vegetation.

Pass a small landslide on the right.

Descend steeply and then climb past a rock outcrop.

Resume the descent through huge koa trees and strawberry guava thickets.

Pass a large native ʻiliahi (sandalwood) tree on the right.

Swing right and then left through uluhe ferns and more guava.

Cross Moanalua Stream to reach a junction with the dirt road (map point K). Turn right on the road. (To the left, the road leads to the start of the power-line trail.)

Almost immediately, reach a junction marked by two boulders on the right. Continue straight on the road. (To the right is the stream trail, which is part of the Kamananui Valley hike.)

Ford the stream six times.

Pass a wide vehicle turnaround area (marker no. 13). On the left, a trail leads up to an overlook of the entire valley.

Reach the original junction by marker no. 12 (map point C).

Follow the road back to Moanalua Valley Park (map point A).

NOTES

Puʻu Keahi a Kahoe is the mist-shrouded peak in back of Kamananui (Moanalua) Valley. The demanding climb to its summit starts and finishes with a pleasant stroll in the valley. In between is a walk on the wild side. If you are an experienced hiker, try the entire loop and find out why it's known as a "wow" hike.

Keahi a Kahoe more than lives up to its expert rating. The trails making up the loop are steep, narrow, and unimproved. The upper sections are slippery, windswept, and frequently socked in. Watch your footing constantly, whether over rock, roots, or mud. Some trail sections may be overgrown with *Clidemia* shrubs and scratchy uluhe ferns. The vegetation can mask narrow spots, making them doubly dangerous.

Puʻu Keahi a Kahoe means the hill of Kahoe's fire. In ancient times, two brothers left their parents and settled on the windward side. Pahu was a fisherman and lived near Kāneʻohe Bay. Kahoe was a *kalo* (taro) farmer in Haʻikū (sharp break) Valley. The two often traded gifts and poi for fish. Stingy Pahu, however, always gave Kahoe the leftover baitfish, rather than the fresh catch. Kahoe eventually learned of his brother's deceit from their sister.

Soon afterward the crops failed, and the fish mysteriously disappeared. Those with some food took to cooking at night to conceal the smoke from their hungry neighbors. Kahoe continued to cook during the day because the smoke from his *imu* (underground oven) appeared only at the very top of the *pali* (cliff) near a pointed peak. Starving Pahu knew the smoke was from *keahi a* Kahoe but did not dare approach his brother for food.

Along the road, look and listen for the white-rumped shama. It is black on top with a chestnut-colored breast and a long black and white tail. The shama has a variety of beautiful songs and often mimics other birds. A native of Malaysia, the shama has become widespread in introduced forests such as this one. Until the 1920s, the owners grazed cattle in the valley, resulting in the destruction of much of the original native vegetation.

Once on Tripler (Kauakaulani) Ridge past the long stretch of guava, look for kōpiko and ʻōhiʻa āhihi trees. Kōpiko is a native member of the coffee family. It has leathery, oblong leaves with a light green midrib. Turn the leaf over to see a row of tiny holes (*piko* or navel) on either side of the midrib. The kōpiko produces clusters of little white flowers and fleshy, orange fruits.

Found only on Oʻahu, ʻōhiʻa ʻāhihi have narrow, pointed leaves with red stems and midribs. Their delicate red flowers grow in clusters and are similar to those of the more common 'ōhi'a. Queen Lili'uokalani mentioned the 'āhihi lehua (blossom) in her haunting love song, "Aloha 'Oe."

Also along the ridge, listen for the Japanese bush warbler (uguisu), a bird often heard but rarely seen. Its distinctive cry starts with a long whistle and then winds down in a series of notes. The bush warbler is olive brown on top with a white breast and a long tail.

More readily seen is the 'amakihi, the most common native forest bird on O'ahu. It is yellowish green with a slightly curved gray bill and feeds on nectar, fruits, and insects. If the native 'ōhi'a trees are in bloom, you may also catch a glimpse of an 'apapane in the forest canopy. It has a red breast and head, black wings and tail, and a slightly curved black bill. In flight, the 'apapane makes a whirring sound as it darts from tree to tree searching for nectar and insects.

Closer to the Ko'olau (windward) summit are the native shrubs pū'ahanui (kanawao) and kūkaemoa (alani). Pū'ahanui, a relative of hydrangea, has large, serrated, deeply creased leaves and clusters of delicate pink flowers. Kūkaemoa (chicken dung) shrubs have curled, dark green leaves, which give off a slight anise odor. The fruits resemble miniature cauliflowers or chicken droppings.

If the weather cooperates, the views all along the summit ridge are spectacular. Over 2,000 feet straight down are Kāne'ohe town and Ho'omaluhia Botanical Garden. You can see the windward coast from Kāne'ohe (bamboo husband) to Waimānalo (potable water) bays. The triple-peaked mountain on the right is Olomana (forked hill). On the way down, the whole of Kamananui Valley spreads out in front of you. In the distance are Pearl Harbor (Pu'uloa) and the Wai'anae (mullet water) Range.

The native plants along the summit are as intriguing as the views are spectacular. Look for lapalapa trees, loulu palms, and 'ohe naupaka shrubs. Lapalapa has roundish leaves arranged in groups of three that flutter in the slightest wind. Early

Hawaiians used the bark, leaves, and purple fruit to make a blue-black dye to decorate their *kapa* (bark cloth). The leaves also make a distinctive lei.

Loulu palms have rigid, fan-shaped fronds in a cluster at the top of a ringed trunk. Early Hawaiians used the fronds for thatch and plaited the blades of young fronds into fans and baskets. 'Ohe naupaka has narrow, pointed leaves growing in clumps at the end of the branches. The distinctive tube-shaped flowers are bright yellow-orange.

There are several variations to the loop as described. You can, of course, do the complete hike in reverse. Intermediates can try either side of the loop and then return the same way. The steep power-line trail near the end of Kamananui Valley Road provides alternate access to Tripler Ridge. The route starts on the left just before the dirt road crosses the stream and ends at a vehicle turnaround.

For a more challenging loop, combine the Pu'u Keahi a Kahoe and Bowman hikes. At the top of Tripler Ridge, turn right along the Ko'olau summit and then descend Bowman. The summit connector is for experienced hikers only, as it is narrow, overgrown, and frequently socked in. For a less difficult outing, try the Kamananui (Moanalua) Valley hike that starts from the same trailhead. The notes section of that hike describes some of the signed and numbered points of interest in the valley.

17

Kamananui
(Moanalua) Valley

TYPE:	Valley
LENGTH:	11-mile round-trip
ELEVATION GAIN:	1,500 feet
DANGER:	Low
SUITABLE FOR:	Novice, Intermediate
LOCATION:	Honolulu Watershed Forest Reserve above Moanalua
TOPO MAP:	Kāneʻohe
ACCESS:	Open

HIGHLIGHTS

This classic stream hike winds through a lovely valley rich in historical sites and legends. Along the way are a small swimming hole, a boulder covered with petroglyphs, and over forty stream crossings. Near the end, a short climb leads to a windward overlook on the Koʻolau summit ridge.

TRAILHEAD DIRECTIONS

At Punchbowl St. get on Lunalilo Fwy. (H-1) heading ʻEwa (west).

Near Middle St. keep left on Moanalua Fwy. (H-201) to ʻAiea.

Take the exit marked Moanalua Valley–Red Hill.

From the off-ramp, turn right on Ala Aolani St. heading into Moanalua Valley.

The road ends at Moanalua Valley Park. The park has restrooms and drinking water.

Park on the street just before the park entrance (elevation 240 feet) (map point A).

BUS: Route 16 to Ala Aolani and Ala Lani Streets on weekday mornings and afternoons only. Walk 0.4 mile along Ala Aolani St. to the park.

ROUTE DESCRIPTION

Enter Moanalua Valley Park and proceed along Kamananui Valley Road, the one-lane dirt/gravel track at the back of the parking lot.

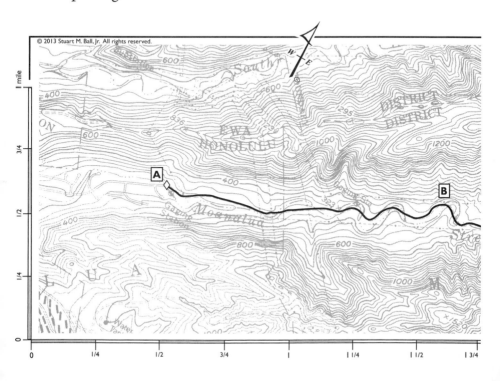

Walk around a locked green gate.

On your left by a huge monkeypod tree, pass a muddy driveway leading to the Douglas Damon house site (marker no. 3 and sign).

Cross Kamananui Stream seven times on stone bridges. The original cobblestones of the old carriage road remain intact on the bridge approaches at the fifth crossing. Look and listen for the white-rumped shama in the introduced forest.

On the right under a mango tree at the seventh crossing is Pōhakukaluahine, a large boulder covered with petroglyphs (map point B) (marker no. 10 and sign).

Around the bend from the petroglyph rock and before the next stream crossing, reach a junction (marker no. 11). Continue straight on the dirt road. (To the right a short loop trail leads up to the May Damon house site and a view up the valley.)

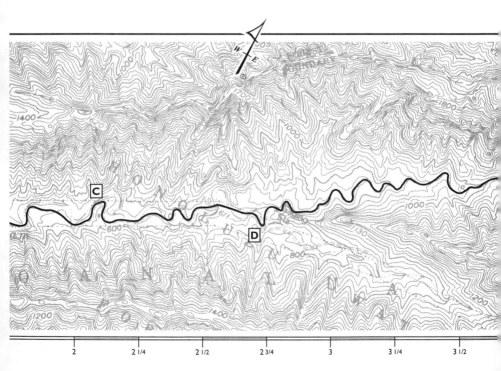

Ford the stream four times. Along the stream are kukui trees and tangled groves of hau.

Reach an obscure junction by marker no. 12 in a grove of strawberry guava. Continue straight on the dirt road. (To the right, a steep route climbs out of the valley to Kauakaulani Ridge above Tripler Hospital.)

Ascend gradually to a wide vehicle turnaround area (map point C). On the right, a short trail leads up to another overlook of the entire valley.

Cross the stream six more times.

After the sixth ford and as the road curves right, look for two boulders on the left and a large koa tree on the right.

Just past the second boulder, reach a signed junction. Turn left off the road onto Kulana'ahane Trail (map point D). (The road continues to the back of the valley.)

Cross the right fork of Kamananui Stream immediately, climb the embankment, and turn left again.

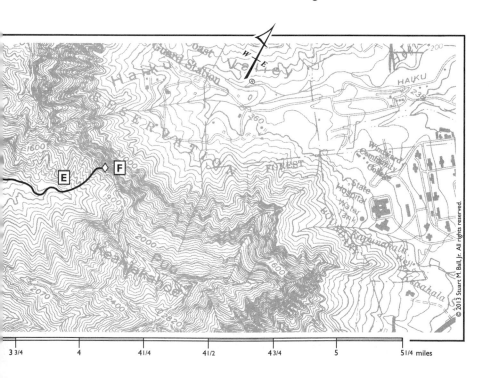

Under a hau tangle, skirt the foot of Keanaakamanō, the middle ridge, which divides the valley into two drainages.

Pass a stream gaging station on the left.

The trail gradually ascends to the head of the valley while fording the left fork of Kamananui Stream twenty-three times.

Just before the second crossing, reach an obscure junction. Keep right and ford the stream. (To the left, the Godek-Jaskulski route ascends the valley wall to the ridgeline above Red Hill.)

After the sixth crossing is a small but delightful pool on the left and another petroglyph rock on the right. Look and listen for the ʻelepaio, an endangered native bird.

Starting at the seventh ford is a series of dense hau groves. Turn sharp right under the hau to reach the eighth crossing and turn sharp right again just after the ninth crossing. Keep your head down!

After the eighteenth crossing is a short open stretch with native hapuʻu tree ferns on the right and a lone native loulu palm on the left. Along the stream, watch for wreckage from a plane crash farther up the valley.

After the nineteenth ford, go over the foot of a small side ridge and around an old Hawaiian house site.

Walk under another hau tangle around the twentieth crossing.

After the twenty-first ford, cross an intermittent side stream.

The stream splits in two. The trail generally hugs the main (left) channel on the island created by the two braids. Lining the route are Chinese ground orchids, which bloom in winter.

The twenty-third ford with a tiny pool and waterfall is a good rest stop before the final climb.

Between the twenty-third and twenty-fourth crossings is a grove of ʻōhiʻa ʻāhihi trees.

At the twenty-fifth crossing, reach an End of Maintained Trail sign. Bear left and up on a rough route that leaves the stream for good (map point E). Listen for the Japanese bush warbler.

Climb steeply up a spur ridge through uluhe ferns and ʻōhiʻa ʻāhihi trees. To the right is a waterfall chute at the head of the stream.

Reach the Koʻolau summit at a saddle with an overlook of Haʻikū Valley (elevation 1,660 feet) (map point F) (UTM 04 0621001E, 2366818N). On the left behind an End of Trail sign, an ʻōhiʻa ʻāhihi and a citrus tree provide some shade.

NOTES

Kamananui (Moanalua) Valley is a classic combination hike that includes a valley stroll, a stream walk, and a ridge climb. Along the valley road are some historical sites. By the stream is a delightful, small swimming hole. At the ridgetop are native plants and windward views. What more could you want?

Interpretive signs and numbered wooden posts mark points of interest along the road. In 1884, Bernice Pauahi Bishop willed the entire *ahupuaʻa* (land division) of Moanalua (two camps) to her husband's business partner, Samuel M. Damon. His son, Douglas, built a luxurious mountain house (marker no. 3) in the valley, which was originally known as Kamananui (great spiritual power). A cobbled carriage road crossed seven ornate bridges and ended at the house of his daughter, May Damon (marker no. 11). For a detailed explanation of those and other sites, pick up the booklet *A Walk into the Past* from Moanalua Gardens Foundation, whose address is listed in the appendix.

Along the road, look and listen for the white-rumped shama. The bird is black on top with a chestnut-colored breast and a long black and white tail. The shama has a variety of beautiful songs and often mimics other birds. A native of Malaysia, the shama has become widespread in introduced forests such as this one. Until the 1920s the owners grazed cattle in the valley, resulting in the destruction of much of the original native vegetation.

At marker no. 10 is Pōhakukaluahine (rock of the old woman), a sacred boulder covered with ancient petroglyphs. Most of the carvings are human stick figures, although a few resemble bird-men. Also on the boulder are a *kōnane* game board and a winding groove suggesting Kamananui Stream.

Pōhakukaluahine received its name from an old story. Many years ago, a small child cried during the consecration of a *heiau* (religious site) in the lower valley. As such an offense to the gods was punishable by death, the grandmother rushed up the valley with the child and hid behind a large boulder. The *mana* (supernatural power) of the rock protected the two from the pursuing warriors. When the noise *kapu* (taboo) was lifted, the grandmother returned the child safely to its parents.

After the vehicle turnaround, start counting stream crossings to home in on the junction with the trail. After the sixth ford, look for the twin boulders and the trail sign on the left. On the trail, watch your footing while rock hopping across the stream. If necessary, slosh through the water. Your boots are eventually going to get wet anyway. As always, do not ford the stream if the water gets much above your knees. Finally, look out for a few wayward mosquitoes.

The stream trail frequently tunnels through tangled hau trees with large, heart-shaped leaves. Their flowers are bright yellow with a dark red center and resemble those of a hibiscus. Early Hawaiians used the wood for kites and canoe outriggers, the bark for sandals, and the sap as a laxative.

While walking along the stream, watch for the ʻelepaio, a small native bird. It is brown on top and white underneath with a black throat and a dark tail, usually cocked. The bird roams the forest understory catching insects on the fly or on vegetation. ʻElepaio are territorial and very curious, which is why you can sometimes see them.

After the last hau tangle, look for the Chinese ground or nun's orchid in winter. Its lovely flowers have tapered petals, which are white on the outside and reddish brown within. The lowest petal is a cream-colored tube with purple marking.

Toward the back of the valley, listen for the Japanese bush warbler (uguisu), a bird often heard but rarely seen. Its distinctive cry starts with a long whistle and then winds down in a series of notes. The bush warbler is olive brown on top with a white breast and a long tail.

On the climb to the saddle, the trail is lined with native ʻōhiʻa ʻāhihi trees found only on Oʻahu. They have narrow, pointed leaves with red stems and midribs. Their delicate red flowers grow in clusters and are similar to those of the more common ʻōhiʻa. Queen Liliʻuokalani mentioned the ʻāhihi lehua (blossom) in her haunting love song, "Aloha ʻOe."

From the saddle along the Koʻolau (windward) summit, the *pali* (cliff) drops straight down into Haʻikū (sharp break) Valley, where the H-3 Freeway runs. The long side ridges enclosing the valley constrict the view somewhat, but you can still see Kāneʻohe (bamboo husband) Bay extending to Mōkapu (taboo district) Peninsula. On the steep side ridge to the right are the Haʻikū Stairs, climbing to a small radar installation on top of Puʻu Keahi a Kahoe (hill of Kahoe's fire).

A short side trip leads to the site of a plane crash on September 2, 1948. To get there, leave the trail at the last stream crossing (no. 23) and walk up the streambed. At a fork, keep right, following the main channel. The wreckage of an F-47N Thunderbolt is strewn along the stream just below an intermittent waterfall with a shallow pool at it base. The Hawaiʻi Air National Guard pilot parachuted to safety from his disabled fighter, whose engine had caught fire. He then hiked out of the valley and was picked up at Moanalua Golf Course.

For a more difficult outing, try the Puʻu Keahi a Kahoe hike that starts from the same trailhead. The route loops along the Koʻolau summit and then descends Keanaakamanō, the middle ridge of Kamananui Valley.

CENTRAL OʻAHU

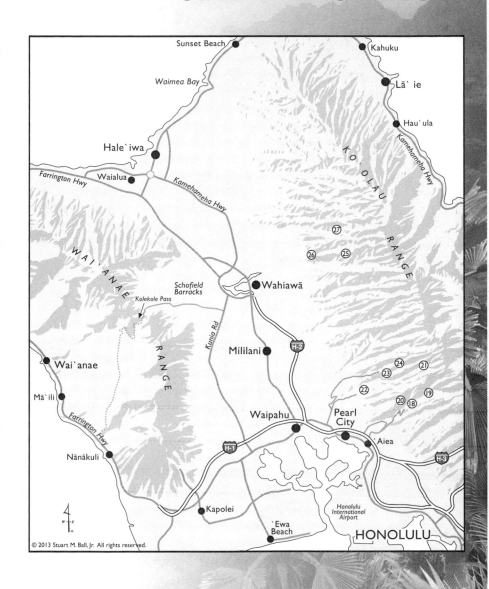

18

'Aiea Loop

TYPE:	Foothill
LENGTH:	5-mile loop
ELEVATION GAIN:	900 feet
DANGER:	Low
SUITABLE FOR:	Novice
LOCATION:	Keaīwa Heiau State Recreation Area above 'Aiea
TOPO MAP:	Waipahu, Kāne'ohe
ACCESS:	Open

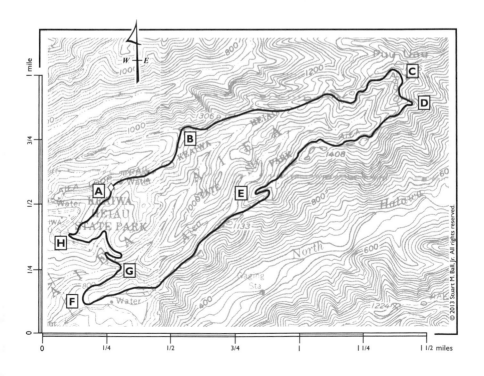

HIGHLIGHTS

This short, pleasant hike winds through the foothills of the
Koʻolau Range. Along the trail are native trees and the site
of a plane crash. Nearby is Keaīwa Heiau, an early Hawaiian
medicine center.

TRAILHEAD DIRECTIONS

At Punchbowl St. get on Lunalilo Fwy. (H-1) heading ʻEwa
(west).

Near Middle St. keep left on Moanalua Fwy. (H-201) to
ʻAiea.

While descending Red Hill, take the exit marked
Hālawa-Stadium.

At the end of the long off-ramp, continue straight on
Ulunē St.

At the road's end, turn right on ʻAiea Heights Dr.

At the first traffic light by the Hawaiʻi Research Center
building, turn left, still on ʻAiea Heights Dr.

Pass ʻAiea High School on the left.

Climb gradually through ʻAiea Heights subdivision.

Reach the entrance to Keaīwa Heiau State Recreation
Area.

Drive past the *heiau* and the camping area to the upper lot
and park there (elevation 1,080 feet) (map point A). At the
trailhead are restrooms and drinking water.

BUS: Route 11 to ʻAiea Heights Dr. and Kaʻamilo St. Walk
2.0 miles along ʻAiea Heights Dr. and through the recreation
area to the trailhead. Route 74 goes farther up ʻAiea Heights
Dr. to Hoapono Pl., but it runs only on weekday mornings and
afternoons.

ROUTE DESCRIPTION

At the back of the upper lot, take the 'Aiea Loop Trail. On the right, look for a plaque honoring the World War II airmen who lost their lives in a plane crash near the return leg of the loop.

Pass a small water tank on the right.

Enter a grove of tall Sydney blue gum trees.

Cross an open, rooty area. On the right is a view of the top of Diamond Head (Lē'ahi) and Honolulu in the distance.

Pass a power-line tower above and to the right. Strawberry guava trees line the trail. Look and listen for the white-rumped shama.

Shortly afterward, reach a junction (map point B). Continue straight on the loop trail. (The side trail to the left leads down to Kalauao Stream and is described in the Kalauao hike.)

Pass a second power-line tower on the left.

Contour on the right side of the ridge. Look for native koa trees below the trail.

Reach a small grassy clearing with a bench. From there is a good view of the Wai'anae Range in the distance. The flat-topped mountain is Ka'ala, the highest point on O'ahu at 4,025 feet.

Continue contouring well below the ridgeline through groves of introduced paperbark and swamp mahogany.

Pass a stand of bamboo down and on the left. Just before the bamboo are several native 'iliahi (sandalwood) trees on the right.

After a long stretch, the trail curves right and climbs over a small landslide. Carved into the cliff above the landslide are some recent graffiti.

Right after the landslide, the trail swings left.

As it begins to curve right again, reach another junction (map point C). Continue on the wide loop trail to the right.

(On the left is the 'Aiea Ridge Trail, which leads to the Ko'olau summit.)

Cross over to the left side of the ridge. You can see the Ko'olau Range through native koa and 'ōhi'a trees. Look for alahe'e, a small native tree with shiny, dark green leaves.

Reach the farthest point of the loop by a large 'ōhi'a tree with exposed roots and a bench (elevation 1,480 feet) (map point D) (UTM 04 0615903E, 2367217N). Around the 'ōhi'a are several 'iliahi trees. Watch for the 'amakihi, a yellowish green native bird.

Along the first part of the return leg are views of North Hālawa Valley and the H-3 Freeway on the left.

Walk under a shady mango tree and then switch to the right side of the ridge.

Descend gradually, well below the ridgeline, through groves of Sydney blue gum.

The trail briefly regains the ridgeline twice.

After stepping down and over a eucalyptus trunk, look for the partially obscured wing section of a B-24J Army Air Corps bomber in the gully on the right. A steep, overgrown trail leads to other wreckage farther down the gully. The gully is marked by two kī (ti) plants near the trail.

Pass a power-line tower above and to the left (map point E) and then a second one after crossing a shallow gully.

Stroll through a grove of Cook pines on a broad trail.

Reach a junction. Keep right on the contour trail. (The eroded trail to the left climbs to a view of Honolulu and Salt Lake.)

Walk under some power lines and through another grove of Cook pines.

As the trail narrows briefly, reach another junction in a stand of white-barked paraserianthes (albizia) trees (map point F). Keep right on the main trail. (The left fork leads to Camp Smith.)

Switchback once and descend into a lush gulch. Look for kukui trees and yellow ginger there.

Cross intermittent 'Aiea Stream (map point G) and climb out of the gulch on a rocky, rooty trail with two switchbacks.

Switchback once again and pass a power-line tower on the left.

The trail levels off and enters the camping area of the park (map point H).

Turn right and climb the steps to the middle parking lot.

Turn right again and walk up the paved road to the upper parking lot (map point A).

NOTES

'Aiea Loop is a very popular novice hike, as the route is reasonably short, mostly shady, and quite scenic. It seems as though everyone who has ever hiked on O'ahu has done the loop. To avoid the crowds, go on a weekday or start early. Many people just walk partway, so the return portion is often less traveled.

The Honolulu Unit of the Civilian Conservation Corps (CCC) built the graded trail in just over three months during 1935. CCC planting crews then reforested the surrounding area with eucalyptus and other introduced trees. Subsequent maintenance has kept the loop wide and well graded for the most part. The only rough section is the short climb out of the gulch near the end of the hike. Watch out for other trail users, such as runners, mountain bikers, and wayward mosquitoes.

An inexpensive interpretive pamphlet, *'Aiea Loop Trail and Kea̅iwa Heiau: Field Site Guide,* is available from Moanalua Gardens Foundation. If possible, pick one up at the foundation office before starting the hike. The address is in the appendix.

After the first viewpoint, the trail is lined with strawberry guava trees (waiawī 'ula'ula). They have glossy, dark green leaves and smooth brown bark. Their dark red fruit is delicious, with a taste reminiscent of strawberries. The guavas usually ripen in August and September. Pickings are slim along the loop trail, however, because of its popularity. The strawberry guava is a native of Brazil but was introduced to Hawai'i from England in the 1800s.

In the forest, look and listen for the white-rumped shama. It is black on top with a chestnut-colored breast and a long black and white tail. The shama has a variety of beautiful songs and often mimics other birds. A native of Malaysia, the shama has become widespread in introduced forests such as this one.

Shortly after the ridge trail junction is a short but lovely stretch of native 'ōhi'a, koa, and alahe'e trees. 'Ōhi'a has oval leaves and clusters of delicate red flowers. Early Hawaiians used the flowers in lei and the wood in outrigger canoes. The hard, durable wood was also carved into god images for *heiau* (religious sites). Koa has sickle-shaped foliage and pale yellow flower clusters. Early Hawaiians made surfboards and outrigger canoe hulls out of the beautiful red-brown wood. Today it is made into fine furniture. Alahe'e has oblong leaves that are shiny and dark green. Its fragrant white flowers grow in clusters at the branch tips. Early Hawaiians fashioned the hard wood into farming tools and hooks and spears for fishing.

At the farthest point of the loop, spend a few moments admiring the nearby native 'iliahi (sandalwood) trees and, perhaps, 'amakihi, a native forest bird. 'Iliahi has small leaves that are dull green and appear wilted. It is partially parasitic, with outgrowths on its roots that steal nutrients from nearby plants. Early Hawaiians ground the fragrant heartwood into a powder to perfume their *kapa*. Beginning in the late 1700s, sandalwood was indiscriminately cut down and exported to China to make incense and furniture, eventually depleting the forest of the tree. The 'amakihi is the most common native forest bird on O'ahu. It is yellowish green with a slightly curved gray bill and feeds on nectar, fruits, and insects.

In a gully on the return leg is a wing section and other wreckage of a Consolidated B-24J Army Air Corps bomber, which crashed on May 5, 1944. Bound for Australia, the aircraft took off from Hickam Field early that morning, failed to make the right turn toward the ocean, and plowed into the wooded ridge above 'Aiea Gulch. A plaque at the trailhead honors the airmen who died in the crash.

In the gulch just above 'Aiea Stream is a grove of kukui trees. Their large, pale green leaves resemble those of the maple with several distinct lobes. Early Polynesian voyagers introduced kukui into Hawai'i. They used the wood to make gunwales and seats for their outrigger canoes. The flowers and sap became medicines to treat a variety of ailments. Early Hawaiians strung the nuts together to make *lei hua* (seed or nut garlands). The oily kernels became house candles and torches for night spearfishing.

After completing the loop hike, stop at Keaīwa (mysterious) Heiau on the way out. The ancient site is a *heiau ho'ōla*, or medical center. There *kāhuna lapa'au* (healers) treated patients with herbs from the surrounding gardens. The *heiau* was probably built in the 1500s and was rededicated in 1951.

The hike is described clockwise. You can, of course, take all or part of the loop in either direction. For a valley walk, take the Kalauao hike that starts from the same trailhead. For a longer, tougher outing, try the 'Aiea Ridge hike that follows the loop partway and then heads to the summit of the Ko'olau (windward) Range.

19

'Aiea Ridge

TYPE:	Ungraded ridge
LENGTH:	11-mile round-trip
ELEVATION GAIN:	1,800 feet
DANGER:	Low
SUITABLE FOR:	Novice, Intermediate, Expert
LOCATION:	Keaīwa Heiau State Recreation Area and 'Ewa Forest Reserve above 'Aiea
TOPO MAP:	Waipahu, Kāne'ohe
ACCESS:	Open

HIGHLIGHTS

This long, wonderful hike follows a mostly open, windswept ridge to the Ko'olau summit. Along the route is an amazing assemblage of native forest plants and some native birds. On the final climb and at the top are magnificent leeward and windward views.

TRAILHEAD DIRECTIONS

At Punchbowl St. get on Lunalilo Fwy. (H-1) heading 'Ewa (west).

Near Middle St. keep left on Moanalua Fwy. (H-2) to 'Aiea.

While descending Red Hill, take the exit marked Hālawa-Stadium.

At the end of the long off-ramp, continue straight on Ulunē St.

At the road's end, turn right on 'Aiea Heights Dr.

At the first traffic light by the Hawai'i Research Center building, turn left, still on 'Aiea Heights Dr.

Pass 'Aiea High School on the left.

Climb gradually through 'Aiea Heights subdivision.

Reach the entrance to Keaīwa Heiau State Recreation Area.

Drive past the *heiau* and the camping area to the upper lot and park there (elevation 1,080 feet) (map point A). At the trailhead are restrooms and drinking water.

BUS: Route 11 to 'Aiea Heights Dr. and Ka'amilo St. Walk 2.0 miles along 'Aiea Heights Dr. and through the recreation area to the trailhead. Route 74 goes farther up 'Aiea Heights Dr. to Hoapono Pl., but it runs only on weekday mornings and afternoons.

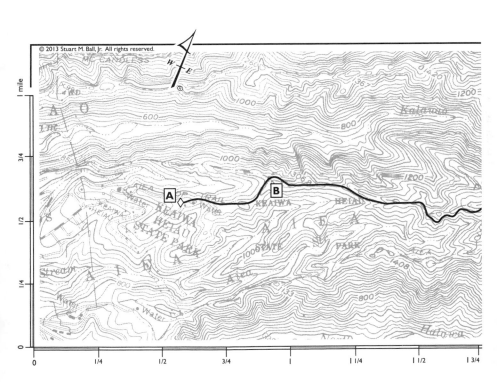

ROUTE DESCRIPTION

At the back of the upper lot, take the 'Aiea Loop Trail.

Pass a small water tank on the right.

Enter a grove of tall Sydney blue gum trees.

Cross an open, rooty area. On the right is a view of the top of Diamond Head (Lē'ahi) and Honolulu in the distance.

Pass a power-line tower above and to the right. Strawberry guava trees line the trail.

Shortly afterward, reach a junction (map point B). Continue straight on the loop trail. (The side trail to the left leads down to Kalauao Stream and is described in the Kalauao hike.)

Pass a second power-line tower on the left.

Contour on the right side of the ridge.

Reach a small grassy clearing with a bench. From there is a good view of the Wai'anae Range in the distance.

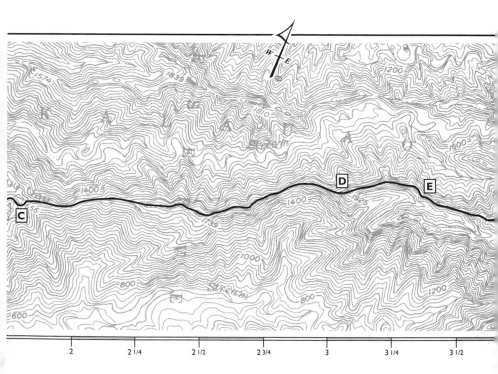

Continue contouring well below the ridgeline through groves of introduced paperbark and swamp mahogany.

Pass a stand of bamboo down and on the left.

After a long stretch, the trail curves right and climbs over a rocky landslide. Carved into the cliff above the landslide are some recent graffiti.

Right after the landslide, the trail swings left.

As it begins to curve right again, reach another junction (map point C). Turn left and up on the 'Aiea Ridge Trail. (The loop trail swings right, descends gradually, and then switches to the left side of the ridge.)

Shortly afterward, turn left at the edge of the ridge.

Almost immediately, go around to the right of Pu'u 'U'au, a large hill on the ridge. Ignore the side trail on the left, which is the return portion of the extended Kalauao loop.

Regain the ridgeline and traverse a relatively level but rooty

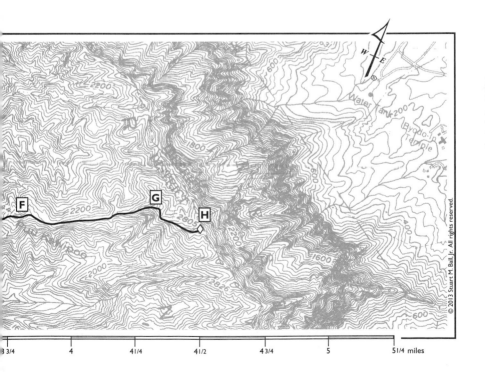

section under native koa and 'ōhi'a trees. Along the trail are native alahe'e trees.

Ascend gradually over several gentle hills through more open forest. Look and listen for the Japanese bush warbler and the native 'apapane and 'amakihi. Watch for a few native 'iliahi (sandalwood) trees.

Contour along the right side of the ridge for a short distance.

The trail bears left and then descends briefly but steeply.

Traverse a lush, more narrow section past native hāpu'u tree ferns and maile shrubs.

Climb gradually, skirting to the left of a large hill (map point D).

Cross a partially open, level stretch through native kōpiko trees. From a small clearing is a magnificent view *mauka* (inland) to the Ko'olau summit.

Descend to a saddle in the ridge (map point E).

Begin the long, gradual climb to Pu'u Kaiwipo'o, the large peak looming ahead.

Pass a small clearing on the right with good views leeward. Look for orange and yellow blossoms on the 'ōhi'a trees nearby.

After a stiff ascent, reach the top of Kaiwipo'o with its magnificent 360-degree view (elevation 2,441 feet) (map point F).

Descend off Kaiwipo'o and then climb gradually over a series of small humps toward the summit. The ridge is open, windswept, and at times narrow. Look for the native shrubs naupaka kuahiwi and pū'ahanui (kanawao).

On the left, reach a flat grassy overlook with a view of the windward side (map point G) (UTM 04 0619555E, 2369138N).

Turn right and down, still on the main ridge, toward a power-line tower. Along the trail are native manono shrubs.

Bear left around the base of the tower.

Climb steadily along the ridge, which levels off near the top.

Reach the Ko'olau summit (elevation 2,805 feet) (map point H) (UTM 04 0619870E, 2369119N) and a sweeping view of the windward coast. Behind the overlook is a native lapalapa tree.

NOTES

'Aiea Ridge offers something for everyone except water babies. The hike starts with a pleasant stroll and ends with a wild climb along an open, windswept ridge. In between are intriguing native plants and a chance at glimpsing some native birds. Go as far as you want and then turn around. The only negatives are the power-line tower near the top and the noise from the H-3 Freeway below.

This hike features two vastly different trails, both worked on by the Civilian Conservation Corps (CCC). The popular 'Aiea Loop Trail was constructed in 1935 to CCC standards— wide and well graded. Deemed a secondary trail, the little-used ridge route received only a minor upgrade in 1936. CCC crews cleared the entire path but only built graded sections around some of the humps in the ridge. The result is a rough, mostly up-and-down trail with a few contour portions. The first half may be overgrown with scratchy uluhe ferns and *Clidemia* shrubs. Watch out especially for narrow sections hidden by vegetation.

On the ridge trail, look for native alahe'e trees and maile shrubs. Alahe'e has shiny, oblong, dark green leaves. Its fragrant white flowers grow in clusters at the branch tips. Early Hawaiians fashioned the hard wood into farming tools and hooks and spears for fishing. Maile has glossy, pointed leaves, tangled branches, and fruit resembling a small olive. The fragrant leaves and bark have been used to make distinctive open-ended lei in both ancient and modern Hawai'i.

Throughout the hike, listen for the Japanese bush warbler (uguisu), a bird often heard but rarely seen. Its distinctive cry starts with a long whistle and then winds down in a series of notes. The bush warbler is olive brown on top with a white breast and a long tail.

More readily seen is the 'amakihi, the most common native forest bird on O'ahu. It is yellowish green with a slightly curved gray bill and feeds on nectar, fruits, and insects. If the native 'ōhi'a trees are in bloom, you may also catch a glimpse of an 'apapane in the forest canopy. It has a red breast and head, black wings and tail, and a slightly curved black bill. In flight, the 'apapane makes a whirring sound as it darts from tree to tree searching for nectar and insects.

Along the gently rolling ridge section are a few 'iliahi (sandalwood) trees. Their small leaves are dull green and appear wilted. 'Iliahi is partially parasitic, with outgrowths on its roots that steal nutrients from nearby plants. Early Hawaiians ground the fragrant heartwood into a powder to perfume their *kapa* (bark cloth). Beginning in the late 1700s, sandalwood was indiscriminately cut down and exported to China to make incense and furniture. The trade ended around 1840 when the forests were depleted of 'iliahi.

In the level stretch before the saddle, look for kōpiko, a native member of the coffee family. The small tree has leathery, oblong leaves with a light green midrib. Turn the leaf over to see a row of tiny holes (*piko* or navel) on either side of the midrib. The kōpiko produces clusters of little white flowers and fleshy, orange fruits.

Take a well-deserved break on top of Pu'u Kaiwipo'o (the skull) and look at the panoramic view. To leeward are Pearl Harbor (Pu'uloa) and the Wahiawā (place of noise) plain. In the distance is the Wai'anae (mullet water) Range with the prominent peaks of Pu'u Kaua (war hill) and Ka'ala (the fragrance), the highest point on O'ahu at 4,025 feet. *Mauka* is the imposing Ko'olau (windward) summit ridge. Along the ridge to the left is flat-topped 'Eleao (plant louse), and to the right, pointed Pu'u Keahi a Kahoe (hill of Kahoe's fire) with a small radar installation on top. Ahead the trail climbs toward a power-line tower.

On the final climb are two more native shrubs, pū'ahanui (kanawao) and ko'oko'olau. Pū'ahanui, a relative of hydrangea, has large, serrated, deeply creased leaves and clusters of delicate pink flowers. Early Hawaiians used the plants for medicinal purposes. The herb ko'oko'olau is related to the daisy and sunflower families. It has pointed, serrated leaves and flower heads with yellow petals. Early Hawaiians steeped the leaves to make a tea used as a tonic.

If you have run out of steam, the wide, grassy overlook makes a good stopping point. For a larger windward view, however, continue to the Ko'olau summit. From there you can see Kāne'ohe (bamboo husband) Bay from Kualoa (long back) to Mōkapu (taboo district) points. In the bay are Mokoli'i (Chinaman's Hat) and Moku o Lo'e (Coconut) Islands. Along the shore are Kahalu'u (diving place) and He'eia fishponds. The pyramid peak on the left is Pu'u 'Ōhulehule (joining of waves hill).

Near the summit overlook is a native lapalapa tree. Its roundish leaves are arranged in groups of three and flutter in the slightest wind. Early Hawaiians used the bark, leaves, and purple fruit to make a blue-black dye to decorate their *kapa.* The leaves also make a distinctive lei.

The 'Aiea Loop and Kalauao hikes also start from the same trailhead. Try the loop hike before taking the 'Aiea Ridge hike. That way you can find the key, unmarked junction with the ridge trail ahead of time. The Kalauao (multitude of clouds) hike descends to the valley of the same name on the left.

20

Kalauao

TYPE:	Valley
LENGTH:	4-mile round-trip
ELEVATION GAIN:	700 feet
DANGER:	Low
SUITABLE FOR:	Novice, Intermediate
LOCATION:	Keaīwa Heiau State Recreation Area and 'Ewa Forest Reserve above 'Aiea
TOPO MAP:	Waipahu, Kāne'ohe
ACCESS:	Open

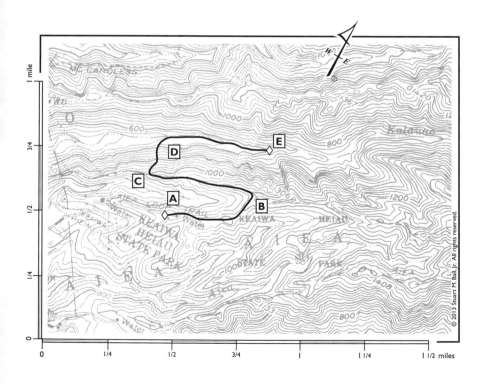

HIGHLIGHTS

A steep descent from a popular trail leads to a lovely, un-crowded valley. Upstream are noisy rapids, quiet pools, and mountain apples. The hike ends at a delightful waterfall with a swimming hole.

TRAILHEAD DIRECTIONS

At Punchbowl St. get on Lunalilo Fwy. (H-1) heading 'Ewa (west).

Near Middle St. keep left on Moanalua Fwy. (H-201) to 'Aiea.

While descending Red Hill, take the exit marked Hālawa-Stadium.

At the end of the long off-ramp, continue straight on Ulunē St.

At the road's end, turn right on 'Aiea Heights Dr.

Pass 'Aiea High School on the left.

Climb gradually through 'Aiea Heights subdivision.

Reach the entrance to Keaīwa Heiau State Recreation Area.

Drive past the *heiau* and the camping area to the upper lot and park there (elevation 1,080 feet) (map point A). At the trailhead are restrooms and drinking water.

BUS: Route 11 to 'Aiea Heights Dr. and Ka'amilo St. Walk 2.0 miles along 'Aiea Heights Dr. and through the recreation area to the trailhead. Route 74 goes farther up 'Aiea Heights Dr., but it runs only on weekday mornings and afternoons.

ROUTE DESCRIPTION

At the back of the upper lot, take the 'Aiea Loop Trail.

Pass a small water tank on the right.

Enter a grove of tall Sydney blue gum trees.

Cross an open, rooty area. On the right is a view of the top of Diamond Head (Lēʻahi) and Honolulu in the distance.

Pass a power-line tower above and to the right.

Almost immediately, the trail curves to the right and then to the left.

After that reverse S curve, reach a junction (map point B). Turn left and down on a side trail. (The ʻAiea Loop Trail continues straight.)

Descend gradually along the side ridge through strawberry guava trees.

Walk under a power-line tower. In the distance to the right is the Waiʻanae Range.

Continue the gradual descent through a narrow corridor of strawberry guavas. The trail is muddy in spots.

Pass a stand of large paperbark trees.

Ironwood trees now line the route. Look for a few native koa trees and pūkiawe shrubs.

Enter a grove of eucalyptus trees on a wider trail.

As the trail levels out briefly, reach a junction marked by a mango tree on the right (map point C). Turn sharp right off the ridge on a narrow trail leading down into Kalauao Valley.

Walk through a corridor of small ironwoods.

Descend steeply through Christmas berry and strawberry guava trees. Watch your footing on the rocky, rooty trail. Look for native lama and alaheʻe trees.

Jog right and then left to avoid a rock face.

Resume the steep descent through mountain apple trees.

Reach a junction at Kalauao Stream (map point D). Turn right heading upstream under kukui and mountain apple trees. (To the left, a less distinct trail leads downstream.) Memorize that junction for the return trip.

Ford the stream eight times. Look and listen for the ʻelepaio, an endangered native bird.

After the first crossing is a huge mango tree on the opposite bank.

After the third is a sheer cliff on the right.

Before the fifth, walk in the streambed briefly.

At the sixth, the stream tumbles over a ledge.

After the eighth crossing, reach a delightful waterfall with a good-sized pool (elevation 600 feet) (map point E) (UTM 04 0614423E, 2367427N). To get to the top of the waterfall, ford the stream and climb up the left side.

NOTES

If you have already done the 'Aiea Loop hike, try this more difficult variation nearby. It is a challenging novice hike because of the steep, rough descent into Kalauao (multitude of clouds) Valley. The very pleasant walk by the stream to the waterfall, however, makes the scramble down and up worthwhile.

During dry weather, the stream, waterfall, and pool disappear. To ensure flowing water, take this hike during the winter or after a heavy rain in summer. Watch your footing on the slippery stream crossings. If necessary, walk in the water rather than rock hopping. As usual with stream hikes, do not attempt the crossings if the water gets much above your knees.

On the side trail past the strawberry guavas, look for native pūkiawe shrubs and koa trees. Pūkiawe has tiny, rigid leaves and small white, pink, or red berries. Koa has sickle-shaped foliage and pale yellow flower clusters. Early Hawaiians made surfboards and outrigger canoe hulls out of the beautiful red-brown wood. Today it is made into fine furniture.

On the steep trail down to the stream are some native lama and alahe'e trees. Lama has oblong, pointed leaves which are dark green and leathery. Its fruits are green, then yellow, and finally bright red when fully ripe. Lama was sacred to Laka, goddess of the hula. Early Hawaiians used the hard, light-colored wood in temple construction and in hula performances.

Alahe'e has shiny, oblong, dark green leaves. Its fragrant white flowers grow in clusters at the branch tips. Early

Hawaiians fashioned the hard wood into farming tools and hooks and spears for fishing.

In Kalauao Valley are groves of mountain apple ('ōhi'a 'ai). The trees have large, oblong, shiny leaves. In spring their purple flowers carpet the trail. The delicious pink or red fruit usually ripens in late July or early August. If none are in reach, shake the tree gently and try to catch the apples as they come down. The species is native to Malaysia and was brought over by early Hawaiians.

While walking along the stream, watch for the 'elepaio, a small native bird. It is brown on top and white underneath with a black throat and a dark tail, usually cocked. The bird roams the forest understory catching insects on the fly or on vegetation. 'Elepaio are territorial and very curious, which is why you can sometimes see them.

After the eighth crossing, a gushing waterfall suddenly appears around a bend in the stream. Shady banyan and mango trees ring an inviting swimming hole. Take the plunge if you are so inclined. Remember to check the depth of the water before jumping from the ledges around the pool.

To make a loop hike, continue upstream from the top of the falls. After crossing the stream five more times, look for an obscure junction. Turn right there and climb a long, steep side ridge back to the 'Aiea Loop Trail at its junction with the 'Aiea Ridge Trail. Turn right on the loop trail to return to the recreation area.

The 'Aiea Loop and 'Aiea Ridge hikes also start from the same trailhead. Try the novice loop hike before taking the Kalauao or the ridge hike. That way you can find the key, unmarked junctions for both those hikes ahead of time.

21

Waimano Ridge

TYPE:	Graded ridge
LENGTH:	15-mile round-trip
ELEVATION GAIN:	1,700 feet
DANGER:	Low
SUITABLE FOR:	Intermediate, Expert
LOCATION:	'Ewa Forest Reserve above Pearl City
TOPO MAP:	Waipahu, Kāne'ohe
ACCESS:	Open

HIGHLIGHTS

This graded trail follows an abandoned irrigation ditch above Waimano Stream and then climbs gradually to the Ko'olau summit. Along the route are some delicious fruit and a good variety of native plants. At the top you look out to Kāne'ohe Bay on the windward side.

TRAILHEAD DIRECTIONS

At Punchbowl St. get on Lunalilo Fwy. (H-1) heading 'Ewa (west).

Near Middle St. keep left on Moanalua Fwy. (H-201) to 'Aiea.

By Aloha Stadium, bear right to rejoin H-1 to Pearl City.

Leave the freeway at exit 10, marked Pearl City–Waimalu.

Turn right on Moanalua Rd. at the end of the off-ramp.

At the third traffic light, turn right on Waimano Home Rd. The road narrows to two lanes.

On the right, look for a guard station at the entrance to Waimano Training School and Hospital.

Park in a dirt/gravel area on the left just before the guard shack and across the road from the Pearl City Cultural Center (elevation 470 feet) (map point A).

BUS: Route 54 to the intersection of Waimano Home Rd. and Hoʻolaulea St. Walk 0.8 mile up Waimano Home Rd. to the trailhead. Route 53 to the intersection of Waimano Home Rd. and Komo Mai Dr. Walk 1.0 mile up Waimano Home Rd. to the trailhead. Route 73 goes all the way to the trailhead, but only on weekdays.

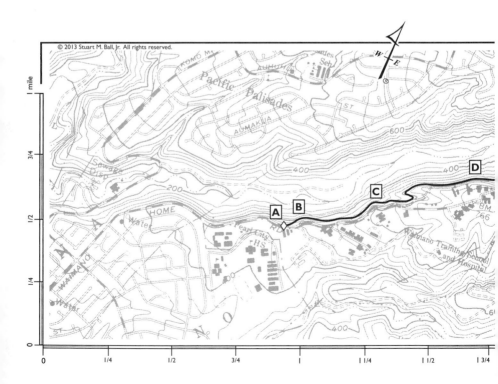

ROUTE DESCRIPTION

Register at the hunter/hiker check-in mailbox across the road from the guard shack.

Follow the path to the left of and along a chain-link fence.

Shortly afterward, reach a signed junction (map point B). Keep right on the Upper Waimano Trail along the fence. (To the left, the Lower Waimano Trail leads down into Waimano Valley.)

Parallel the fence and the road, passing several guardrails.

Across from the Department of Land and Natural Resources (DLNR) Oʻahu Baseyard, turn left and down, leaving the road behind (map point C).

An abandoned irrigation ditch appears on the right.

Jump over a narrow concrete spillway.

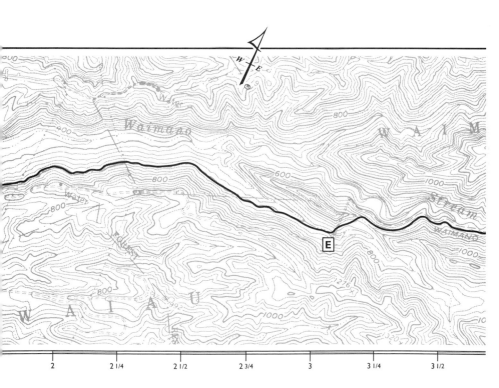

Swing left and cross over the top of an eroded side ridge through eucalyptus trees. In the distance is a good view of the Wai'anae Range.

Contour along the right side of Waimano Valley. Watch for native lama trees interspersed with strawberry guava and Christmas berry trees.

The ditch reappears on the right and then periodically disappears into short tunnels.

Reach a signed junction (map point D). Continue straight on the upper trail. (To the left, the lower trail leads down to the floor of Waimano Valley.)

Negotiate a rock face covered with slippery roots. Cables may be provided for assistance. You can use the short tunnels on the right to bypass this rock face and the next one.

Break out into the open briefly and descend another rock face, perhaps with the aid of a rope.

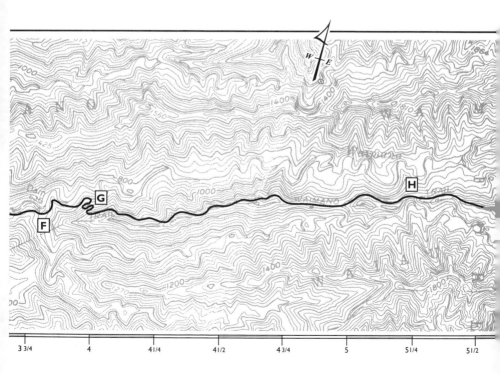

Pass a lone banyan tree and several large mango trees.

Descend gradually to a tributary of Waimano Stream and a signed junction (map point E). Keep left and ford the stream. (The trail to the right climbs out of the valley back to Waimano Training School and Hospital.)

After crossing, bear right upstream.

Leave the stream behind and climb a low side ridge on the left with the help of two switchbacks.

Cross over the ridgeline at a grassy clearing with a covered picnic table. Nearby are some large koa and lama trees.

Descend briefly to a bamboo grove and then contour along the left side of the ridge well above Waimano Stream. Look for Chinese ground orchids, which bloom in winter.

Descend gradually to the stream through mountain apple groves and hau tangles. By the stream are the remains of a dam and intake for the irrigation ditch.

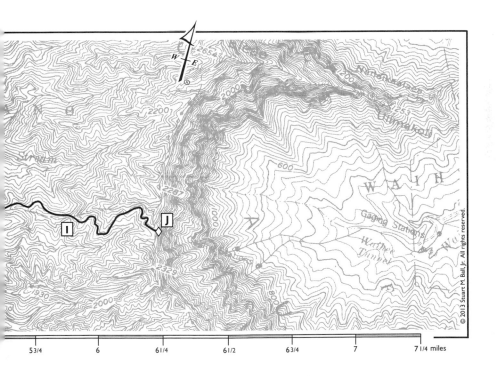

Almost immediately, Waimano Stream forks (map point F). Cross the right fork and take the trail heading upstream along the right side of the left fork (got it?).

Climb steadily up the ridge, switchbacking four times (map point G). Ornamental kī (ti) plants and stands of tall palm trees line the route. As the trail levels off and turns a corner, look for several 'iliahi (sandalwood) trees with their droopy leaves.

Resume contouring near the top of the ridge through large koa and 'ōhi'a trees. Look for kōpiko trees in the understory and the 'amakihi, a yellowish green native bird in the canopy.

Reach the top of the ridge in a saddle.

Leave the ridgeline and contour on its left side. The trail is lined with native naupaka kuahiwi shrubs.

After going around a small hump, gain the ridgeline once again.

Almost immediately, reach an obscure junction (map point H). Continue straight on the contour trail. (To the right, a short, steep trail leads down to the right fork of Waimano Stream. On the far bank is a collapsed cabin probably built by the U.S. Army during World War II.)

Climb gradually, working into and out of every side gulch.

Switchback once to gain the ridgeline and cross over to its right side (map point I).

Ascend steadily, weaving in and out of the side gullies just below the top of the ridge. Watch for Philippine or wind orchids and kōpiko trees along the trail.

Reach the Ko'olau summit in a saddle just to the right of a large landslide (elevation 2,160 feet) (map point J) (UTM 04 0616705E, 2371552N). Nearby is an End of Trail sign.

NOTES

Don't be put off by the high mileage of this hike. The well-designed trail makes for steady, pleasant walking through some very wild country. The miles just seem to fly by, and before you know it you're at the Koʻolau summit. Start early to have time to check out the native plants and birds and to enjoy a delicious guava or mountain apple in season.

The Upper Waimano Trail originally served as an access route to a water ditch and tunnel system built by the Honolulu Plantation Company in 1912. The ditch started at its intake by a small dam along Waimano Stream and ended at a reservoir that gradually delivered the water to irrigate the company's sugarcane fields above Pearl City. In 1934–1935, the Honolulu Unit of the Civilian Conservation Corps (CCC) renovated the plantation trail and extended the path from the ditch intake all the way to the summit.

That combination ditch and CCC trail remains the best preserved of the Koʻolau ridge trails of that era. The footpath is graded, wide, and easy to follow for the most part. Pay particular attention to the directions at the two stream crossings. Watch your step on the two rock faces. From the stream to the final switchback, the trail may be somewhat overgrown with scratchy uluhe ferns and various introduced shrubs.

Lining the initial trail section are strawberry guava (waiawī ʻulaʻula) trees whose tasty, dark red fruit usually ripen in August and September. Farther along are native lama trees. Their oblong, pointed leaves are dark green and leathery. The fruits are green, then yellow, and finally bright red when fully ripe. Lama was sacred to Laka, goddess of the hula. Early Hawaiians used the hard, light-colored wood in temple construction and in hula performances.

On the gradual descent to the stream and the ditch intake are groves of mountain apple (ʻōhiʻa ʻai). The trees have large, oblong, shiny leaves. In spring their purple flowers carpet the trail. The delicious pink or red fruit usually ripens in late July or early August. If none are in reach, shake the tree gently and try to catch the apples as they come down. The species is native to Malaysia and was brought over by early Hawaiians.

After crossing Waimano (many waters) Stream, watch for the native shrub naupaka kuahiwi. It has light green, pointed leaves and half-flowers. Initially the naupaka along the trail has toothed leaves and white flowers. Closer to the summit, a slightly different variety appears, with smoother leaf margins and purple streaks in the flowers.

Along the switchback section are ornamental kī (ti) plants and king palms originally planted in 1936 by Colin Potter, superintendent of Foster Botanical Gardens. Beyond the switchbacks, look for the ʻamakihi, the most common native forest bird on Oʻahu. It is yellowish green with a slightly curved gray bill and feeds on nectar, fruits, and insects.

Along the final stretch is the native shrub kōpiko. It is a member of the coffee family and has leathery, oblong leaves with a light green midrib. Turn the leaf over to see a row of tiny holes (*piko* or navel) on either side of the midrib. The kōpiko produces clusters of little white flowers and fleshy, orange fruits.

From the summit viewpoint you can look straight down into Waiheʻe (octopus liquid) Valley. In back is Kāneʻohe (bamboo husband) Bay stretching to Mōkapu (taboo district) Point. By the bay is Kahaluʻu (diving place) Fishpond and a wooded hill known as Māʻeliʻeli (digging). Along the summit ridge to the right is the massive unnamed peak at the head of Waimalu (sheltered water) drainage. To the left past the landslide scar is the summit of ʻEleao (plant louse).

Below and to the left of the lookout are native loulu palms. They have rigid, fan-shaped fronds in a cluster at the top of a ringed trunk. Early Hawaiians used the fronds for thatch and plaited the blades of young fronds into fans and baskets. In back of the overlook is a native ʻōhiʻa tree with clusters of salmon-colored flowers.

For a much shorter loop walk, take the Waimano Valley hike that starts from the same trailhead. For a longer, more challenging route, connect the Waimano Ridge and Mānana hikes. Go up Waimano, turn left along the Koʻolau summit ridge, and then go down Mānana. The 1-mile summit section is for experienced hikers only, as the trail there is rough, narrow, overgrown, and frequently socked in.

22

Waimano Valley

TYPE:	Valley
LENGTH:	2-mile loop
ELEVATION GAIN:	400 feet
DANGER:	Low
SUITABLE FOR:	Novice
LOCATION:	'Ewa Forest Reserve above Pearl City
TOPO MAP:	Waipahu
ACCESS:	Open

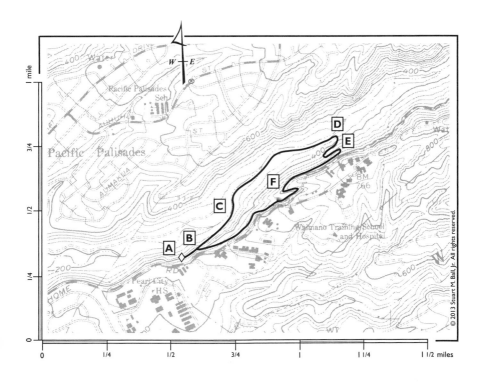

HIGHLIGHTS

This loop hike samples a short stretch of a tranquil, lovely valley. Smooth, reflective water alternates with shallow rapids in the stream there. The return route follows an abandoned irrigation ditch along the side of the valley.

TRAILHEAD DIRECTIONS

At Punchbowl St. get on Lunalilo Fwy. (H-1) heading 'Ewa (west).

Near Middle St. keep left on Moanalua Fwy. (H-201) to 'Aiea.

By Aloha Stadium, bear right to rejoin H-1 to Pearl City.

Leave the freeway at exit 10, marked Pearl City–Waimalu.

Turn right on Moanalua Rd. at the end of the off-ramp.

At the third traffic light, turn right on Waimano Home Rd. The road narrows to two lanes.

On the right, look for a guard station at the entrance to Waimano Training School and Hospital.

Park in a dirt/gravel area on the left just before the guard shack and across the road from the Pearl City Cultural Center (elevation 470 feet) (map point A).

BUS: Route 54 to the intersection of Waimano Home Rd. and Ho'olaulea St. Walk 0.8 mile up Waimano Home Rd. to the trailhead. Route 53 to the intersection of Waimano Home Rd. and Komo Mai Dr. Walk 1.0 mile up Waimano Home Rd. to the trailhead. Route 73 goes all the way to the trailhead, but only on weekdays.

ROUTE DESCRIPTION

Register at the hunter/hiker check-in mailbox across the road from the guard shack.

Follow the path to the left of and along a chain-link fence.

Shortly afterward, reach a signed junction (map point B). Bear left on the Lower Waimano Trail heading into the valley. (The trail along the fence is the upper trail, which is the return portion of the loop.)

Pass a wooden signpost on the right.

Descend gradually down the side of the ridge on an old, sometimes grassy plantation road. Look and listen for the white-rumped shama.

Walk under arching Christmas berry and Java plum trees.

On the valley floor, reach a junction by three large mango trees (map point C). Continue straight on the wide road upstream. (To the left, a narrow hunters' route heads downstream.)

Keep a tangled hau grove on the left. Ignore several side trails leading down to the stream.

The trail edges close to Waimano Stream and parallels it. Watch your step on a short, rocky section near the water.

Pass a line of small palms on the left.

After another hau tangle, climb very gradually underneath huge white-barked paraserianthes (albizia) trees.

Soon afterward, reach a junction in a clearing marked by two mango trees and a line of rocks (map point D) (UTM 04 0609825E, 2369602N). Turn right uphill on a wide trail. (The narrow hunters' route straight ahead continues up the valley.)

As the trail narrows, work left initially and then straight up the side of the ridge.

Turn right on a graded trail, which climbs the side of the valley on three switchbacks.

Halfway up the ridge, reach a junction with the Upper Waimano Trail (map point E). Turn sharp right on it. (To the left, the trail goes all the way to the Koʻolau summit.)

An abandoned irrigation ditch comes in on the left and parallels the trail. Periodically, the ditch disappears into short tunnels. The trail is narrow in spots and may be slippery when wet.

Contour through strawberry guava and Christmas berry trees. Watch for an occasional native lama tree.

Climb gradually through swamp mahogany, a variety of eucalyptus.

Swing left and cross over the top of an eroded side ridge (elevation 640 feet) (map point F). In the distance is a good view of the Wai'anae Range.

Descend into a side gully. The ditch reappears on the left.

Step over a narrow concrete spillway.

As the ditch trail ends, turn right along the fence by Waimano Home Rd.

Reach the junction with the lower trail (map point B) and, shortly afterward, the guard shack (map point A).

NOTES

Waimano (many waters) Valley is the perfect afternoon outing for beginning hikers. The loop is short and scenic and mainly wide and well graded. Watch your footing, however, on the slippery rocks by the stream and on several narrow spots by the ditch. After heavy rain, the valley section may be muddy, with some mosquitoes.

The hike mostly follows maintenance routes developed by the Honolulu Plantation Company around 1912. The initial road section once connected with a rail line built partway into the valley for easier harvesting of sugarcane. The return portion traces the access trail for the Waimano Ditch. Abandoned just after World War II, the ditch channeled water from the stream to the company's upper-level fields above Pearl City.

The first and last sections of the loop are lined with strawberry guava trees (waiawī 'ula'ula). They have glossy, dark green leaves and smooth brown bark. Their dark red fruit is delicious, with a taste reminiscent of strawberries. The guavas usually ripen in August and September. The strawberry guava is a native of Brazil but was introduced to Hawai'i from England in the 1800s.

On the descent into the valley, look and listen for the white-rumped shama. It is black on top with a chestnut-colored breast and a long black and white tail. The shama has a variety of beautiful songs and often mimics other birds. A native of Malaysia, the shama has become widespread in introduced forests such as this one.

Along the stream are tangled groves of hau trees with large, heart-shaped leaves. Their flowers are bright yellow with a dark red center and resemble those of a hibiscus. Early Hawaiians used the wood for kites and canoe outriggers, the bark for sandals, and the sap as a laxative.

In the valley the unmarked junction with the return route uphill is not immediately obvious. Look for the two mango trees and the line of rocks. Beyond the junction, the hunters' route along the stream becomes narrow and overgrown.

On the return contour section are native lama trees. Their oblong, pointed leaves are dark green and leathery. The fruits are green, then yellow, and finally bright red when fully ripe. Lama was sacred to Laka, goddess of the hula. Early Hawaiians used the hard, light-colored wood in temple construction and in hula performances.

For a much longer outing, take the Waimano Ridge hike that starts from the same trailhead. That 15-mile graded route follows the ditch to its intake and then climbs to the Ko'olau summit. Go as far as you want and then turn around.

23

Waimano Pool

TYPE:	Valley
LENGTH:	3-mile round-trip
ELEVATION GAIN:	700 feet
DANGER:	Low
SUITABLE FOR:	Novice, Intermediate
LOCATION:	'Ewa Forest Reserve above Pacific Palisades
TOPO MAP:	Waipahu
ACCESS:	Open

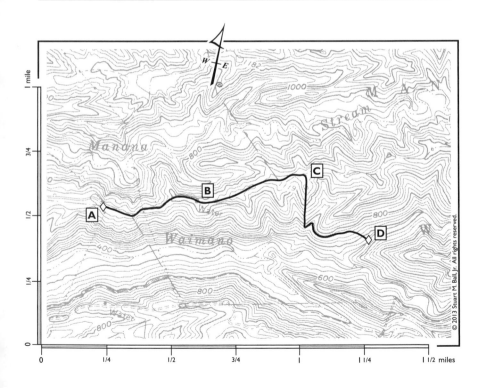

HIGHLIGHTS

This short, popular hike leads into lush Waimano Valley. Awaiting you along the stream are two deep swimming holes backed by a cascading waterfall. On the return, take your time climbing "Cardiac Hill."

TRAILHEAD DIRECTIONS

At Punchbowl St. get on Lunalilo Fwy. (H-1) heading ʻEwa (west).

Near Middle St. keep left on Moanalua Fwy. (H-201) to ʻAiea.

By Aloha Stadium, bear right to rejoin H-1 to Pearl City.

Leave the freeway at exit 10, marked Pearl City–Waimalu.

Turn right on Moanalua Rd. at the end of the off-ramp.

At the third traffic light, turn right on Waimano Home Rd.

At the third traffic light and just before the road narrows to two lanes, turn left on Komo Mai Dr.

The road descends into Waimano Valley and then climbs the next ridge.

Drive through Pacific Palisades subdivision to the end of the road.

Park on the street just before a turnaround circle (elevation 960 feet) (map point A).

BUS: Route 53 to Komo Mai Dr. and ʻAuhuhu St. Walk 0.4 mile along Komo Mai Dr. to the trailhead.

ROUTE DESCRIPTION

At the back of the circle, walk through an opening in the fence next to a gate.

Register at the hunter/hiker check-in mailbox on the right.

Proceed up the one-lane paved road through a grove of ironwood trees. In the distance on the left is the Waiʻanae Range.

On the right, pass a water tank at the road's end (map point B).

Continue straight on the Mānana Trail through a eucalyptus forest.

Pass a utility tower on the left.

Stroll through a pleasant level section on top of the ridge.

As the trail splits, keep left, avoiding the grassy area on the right.

In a rooty clearing, keep left and down to continue on the main ridge. Ignore the trail leading down a side ridge on the right.

While contouring to the right of a hump in the ridge, the trail forks. Keep right on the lower trail (map point C).

Shortly afterward, pass a signed junction on the left. Keep right onto a side ridge leading down to Waimano Valley. (The left fork is the continuation of the Mānana Trail, which follows the main ridge all the way to the Koʻolau summit.)

The trail ascends briefly to a small rooty knoll (elevation 1,120 feet). In the distance is the Koʻolau Range.

Descend steeply along the eroded side ridge. Watch your step on the exposed roots and loose soil.

Partway down the ridge, turn left in a strawberry guava grove.

Descend, steeply at times, into a small gulch and cross the intermittent stream there. The trail becomes narrow and muddy.

Contour along the side of Waimano Valley through strawberry guava and kī (ti) plants.

Descend steadily on a rough, rocky trail past several native lama trees.

After passing a small rock cliff, enter a stand of mountain apple trees.

Reach a junction. Turn left and resume contouring above Waimano Stream. (The trail to the right descends to the stream and a pleasant spot under a mango tree.)

Break out into the open briefly by native 'ōhi'a trees and a lone palm tree. Below, Waimano Stream splits in two.

Bear right and descend straight down toward the stream.

Reach the left fork of the stream at the lower pool (elevation 540 feet) (map point D) (UTM 04 0611702E, 2370389N). A narrow, slippery trail leads upstream to the upper pool at the base of a waterfall and to the top of the falls.

NOTES

Waimano Pool is a popular outing because of its short length and its main attraction: two good-sized swimming holes. Take this hike during the wet season (November–April). After a good rain, the stream keeps the pools full of cool, clear water. During summer the flow often slows to a trickle, leaving the pools shallow and stagnant. Whenever you go, be prepared to meet some pesky mosquitoes.

The initial hike section along the main ridge follows the well-groomed Mānana Trail, opened up in 1965. Two years later, Pacific Palisades residents Kazuo and Misao Yamaguchi developed a rough, muddy route down to the pools and a waterfall along Waimano (many waters) Stream. The short spur descends a steep side ridge, informally and affectionately known as "Cardiac Hill." Watch your footing on the way down; take your time on the way up. Although suitable for novices, the complete hike may prove difficult for an out-of-shape beginner because of the narrow, slippery trail and the steep climb on the return.

Along the main ridge and in the valley are strawberry guava trees (waiawī 'ula'ula). They have glossy, dark green leaves and smooth brown bark. Their dark red fruit is 'ono (delicious), with a taste reminiscent of strawberries. The guavas usually ripen in August and September; however, pickings may be slim along the trail because of its popularity. The strawberry guava is a native of Brazil but was introduced to Hawai'i from England in the 1800s.

As the trail contours above the stream, look for kī (ti) plants. They have shiny leaves 1–2 feet long that are arranged spirally in a cluster at the tip of a slender stem. Early Polynesian voyagers introduced ti to Hawai'i. They used the leaves for house thatch, skirts, sandals, and raincoats. Food to be cooked in the *imu* (underground oven) was first wrapped in ti leaves. A popular sport with the commoners was *ho'ohe'e kī* or ti-leaf sledding. The sap from ti plants stained canoes and surfboards.

On the final descent, watch for native lama trees. Their oblong, pointed leaves are dark green and leathery. The fruits are green, then yellow, and finally bright red when fully ripe. Lama was sacred to Laka, goddess of the hula. Early Hawaiians used the hard, light-colored wood in temple construction and in hula performances.

In the brief clearing just above the stream are several native 'ōhi'a trees. They have oval leaves and clusters of delicate red flowers. Early Hawaiians used the flowers in lei and the wood in outrigger canoes. The hard, durable wood was also carved into god images for *heiau* (religious sites).

The hike ends at two delightful swimming holes separated by a miniature cascade. In back of the upper pool is a larger waterfall. The lower pool offers easier access for a cooling dip. Nonswimmers can hike upstream to a breezy overlook at the top of the falls.

Overhanging the pools are some kukui trees. Their large, pale green leaves resemble those of the maple with several distinct lobes. Early Polynesian voyagers introduced kukui into Hawai'i. They used the wood to make gunwales and seats for their outrigger canoes. The flowers and sap became medicines to treat a variety of ailments. Early Hawaiians strung the nuts together to make *lei hua* (seed or nut garlands). The oily kernels became house candles and torches for night spearfishing.

For a nearby ridge outing, try the Mānana hike that starts from the same trailhead. The route is suitable for everyone; go as far as you want and then turn around.

24

Mānana

TYPE:	Ungraded ridge
LENGTH:	12-mile round-trip
ELEVATION GAIN:	1,700 feet
DANGER:	Low
SUITABLE FOR:	Novice, Intermediate, Expert
LOCATION:	‘Ewa Forest Reserve above Pacific Palisades
TOPO MAP:	Waipahu, Kāne‘ohe
ACCESS:	Open

HIGHLIGHTS

This long, splendid ridge hike leads deep into the wild Ko‘olau Mountain Range. Along the way is an incredible variety of native dryland and rain forest plants. Lofty lookouts, en route and at the summit, provide stunning views of leeward and windward O‘ahu.

TRAILHEAD DIRECTIONS

At Punchbowl St. get on Lunalilo Fwy. (H-1) heading ‘Ewa (west).

Near Middle St. keep left on Moanalua Fwy. (H-201) to ‘Aiea.

By Aloha Stadium, bear right to rejoin H-1 to Pearl City.

Leave the freeway at exit 10, marked Pearl City–Waimalu.

Turn right on Moanalua Rd. at the end of the off-ramp.

At the third traffic light, turn right on Waimano Home Rd.

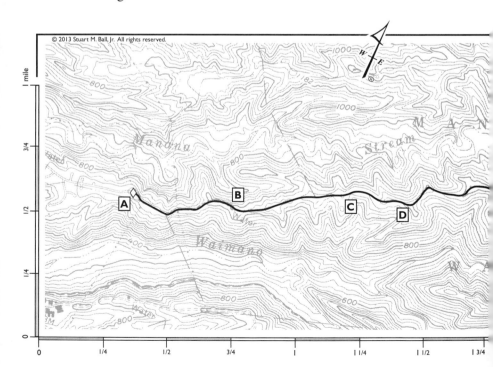

At the third traffic light and just before the road narrows to two lanes, turn left on Komo Mai Dr.

The road descends into Waimano Valley and then climbs the next ridge.

Drive through Pacific Palisades subdivision to the end of the road.

Park on the street just before a turnaround circle (elevation 960 feet) (map point A).

BUS: Route 53 to Komo Mai Dr. and ʻAuhuhu St. Walk 0.4 mile along Komo Mai Dr. to the trailhead.

ROUTE DESCRIPTION

At the back of the circle, walk through an opening in the fence next to a gate.

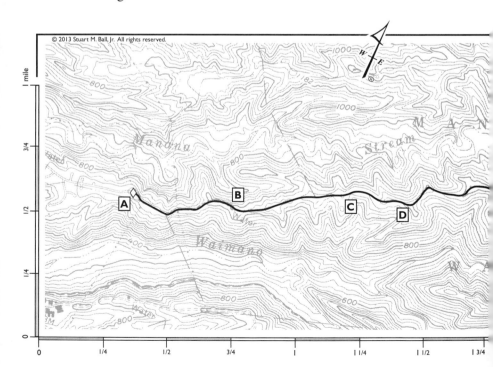

Register at the hunter/hiker check-in mailbox on the right.

Proceed up the one-lane paved road through a grove of ironwood trees.

On the right pass a water tank at the road's end (map point B).

Continue straight on the Mānana Trail through a eucalyptus forest.

Pass a utility tower on the left.

Stroll through a pleasant level section on top of the ridge.

As the trail splits, keep left, avoiding the small grassy area on the right.

In a rooty clearing, keep left and down to continue on the main ridge. Ignore the trail leading down a side ridge on the right.

While contouring to the right of a small hump in the ridge, the trail forks. Keep left on the upper trail (map point C).

Shortly afterward, reach a signed junction. Keep left around the hump on the main ridge. (The right fork leads down a side

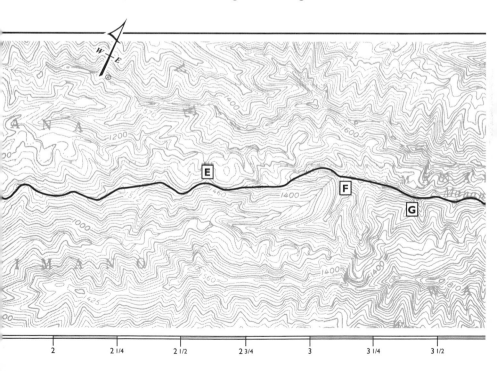

ridge into Waimano Valley and is described in the Waimano Pool hike.)

Climb gradually through a grove of brush box trees.

The trail forks in another rooty area. Bear left and down to stay on the ridgetop (map point D).

Break out into the open. *Mauka* (inland) is a view of the entire ridge to be climbed.

Traverse a narrow, eroded stretch with plastic steps. Watch your footing, especially if the ground is wet.

The trail becomes a grassy avenue lined with introduced pines and the stumps of paperbark trees. Look for native koa and 'iliahi (sandalwood) trees and the native shrub naupaka kuahiwi.

On the left, a side trail climbs to a small knob and then rejoins the main route.

Descend a steep eroded section to the right of a flat, grassy viewpoint.

Pass a covered picnic table on the right.

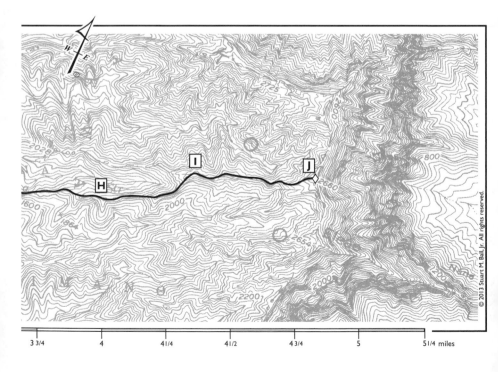

Stroll through a lovely rolling ridge section with more koa and ʻiliahi trees.

Climb steeply to the first really distinct knob in the ridge (map point E).

Descend the next dip and ascend steeply to the next hump. The native vegetation gradually changes from dryland to rain forest. Along the route are ʻōhiʻa and kōpiko trees and hāpuʻu tree ferns.

Cross a short level section.

Climb very steeply to another knob, where a long side ridge comes in on the right (map point F).

The trail narrows and becomes rough and rooty.

Cross another level section, descend briefly, and then ascend a flat, cleared hill used occasionally as a helipad (map point G). There is a view in all directions. To leeward is Pearl Harbor (Puʻuloa) and the Waiʻanae Range. On the left is a native lapalapa tree with its fluttering leaves.

Traverse a long series of small but steep knobs in the ridge.

Cross a level muddy section.

Ascend steeply to a large hill with a small clearing on top (map point H). From there is a commanding view of the ridge ahead.

Swing left and climb steadily. The vegetation becomes stunted, and the wind picks up.

Curve right toward the Koʻolau summit as a long side ridge comes in on the left (map point I).

The main ridge narrows significantly.

Traverse a series of small humps. On the left are several native loulu palms.

The ridge broadens and levels briefly through low-lying sedge.

Cross a second series of humps on the narrow ridge.

Pass a waterfall chute down and on the right.

Climb steadily through increasing vegetation.

Reach the Koʻolau summit at a massive knob (elevation 2,660 feet) (map point J) (UTM 04 0616532E, 2373093N).

NOTES

The Mānana hike offers some of the finest ridge walking on the island. Along the route are some intriguing native plants and a chance at glimpsing some native birds. The last mile of the open, windswept ridge is wild and wonderful. Mist frequently settles over the summit area, reducing visibility and creating a dark, eerie atmosphere.

The 6-mile trail was a project of Charles (Charlie) Nakamura and several friends, all members of the Hawaiian Trail and Mountain Club. In 1965, they started clearing the ridge route *mauka* of the recently built Pacific Palisades subdivision. The group finally reached the Koʻolau summit in 1969. Named after the stream and *ahupuaʻa* (land division) north of the ridge, the new Mānana Trail quickly became popular with hikers of all abilities. Novices strolled to the picnic table. Intermediate hikers continued to the helipad, and experts headed for the summit.

Although not graded, the trail is wide and clear to the distinct knob beyond the picnic table. Watch your step, however, on the two eroded sections. Farther *mauka* (inland) the route becomes rough, steep, narrow, and muddy, although rarely all at the same time. Between the helipad and the final climb, the trail may be overgrown with scratchy uluhe ferns and *Clidemia* shrubs.

On the initial trail section, remember to keep left along the main ridge. Ignore the side trails leading down into Waimano (many waters) Valley on the right. Also, watch for mountain bikers, especially in the afternoon. Portions of the trail in this section are lined with strawberry guava (waiawī ʻulaʻula) trees whose tasty, dark red fruit usually ripens in August and September.

After leaving the introduced forest, the route winds through a lovely open stretch still recovering from a fire in 1972. Making a comeback are the native trees koa and ʻiliahi. Koa has sickle-shaped foliage and pale yellow flower clusters.

Early Hawaiians made surfboards and outrigger canoe hulls out of the beautiful red-brown wood. Today it is made into fine furniture.

'Iliahi or sandalwood has small, dull green leaves that appear wilted. The tree is partially parasitic, with outgrowths on its roots that steal nutrients from nearby plants. Early Hawaiians ground the fragrant heartwood into a powder to perfume their *kapa* (bark cloth). Beginning in the late 1700s, 'iliahi was indiscriminately cut down and exported to China to make incense and furniture. The trade ended around 1840 when the forests were depleted of the tree.

Farther along the ridge is the native rain forest, dominated by 'ōhi'a trees and hāpu'u tree ferns. 'Ōhi'a has oval leaves and clusters of delicate red flowers. Early Hawaiians used the flowers in lei and the wood in outrigger canoes. The hard, durable wood was also carved into god images for *heiau* (religious sites). Beneath the 'ōhi'a are hāpu'u tree ferns with delicate sweeping fronds. Their trunks consist of roots tightly woven around a small central stem. The brown fiber covering the young fronds of hāpu'u is called *pulu*.

At the helipad is a magnificent lapalapa tree. Its roundish leaves are arranged in groups of three and flutter in the slightest wind. Early Hawaiians used the bark, leaves, and purple fruit to make a blue-black dye to decorate their *kapa*. The leaves also make a distinctive lei.

Beyond the helipad, watch for 'apapane and 'amakihi, two colorful native birds. The 'apapane has a red breast and head, black wings and tail, and a slightly curved black bill. In flight, the bird makes a whirring sound as it darts among the 'ōhi'a searching for insects and nectar. The 'amakihi is yellowish green with a slightly curved gray bill and feeds on nectar, fruits, and insects. It is the most common native forest bird on O'ahu.

On the final climb, look for the native loulu palm, emerging out of the mist. It has rigid, fan-shaped fronds in a cluster at the top of a ringed trunk. Early Hawaiians used the fronds for thatch and plaited the blades of young fronds into fans and baskets.

As you near the top, listen for the Japanese bush warbler (uguisu), a bird often heard but rarely seen. Its distinctive cry starts with a long whistle and then winds down in a series of notes. There seems to be at least one bush warbler at the top of every Koʻolau ridge trail.

The view from the summit lookout is exceptional, weather permitting. Kaʻalaea (reddish earth) Valley lies 2,000 feet below. The windward coast stretches from Kualoa (long back) to Makapuʻu (bulging eye) points. In Kāneʻohe (bamboo husband) Bay you can see three enclosed fishponds: Mōliʻi (small section), Kahaluʻu (diving place), and Heʻeia, from left to right. On the left are four windward valleys: Waiāhole, Waikāne, Hakipuʻu (hill broken), and Kaʻaʻawa (the wrasse fish). Dominating those valleys is the massive peak Puʻu ʻŌhulehule (joining of waves hill). In the distance to the right is triple-peaked Olomana (forked hill).

For a shorter valley outing, take the Waimano Pool hike that starts from the same trailhead. For a longer, more challenging route, connect the Mānana and Waimano Ridge hikes. Go up Mānana, turn right along the Koʻolau summit ridge, and then go down Waimano. The 1-mile summit section is for experienced hikers only, as the trail there is rough, narrow, overgrown, and frequently socked in.

Crossing the arch. Koko Crater hike. (PHOTO BY JOHN HOOVER.)

White-rumped shama.
(PHOTO BY NATHAN YUEN.)

Reaching the top. Kuliouou Ridge hike. (PHOTO BY KELVIN LU.)

Climbing Keanaakamanō, the misty middle ridge of Kamananui Valley. Pu'u Keahi a Kahoe hike. (PHOTO BY KELVIN LU.)

Koki'o ke'oke'o, the native white hibiscus. Makiki-Tantalus hike. (PHOTO BY NATHAN YUEN.)

Kulanaʻahane trailhead. Kamananui (Moanalua) Valley hike.
(PHOTO BY NATHAN YUEN.)

LEFT: *Chinese ground orchid. Kamananui (Moanalua) Valley hike.*
(PHOTO BY NATHAN YUEN.)

OPPOSITE PAGE: *Heading for the summit through native koa forest. Mānana hike.* (PHOTO BY NATHAN YUEN.)

Native orange ōhiʻa lehua. Schofield-Waikāne hike.
(PHOTO BY NATHAN YUEN.)

LEFT: *Native land snail. Poamoho hike.*
(PHOTO BY NATHAN YUEN.)

OPPOSITE PAGE:
Loulu palms at the Koʻolau summit. Schofield-Waikāne hike. (PHOTO BY
NATHAN YUEN.)

ABOVE: *At the swimming hole. Maunawili Falls hike.* (PHOTO BY RICHARD BAILEY.)

OPPOSITE PAGE: *Second and third peaks. Olomana hike.*
(PHOTO BY LYNNE MASUYAMA.)

ABOVE: *Ko'olau cascades after a heavy rain. Likeke hike.* (PHOTO BY KELVIN LU.)

OPPOSITE PAGE: *Ko'olau cliffs and waterfall chutes. Maunawili hike.*
(PHOTO BY DEBORAH UCHIDA.)

Crossing Kahawainui Stream. Kahana Valley hike.
(PHOTO BY LYNNE MASUYAMA.)

Under the towering canyon walls. Koloa Gulch hike.
(PHOTO BY RICHARD BAILEY.)

Descending a rock face. Pu'u Manamana hike. (PHOTO BY JOHN HOOVER.)

At Black Junction.
Pūpūkea Summit hike.
(PHOTO BY RICHARD BAILEY.)

Native koliʻi. Waiʻanae-Kaʻala hike. (PHOTO BY NATHAN YUEN.)

All to yourself. Kahuku Shoreline hike. (PHOTO BY KELVIN LU.)

Tide pools along the rugged leeward coast. Ka'ena Point hike. (PHOTO BY NATHAN YUEN.)

25

Schofield-Waikāne

TYPE:	Graded ridge
LENGTH:	14-mile round-trip
ELEVATION GAIN:	1,200 feet
DANGER:	Low
SUITABLE FOR:	Novice, Intermediate, Expert
LOCATION:	'Ewa Forest Reserve above Wahiawā
TOPO MAP:	Hau'ula
ACCESS:	Conditional; open to individuals and outdoor organizations with permission. Write Directorate of Public Works, Real Estate Branch, 947 Wright Ave, Wheeler Army Airfield, Schofield Barracks, HI 96857–5000.

HIGHLIGHTS

This rugged hike follows an old army trail that traverses the Ko'olau Range. The route pushes through some very wild and remote country in central O'ahu. Along the way are awesome overlooks, a variety of native plants, and some native birds.

TRAILHEAD DIRECTIONS

At Punchbowl St. get on Lunalilo Fwy. (H-1) heading 'Ewa (west).

Near Middle St. keep left on Moanalua Fwy. (H-201) to
'Aiea.

By Aloha Stadium, bear right to rejoin H-1 to Pearl City.

Take the H-2 Freeway north (exit 8A) to Wahiawā.

Get off H-2 at Wahiawā (exit 8, Rte. 80 north).

At the end of the off-ramp, merge into Kamehameha Hwy.

Cross Wilson Bridge and enter Wahiawā town.

At the third traffic light, turn right on California Ave.

The road narrows to two lanes.

Pass Leilehua High School on the right.

The road jogs right and then left.

Park at the end of California Ave. near its intersection
with Puninoni St. (elevation 1,240 feet) (map point A). Leave
plenty of room for the bus to get by.

BUS: Route 62 to the trailhead.

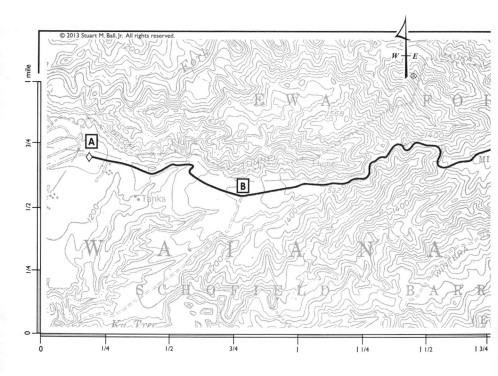

ROUTE DESCRIPTION

Walk to the small turnout at the end of California Ave.

Pick up the trail starting between a yellow metal barrier and a chain-link fence surrounding two green water tanks.

The trail splits at the corner of the fence; take the right fork.

Angle to the right through a grove of paperbark trees.

The trail swings right, through strawberry guava trees along the edge of a drop-off.

Turn right toward a dirt road visible from the trail.

Turn left onto the dirt road, which leads into the East Range, an army training area. Memorize that junction for the return trip.

Immediately pass a large clearing and tower used for rappel instruction.

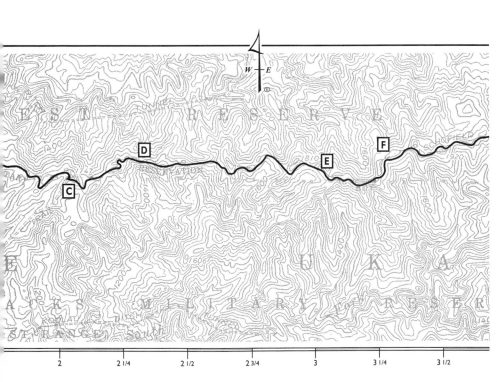

Stroll through a shady eucalyptus grove and then begin to climb.

As the road curves left, reach a junction with a narrow dirt road. Keep left on the main road.

Reach a second junction (map point B). Again, keep left on the dirt road heading toward the mountains. (The graveled, well-traveled road to the right heads down to the South Fork of Kaukonahua Stream and then exits the East Range by Wheeler Airfield.)

The road ascends gradually with an occasional dip.

Climb steeply around two humps in the ridge.

About two miles in, the road curves right and climbs past a third hump.

Just past the hump, reach a signed junction. Turn left onto the Schofield-Waikāne Trail (map point C). (To the right, the road heads down and back toward Wheeler Airfield.)

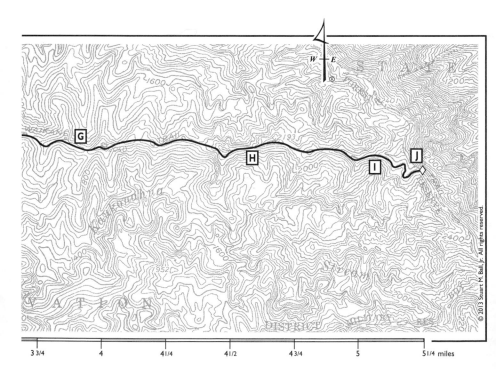

Descend briefly on plastic steps and then switchback left.

Cross a deep, narrow cut in the ridge on a short walkway.

Contour on the left and then on the right side of the ridge. Along the trail are the magnificent native rain forest trees koa and 'ōhi'a. Begin looking for two native birds, 'apapane and 'amakihi.

Reach a junction (map point D). Take the right fork heading up the ridge. (The left fork leads down to the abandoned intake of the Mauka Ditch and some good swimming holes along the North Fork of Kaukonahua Stream.)

Contour mostly along the right side of the up-and-down ridge. The trail occasionally switches to the left side or goes along the top of the ridge.

Climb steeply up a natural rock stairway on the right side of the ridge.

On the right, pass two large side ridges forming a pocket valley (map point E). Look back to see the Wai'anae Range in the distance. To the right of Kolekole Pass are the summits of Kalena and Ka'ala.

Pass two more side ridges on the right (map point F). In the valley formed by the ridges are 'ōhi'a trees with red, yellow, and orange flowers.

Continue contouring on the right side of the ridge for a long stretch. The trail becomes rough and narrow. Look for the native tree kōpiko and listen for the Japanese bush warbler with its distinctive, extended song.

Pass another pair of side ridges (map point G).

Cross a relatively level section on top of the ridge. The vegetation is lower there because of the wind.

Climb steadily now, following the crest of the ridge (map point H). The trail contours to the right twice and to the left once to skirt humps in the ridge. Look for native loulu palms and 'ōlapa trees with their fluttering leaves.

Begin the last contour section around the right side of a large peak along the summit ridge (map point I).

Step on some metal roofing, all that's left of an old cabin blown down in 1963.

On the right just before the top, pass a small open area with good views of the Wai'anae Range.

Reach the Ko'olau summit (elevation 2,320 feet) (map point J) (UTM 04 0613259E, 2378724N) and the junction with the Ko'olau Summit Trail.

NOTES

Schofield-Waikāne is a rugged ridge hike that penetrates deep into the central Ko'olau (windward) Range. The trail traverses country so wild that it's hard to believe you're on populous O'ahu. Remote overlooks en route and at the summit offer green views in all directions. Get an early start because of the high mileage and the rough, overgrown trail.

The Schofield-Waikāne Trail started out as a plantation ditch trail and then became an army route connecting Schofield Barracks with the windward side. In 1900, Waialua Agricultural Company built the initial section along the ridge to gain access to the intake of the Mauka Ditch along Kaukonahua Stream. The army extended the trail to the Ko'olau Summit in 1912 and built the Waikāne section in 1923. The wide, graded path was suitable for horses and mules.

In the mid 1930s, the Civilian Conservation Corps reconstructed deteriorated sections of the army route. Since then the trail has gradually fallen into disrepair. Although still graded, the treadway has many uneven and narrow spots because of slippage and erosion through the years. Uluhe ferns and other vegetation growing on the high side of the trail tend to force you downslope. Watch your footing constantly; expect to fall down a few times and get muddy and wet.

For the most part, the trail winds through magnificent native rain forest dominated by 'ōhi'a and koa trees. 'Ōhi'a has oval leaves and clusters of delicate red, yellow, or orange flowers. Early Hawaiians used the flowers in lei and the wood in outrigger canoes. The hard, durable wood was also carved into god images for *heiau* (religious sites). Koa has sickle-shaped foliage and pale yellow flower clusters. Early Hawaiians made surfboards and outrigger canoe hulls out of the beautiful red-brown wood. Today it is made into fine furniture.

In the understory is kōpiko, a native member of the coffee family. The small tree has leathery, oblong leaves with a light green midrib. Turn the leaf over to see a row of tiny holes (*piko* or navel) on either side of the midrib. The kōpiko produces clusters of little white flowers and fleshy, orange fruits.

In the forest canopy, watch for the ʻamakihi, the most common native forest bird on Oʻahu. It is yellowish green with a slightly curved gray bill and feeds on nectar, fruits, and insects. If the ʻōhiʻa are in bloom, you may glimpse the scarce ʻapapane. It has a red breast and head, black wings and tail, and a slightly curved black bill. In flight, the ʻapapane makes a whirring sound as it darts from tree to tree searching for insects and nectar.

As the vegetation opens up, look for the native loulu palm. It has rigid, fan-shaped fronds in a cluster at the top of a ringed trunk. Early Hawaiians used the fronds for thatch and plaited the blades of young fronds into fans and baskets.

Also along the open ridge is the native ʻōlapa tree. Its leaves are opposite and oblong, and flutter in the slightest wind. In a special hula stance named after the tree, dancers mimic the exquisite movements of the leaves. Early Hawaiians used the bark, leaves, and purple fruit to make a blue-black dye to decorate their *kapa* (bark cloth).

On the final stretch, look closely for the native shrub ʻōhelo. It has rounded, toothed leaves and delicious red berries, about the size of blueberries. According to legend, ʻōhelo is sacred to Pele, goddess of fire. She changed her dead sister, Kaʻōhelo, into the shrub and named it after her.

Weather permitting, the view from the summit lookout is one of the best on the island. Directly below the *pali* (cliff) are five undeveloped valleys: from left to right, Punaluʻu (coral dived for), Kahana (cutting), Kaʻaʻawa (the wrasse fish), Hakipuʻu (hill broken), and Waikāne (Kāneʼs water). Puʻu ʻŌhulehule (joining-of the-waves hill) is the impressive mountain dead ahead. To the right, the Koʻolau Summit Trail hugs the *pali* and then works leeward behind Puʻu Kaʻaumakua (the family god). You can also make out the continuation of the Schofield-Waikāne Trail as it descends the windward slopes into Waikāne Valley.

There are two attractive variations to the route as described. For a shorter, novice hike, take the original plantation trail at map point D down to Kaukonahua (place his testicles) Stream. Walk up or downstream to find a swimming hole to your liking. Total distance round-trip is about 6 miles. For a more challenging outing, connect the Schofield-Waikāne and Poamoho hikes. At the top of Schofield-Waikāne, turn left on the Koʻolau Summit Trail and then go down Poamoho. The 2-mile summit section is for experienced hikers only, as the trail there is rough, narrow, and frequently socked in.

26

Wahiawā Hills

TYPE:	Foothill
LENGTH:	4-mile loop
ELEVATION GAIN:	1,300 feet
DANGER:	Low
SUITABLE FOR:	Intermediate
LOCATION:	Ewa Forest Reserve above Wahiawā
TOPO MAP:	Hauʻula
ACCESS:	Open

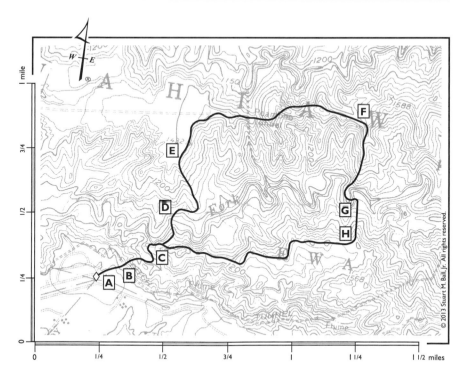

HIGHLIGHTS

This intricate loop traverses the Koʻolau foothills above Wahiawā. In the process, you cross two streams twice and climb and
descend two ridges. The reward for all this meandering is a
cooling dip in a delightful stream pool.

TRAILHEAD DIRECTIONS

At Punchbowl St. get on Lunalilo Fwy. (H-1) heading ʻEwa
(west).

Near Middle St. keep left on Moanalua Fwy. (H-201) to
ʻAiea.

By Aloha Stadium, bear right to rejoin H-1 to Pearl City.

Take the H-2 Freeway north (exit 8A) to Wahiawā.

Get off H-2 at Wahiawā (exit 8, Rte. 80 north).

At the end of the off-ramp, merge into Kamehameha Hwy.

Cross Wilson Bridge and enter Wahiawā town.

At the third traffic light, turn right on California Ave.

The road narrows to two lanes.

Pass Leilehua High School on the right.

The road jogs right and then left.

Park at the end of California Ave. near its intersection
with Puninoni St. (elevation 1,240 feet) (map point A). Leave
plenty of room for the bus to get by.

BUS: Route 62 to the trailhead.

ROUTE DESCRIPTION

Walk to the small turnout at the end of California Ave.

Pick up the trail starting between a yellow metal barrier
and a chain-link fence surrounding two green water tanks.

The trail splits at the corner of the fence; take the right fork.

Angle to the right through a grove of paperbark trees. Ignore side paths on the left and right.

The trail swings right, along the edge of a drop-off.

Shortly afterward, reach an obscure junction (map point B). Turn left and descend steeply down a side ridge on a rooty trail.

As the gradient levels, bear left off the ridge onto a graded path known as the Mauka Ditch Trail.

Descend gradually into a gulch with a small stream.

The trail forks just downstream of a tiny waterfall. Turn left and cross the stream.

Climb the opposite bank on two short switchbacks.

Bear left and gradually ascend out of the gulch. Duck under several huge tree trunks across the trail.

Reach a junction at the top of a side ridge (map point C). Continue straight across the ridge on the graded contour trail. (Memorize that junction well, as the ungraded trail to the right and up is the return portion of the loop.)

As the trail crosses a second side ridge, reach another junction. This time, turn left down the side ridge on an ungraded trail. (The contour trail continues straight across the side ridge.)

Descend steadily along the side ridge through eucalyptus trees.

As the side ridge ends, bear right and down to reach the North Fork of Kaukonahua Stream (map point D).

Ford the wide stream carefully, walk upstream briefly, and climb the bank.

Jog right and then left to pick up a side ridge just upstream of the crossing.

Ascend the side ridge through strawberry guavas and eucalyptus.

Reach a junction on top of the main ridge (map point E). Turn right, heading *mauka* (inland).

Stroll through paperbark trees on the broad ridge. Keep to the right along its edge.

Break out into the open through a stretch of uluhe ferns. Look for native 'ōhi'a trees on the right.

Reach a junction with a dirt road near a traveler's palm and a small stand of bamboo. Turn right on the road. (The obscure trail across the road leads down to Poamoho Stream.)

Enter a eucalyptus forest. The road eventually narrows to a trail, which continues to follow the main ridge. Ignore makeshift trails down side ridges on both the left and right. Look for the native lily, 'uki'uki, in the understory.

In a grove of paperbark trees, bear left to bypass a hump in the ridge.

Shortly afterward, the ridge levels and then climbs slightly to a breezy lookout (elevation 1,480 feet) (map point F) (UTM 04 0606524E, 2379940N). *Mauka* is a good view of the Ko'olau summit.

At the lookout, turn right down a side ridge. Look for the native shrub pūkiawe.

The ridge splits into two fingers; take the right one.

Descend steeply toward the North Fork of Kaukonahua Stream and cross a narrow neck. The stream makes a sharp bend around the end of the ridge and so is visible on both sides.

Shortly afterward, reach a junction. Turn right and descend to a long, deep, and inviting pool.

When you've had enough swimming and sunning, retrace your steps to the junction and turn right to continue along the finger ridge.

Bear left across the tip of the finger and descend to the stream.

Ford it just below another pool, somewhat smaller than the first (map point G).

Bear right and climb steeply up a side ridge. Look back for a view of Ka'ala, the flat-topped peak in the Wai'anae Range.

Reach the top of the main ridge (map point H) (UTM 04 0606556E, 2379245N) and turn right along it.

Follow the near edge of the broad ridge through native 'ōhi'a and koa trees.

Enter a long stretch of eucalyptus forest. Watch for the native shrub maile along the up-and-down ridge.

Swing right and descend as the ridge narrows.

Reach the familiar junction ending the loop (map point C). Turn sharp left on the graded Mauka Ditch Trail into the gulch and retrace your steps back to the end of California Ave.

NOTES

Wahiawā (noisy place) Hills is a meandering loop hike bisected by magnificent Kaukonahua Stream. The route was cobbled together from old trails and dirt roads of varying difficulty in the late 1970s. Watch your step on the slippery downhill sections at the start of the hike. The side ridges and the main ridge on the return may be overgrown with scratchy uluhe ferns. A few mosquitoes may lurk along the stream.

The graded trail before and after the side stream is a remnant section of the Mauka Ditch Trail, built in 1900. The route contoured along Kaukonahua Stream for 12 miles to provide access to the ditch and its intake and tunnels. The ditch delivered stream water to Wahiawā colony for domestic and agricultural use.

Much of the hike passes through stands of paperbark and eucalyptus trees planted in the 1930s and 1940s for reforestation. You can easily recognize paperbark by its spongy white bark. The eucalyptus along the trail comes in several varieties. Sydney blue gum has smooth blue-gray bark and very narrow, pointed leaves. Swamp mahogany has spongy reddish brown bark and slightly wider leaves. Ironbark has black or gray bark, heavily furrowed.

Approach powerful Kaukonahua (place his testicles) Stream with some caution. Watch your footing while fording, as the streambed is very uneven. As always, do not venture across if the water is much above your knees. If you are caught on the far side, wait until the stream goes down. Kaukonahua is the longest stream in the state and has a huge watershed. The debris on the shrubs and trees lining the banks gives you a good idea of how high the water can get during a sudden heavy rainstorm.

On the main ridge going out, look for the native lily 'uki'uki. It has long, slender, shiny leaves with a central vein. The plant produces a stalk with small pale blue to white flowers, followed by blue or purple berries. Early Hawaiians used the berries to make a blue dye and the leaves as cordage in house construction.

Near the second Kaukonahua crossing are two inviting swimming holes above and below a sharp bend in the stream. Take a dip in the cool, clear water before climbing the hot, open ridge on the return.

Native 'ōhi'a and koa trees make a brief appearance along the main ridge going back. 'Ōhi'a has oval leaves and clusters of delicate red flowers. Early Hawaiians used the flowers in lei and the wood in outrigger canoes. The hard, durable wood was also carved into god images for *heiau* (religious sites). Koa has sickle-shaped foliage and pale yellow flower clusters. Early Hawaiians made surfboards and outrigger canoe hulls out of the beautiful red-brown wood. Today it is made into fine furniture.

As you approach the end of the loop, look for maile, a twining native shrub, under the eucalyptus. Maile has shiny, pointed leaves, tangled branches, and fruit resembling a small olive. The fragrant leaves and bark have been used to make distinctive open-ended lei in both ancient and modern Hawai'i.

There are several longer variations to the basic loop, but all are obscure and complicated. You can, of course, walk the route in the opposite or counterclockwise direction if you are good at following directions in reverse. For a much longer ridge outing, try the Schofield-Waikāne hike that starts from the same trailhead.

27

Poamoho

TYPE:	Graded ridge
LENGTH:	7-mile round-trip
ELEVATION GAIN:	600 feet
DANGER:	Low
SUITABLE FOR:	Novice, Intermediate, Expert
LOCATION:	Kawailoa and ʻEwa Forest Reserves above Helemano
TOPO MAP:	Hauʻula
ACCESS:	Conditional; open on weekends and holidays to individuals with a four-wheel drive vehicle and a permit from the Forestry and Wildlife-Oʻahu Division. For more information, see Appendix: Hiking and Camping Information Sources.

HIGHLIGHTS

This scenic ridge hike is the shortest route to the Koʻolau summit in central Oʻahu. Along the way are native birds and a large variety of native plants. From the windy lookout at the top is one of the best views on the island.

TRAILHEAD DIRECTIONS

At Punchbowl St. get on Lunalilo Fwy. (H-1) heading ʻEwa (west).

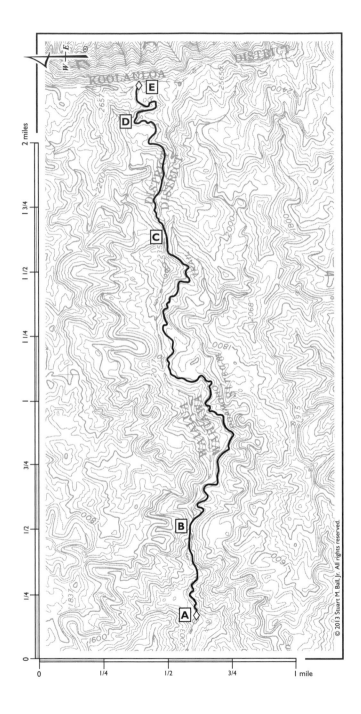

Near Middle St. keep left on Moanalua Fwy. (H-201) to 'Aiea.

By Aloha Stadium, bear right to rejoin H-1 to Pearl City.

Take H-2 Freeway (exit 8A) to Wahiawā.

As the freeway ends, continue on Rte. 99 north (Wilikina Dr.), bypassing Wahiawā.

Pass Schofield Barracks on the left.

The road narrows to two lanes, dips, and then forks. Take the right fork toward the North Shore (Kamananui Rd., but still Rte. 99 north).

At the road's end, turn left on Kamehameha Hwy. (Rte. 99).

Pass Dole and Helemano Plantations on the right.

At the first traffic light, turn right on Pa'ala'a Uka Pūpūkea Rd. toward Helemano Military Reservation.

On the right, look for a paved parking lot just before the reservation entrance station. Before reaching the lot, turn right on a dirt road known as Poamoho Hele Loa.

Immediately reach a locked yellow gate. Reset your trip odometer (0.0 mile). Register at the hunter/hiker check-in mailbox on the right just past the gate.

After proceeding through the gate, keep the fence on the right and circle around the reservation housing area on the one-lane road. Watch for rock speed bumps.

At the back of the reservation, bear right and then reach a second locked gate (1.6 miles).

Reach a third locked gate (2.1 miles).

Climb gradually through abandoned agricultural fields. The road jogs right and then left past a covered storage area.

Pass a grassy parking area on the right (4.5 miles).

Descend briefly and then switchback twice to gain altitude gradually. Ignore less-traveled roads coming in on the right.

Pass a Public Hunting Area sign (5.2 miles).

Reach a small, eroded parking area at the road's end (6.1 miles) (map point A) (elevation 1,900 feet).

BUS: None within reasonable walking distance of the trailhead.

ROUTE DESCRIPTION

At the far end of the parking area, proceed along the wide, graded Poamoho Trail.

Thread through a wooden barrier to thwart bikers.

Descend gradually along the right side of a ridge.

Cross over to the left side. To the right, a short side trail leads to a bench with an overlook of the Wai'anae Range.

Switch to the right side again (map point B). Look for the native shrub naupaka kuahiwi on the high side of the trail.

Contour for a long stretch through strawberry guava and native koa and 'ōhi'a trees. The 'ōhi'a have delicate red, yellow, or salmon-colored blossoms. Watch for the native birds 'apapane and 'amakihi and listen for the Japanese bush warbler.

Cross two small gullies on a plank bridge and pass another bench and an automated weather station on the left. From the bench is a good view of winding Poamoho Stream.

As the ridge narrows, the trail follows the crest briefly and then switches to the left side of the ridge just past an End of Maintained Trail sign (map point C). Look for a waterfall on the right below.

Cross over to the right side briefly and then resume contouring on the left side. Along the now narrow and deeply rutted trail are native manono trees, na'ena'e shrubs, and mint herbs.

Cross a small gully on another plank bridge.

Work up a side gulch above a small tributary of Helemano Stream (map point D). Look for native pū'ahanui (kanawao) shrubs and loulu palms.

After passing a grassy campsite on the right, descend briefly to the stream and ford it.

Turn left downstream and resume the gradual climb.

Cross over to the right side of a ridge.

Traverse a more open windswept area. Watch for koli'i, a native *Lobelia*.

Bear right to cross a grassy strip with another small weather station. On the left and above are the remains of an enclosure to protect native snails.

Reach a junction with the Koʻolau Summit Trail by two warning signs and a stone memorial to Geraldine Cline.

Keep the memorial on the left and ascend a small, grassy hump to reach the Koʻolau summit (elevation 2,500 feet) (map point E) (UTM 04 0611722E, 2381683N).

NOTES

The magnificent Poamoho Trail winds along the ridge between Helemano and Poamoho Streams through the rugged Koʻolau wilderness in central Oʻahu. The hike is relatively short because of the improved access route developed in 2007 by Na Ala Hele, the state trail program. Start early, however, to have plenty of time to drive the long approach road and to enjoy the native plants and splendid views along the trail.

While you are safely negotiating the dirt access road in your four-wheel-drive vehicle, consider that early travelers on this remote ridge had to contend with a band of cannibals, according to Hawaiian lore. Led by chief Kalo ʻAi Kanaka, the man-eaters built a *heiau* (religious site) and dwellings at an idyllic, secluded, and strategic spot. *Makai* (seaward), the ridge narrowed considerably, forcing woodcutters and windward wayfarers to pass close to the chief's house. The band nabbed the unfortunate ones, roasted them in an *imu* (underground oven), and carved them on a large flat stone or *ipu kai* (meat platter).

The Wahiawā Camp of the Civilian Conservation Corps built the Poamoho Trail during the spring and summer of 1934. Since then, periodic maintenance has kept the lower and middle sections wide and well graded for the most part. The upper part, however, is deeply rutted and very slippery.

Watch your footing constantly; expect to fall down a few times and get muddy and wet. Novices can go as far as they like and then turn around.

On the trail, watch for the native shrub naupaka kuahiwi. It has light green, pointed leaves and half-flowers. Initially the naupaka along the trail has toothed leaves and white flowers. Closer to the summit, a slightly different variety appears with smoother leaf margins and purple streaks in the flowers.

Throughout the hike, listen for the Japanese bush warbler (uguisu), a bird often heard but rarely seen. Its distinctive cry starts with a long whistle and then winds down in a series of notes. The bush warbler is olive brown on top with a white breast and a long tail. If the 'ōhi'a are in bloom, you may glimpse the native 'apapane. It has a red breast and head, black wings and tail, and a slightly curved black bill. In flight, the 'apapane makes a whirring sound as it darts from tree to tree searching for insects and nectar.

On the upper section, look for native mint herbs, na'ena'e shrubs, and manono trees. The viny mint has square stems and pointed, toothed leaves with red veins, but little aroma. The lovely white flowers are about an inch long with an extended lower lip. Na'ena'e has narrow, shallowly toothed leaves grouped near the branch tips. Its purple-green flower heads are displayed in cone-shaped clusters. Manono has thick, glossy, oblong leaves with purple stems, small yellow-green flowers shaped like anchors, and purple-black fruits.

Along the small stream near the summit are native pū'ahanui (kanawao) shrubs and loulu palms. A relative of hydrangea, pū'ahanui has large, serrated, deeply creased leaves and clusters of delicate pink flowers. The shrub is a favorite habitat of the endangered Hawaiian land snail. Early Hawaiians used the plants for medicinal purposes. Loulu palms have rigid, fan-shaped fronds in a cluster at the top of a ringed trunk. Early Hawaiians used the fronds for thatch and plaited the blades of young fronds into fans and baskets.

After crossing the stream, watch for koli'i, an unusual native *Trematolobelia*. It has a single woody stem with triangular leaf scars. Its long, slender leaves are arranged in a rosette resembling a dry mop head. A circle of horizontal stalks from the rosette bears lovely scarlet tubular flowers in November. After flowering, the entire plant dies, leaving a ring of seed capsules.

At the Ko'olau (windward) summit is one of the great viewpoints on the island. You can look straight down into green Punalu'u (coral dived for) and Kahana (cutting) valleys. Separating the two is the summit of Pu'u Piei. The pyramid peak on the right is Pu'u 'Ōhulehule (joining of waves hill). In front of it and partially hidden is Ka'a'awa Valley. Beyond, the windward coast stretches from Mōkapu (taboo district) to Makapu'u (bulging eye) points. To leeward you can see the Wai'anae (mullet water) Range. From left to right along its summit ridge are Pu'u Kaua (war hill), Kolekole (raw) Pass, Kalena (the lazy one), and flat-topped Ka'ala (the fragrance), the highest mountain on O'ahu.

Before the viewpoint is the junction with the Summit Trail, an 18.5-mile footpath along the top of the Ko'olau Range for experienced hikers only. Turn right to reach the Poamoho Cabin, a half mile away, and the Schofield-Waikāne Trail. Turn left to get to Lā'ie Trail and the Pūpūkea (white shell) Summit hike. The mileage to each trail junction is listed on a plaque in the stone memorial, erected in 1978 by friends and relatives of Geraldine Cline. A beloved member of the Hawaiian Trail and Mountain Club and the Sierra Club, she died tragically in an automobile accident.

WINDWARD SIDE

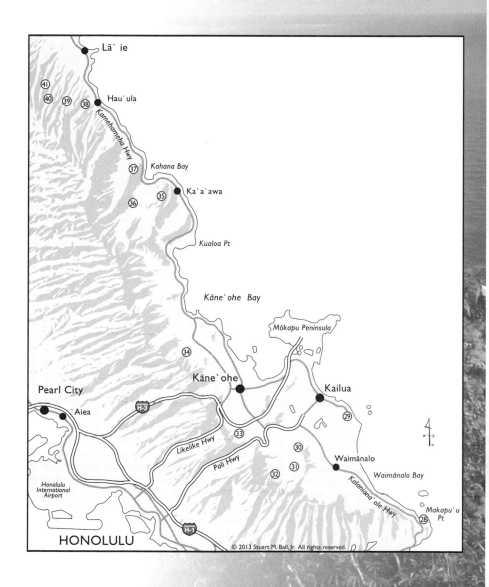

28

Makapu'u Point

TYPE:	Ungraded ridge
LENGTH:	3-mile loop
ELEVATION GAIN:	600 feet
DANGER:	Low
SUITABLE FOR:	Novice, Intermediate
LOCATION:	Makapu'u Point State Wayside Park
TOPO MAP:	Koko Head
ACCESS:	Open

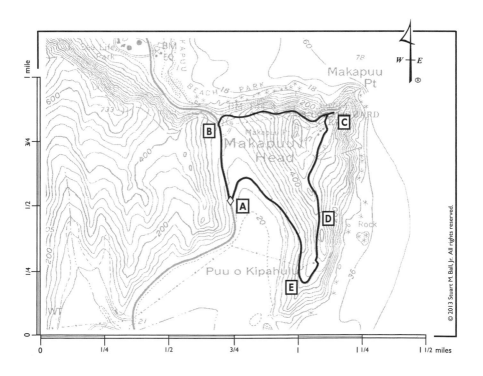

HIGHLIGHTS

This short, scenic loop climbs the windswept cliffs above the easternmost point on the island. Along the way are remnant fortifications, a lighthouse, and some rock scrambling. From ocean overlooks, you can often see humpback whales and colonies of seabirds.

TRAILHEAD DIRECTIONS

At Ward Ave. get on Lunalilo Fwy. (H-1) Koko Head bound (east).

As the freeway ends, continue straight on Kalanianaʻole Hwy. (Rte. 72).

The highway narrows to two lanes just past Koko Marina Shopping Center.

Pass Hanauma Bay Nature Preserve and Sandy Beach Park on the right and Hawaiʻi Kai Golf Course on the left.

The road swings left and begins the climb to Makapuʻu lookout.

By the Kaiwi Shoreline sign, turn right into the main parking lot for the Makapuʻu Point hike and leave your car there (elevation 40 feet) (map point A).

BUS: Route 22, 23, or 57 to Sea Life Park. Walk 0.5 mile along Kalanianaʻole Hwy. to Makapuʻu lookout. (This is the most dangerous part of the hike because of the heavy traffic on the narrow road.)

ROUTE DESCRIPTION

Walk back up the access road toward the highway.

As the road swings left, turn right onto a makeshift trail that leads through a grassy, rocky area to the Makapuʻu lookout parking lot (map point B). If you miss the trail, walk along the highway to the lookout.

At the far end of the parking lot, climb two short flights of stairs to the upper viewing area.

Step between the railing and a rock wall and proceed along the edge of the cliff on a makeshift trail. Look for the low-lying native shrub ʻilima papa with its delicate yellow-orange flowers.

Pass three walled-up observation bunkers below and on the left.

Climb steadily along the cliff edge past a fourth bunker. As necessary, work right to avoid steep rock faces. Watch for *Schiedea globosa,* a prostrate native subshrub with narrow, somewhat fleshy leaves.

Pass a line of stunted ironwood trees on the left. The top of Makapuʻu Point Lighthouse appears dead ahead.

Reach a relatively flat, grassy area. In back is a rock face used by climbers.

Resume the steady ascent, roughly paralleling a water pipe and a utility line.

Pass a huge pānini cactus on the right.

Work left around the front of the cliff past some more ironwoods.

Pass a concrete water tank on the right. From there a short trail leads to the top of Makupuʻu Head (elevation 647 feet).

Descend briefly to a paved road and turn left on it.

Pass a memorial plaque honoring nine World War II airmen whose Catalina seaplane crashed nearby in 1942.

The road narrows to a path that climbs to a lookout (map point C) (UTM 04 0639952E, 2356980N). In season, look for humpback whales below and frigate birds above.

From the lookout, retrace your steps back to the road.

In a level area, reach a junction. Turn left and down. (The road straight ahead soon ends and becomes a rough trail that ascends to the top of Makapuʻu Head.)

Descend along the crest of a ridge past night-blooming cereus and native milo trees.

Reach a junction with a gravel road. Continue straight on the main road. (The gravel road to the left leads past a red-roofed structure to the Makapuʻu Point Lighthouse, which is strictly off-limits to the public.)

Just before a hump on the left, reach a junction marked by a whale sign (map point D). Continue straight on the paved road. (To the left, an obscure trail marked with white paint descends steeply down the cliff to some tide pools and a double blowhole along the rocky shoreline.)

The road leaves the ridgeline at Puʻu o Kāpahulu and curves right through scrub kiawe trees.

Walk past an open black gate. Along the coast to the left is a prominent rock formation known as Pele's Chair.

Reach the main parking lot, which is lined with native naupaka kahakai shrubs (map point A).

NOTES

Makapuʻu (bulging eye) Point is a very popular hike with tourists and locals alike. Most people walk up and back on the paved road from the main parking lot. If you are a novice hiker, that's exactly what you should do. More experienced hikers can try the loop route described above. It starts with a steep scramble along the edge of the Makapuʻu cliffs and ends with the pleasant stroll down the road.

Take this hike during winter (November–April) to see migrating humpback whales. The temperature is also cooler then, and the sun is less intense. Start early or late, or go on a weekday to avoid the crowds. Don't forget the two essentials for this hike: sunscreen and binoculars.

Near the start of the trail is the low-lying native shrub ʻilima papa. It has oblong, serrated leaves, about 1 inch long. The yellow-orange flowers strung together have been used to make regal lei in both ancient and modern Hawaiʻi.

On the climb up, look out for the thorny pānini (prickly

pear cactus). It has red or yellow flowers and a delicious, dark red, pear-shaped fruit. Wear gloves when handling the fruit, as the skin has small bristles. Don Marin, a Spaniard and advisor to King Kamehameha I, introduced pānini from Mexico in the early 1800s.

From the *makai* (seaward) lookout is a magnificent view along the windward coast to Mōkapu (taboo district) Point. Below are Makapuʻu Beach and Sealife Park. Beyond is the broad sweep of lovely Waimānalo (potable water) Bay. The two islands offshore, Mānana and Kāohikaipu (Mokuhope), are state seabird sanctuaries. On a clear day, you can see the neighbor islands of Molokaʻi and Maui across Kaiwi (the bone) Channel.

While at the lookout, scan the ocean for humpback whales. They migrate from the North Pacific to the Hawaiian Islands, arriving in October and leaving in May. The whales congregate off the leeward coast of Maui and occupy themselves calving, nursing, breeding, and generally horsing around.

From the lookout you can also see frigate birds and tropic birds soaring overhead. Frigate birds are large, mostly black seabirds with slender wings and a forked tail. Early Hawaiians called them ʻiwa, or thief, because they often forced other seabirds to drop their food, which the ʻiwa would then catch in midair. The red-tailed tropic bird, or koaʻe ʻula, is white with a black eye patch and two central tail feathers elongated into streamers. Tropic birds feed by diving into the ocean for fish and squid. They nest in burrows or rock crevices on nearby Mānana island.

The Makapuʻu Lighthouse nestles on a shelf below the top of the cliffs. Completed in late 1908, the 35-foot tower houses the largest lighthouse lens in the United States, The kerosene lamp inside the lens was first lit on October 1, 1909. During World War II, James Jones, author of the novel *From Here to Eternity,* helped build five pillboxes on Makapuʻu Head in November 1941. After the Pearl Harbor attack on December 7, he and fellow soldiers occupied those fortifications with machine guns and rifles to deter an anticipated Japanese invasion.

The short side trip to the top of Makapu'u Head is well worthwhile. A makeshift trail starts from the water tank, parallels a water pipe, and then angles left to the summit (elevation 647 feet). From the bunker there, you can see the Ko'olau (windward) Range gradually rising to a flat-topped mountain, Pu'u o Kona (hill of leeward). On the leeward side are Koko Crater (Koheleplepe), Hanauma Bay, and, in the distance, Diamond Head (Lē'ahi).

On the way down, watch for native milo trees with glossy, heart-shaped leaves and yellow flowers. Hawaiian craftsmen carved the rich reddish brown wood into bowls, dishes, and platters. The fruit is a flattened globe and produces a yellow-green dye.

As the road heads *mauka* (inland), look left along the coast for a prominent rock formation resembling a chair. According to legend, Pele, the goddess of fire, rested there before leaving O'ahu for Maui and the Big Island. The Makapu'u cliffs were also the site of Mālei, another ancient stone. It was a physical representation of the goddess Mālei, who watched over the uhu (parrot fishes) of Makapu'u Point. Fishermen left offerings by the stone or sang to it to insure a good catch. The stone disappeared many years ago and has never been found.

29

Ka'iwa Ridge

TYPE:	Ungraded ridge
LENGTH:	2-mile round-trip
ELEVATION GAIN:	600 feet
DANGER:	Low
SUITABLE FOR:	Novice
LOCATION:	Windward side above Lanikai
TOPO MAP:	Mōkapu
ACCESS:	Open

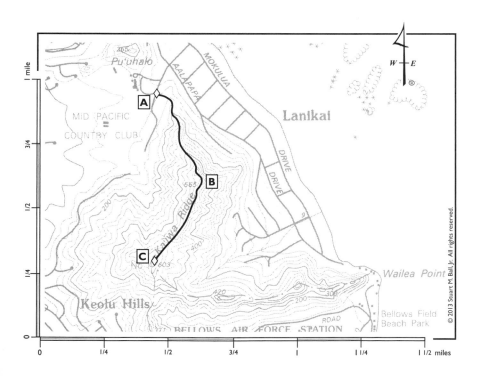

HIGHLIGHTS

This short, steep hike climbs a dry, windy ridge above Lanikai. From the observation bunkers are magnificent views
of the windward coast and the Koʻolau cliffs. The outing is
especially fine in the morning for sunrise or in the evening for
moonrise.

TRAILHEAD DIRECTIONS

At Punchbowl St. get on Pali Hwy. (Rte. 61 north) heading up
Nuʻuanu Valley.

Go under the Pali through the twin tunnels.

At the first traffic light (Castle Junction), continue straight
on Kalanianaʻole Hwy. (still Rte. 61).

By Castle Medical Center, continue straight on Kailua Rd.

In Kailua town, the road forks after crossing a small bridge.
Keep left onto Kuʻulei Rd.

At the road's end, turn right on S. Kalaheo Ave.

After passing Kalapawai Market, the road jogs left, crosses
Kaʻelepulu Stream, and becomes Kawailoa Rd.

Pass Kailua Beach Park on the left. The park has restrooms
and drinking water.

Turn left on Alala Rd. at a stop sign.

Enter Lanikai and keep right on one-way ʻAʻalapapa Dr.

Take the second right on Kaʻelepulu Dr.

Pass the entrance to Mid-Pacific Country Club on the
right.

Park on the right by the country club fence before reaching
the gated community of Bluestone (elevation 80 feet) (map
point A).

BUS: Route 70 to ʻAʻalapapa Dr. and Kaʻelepulu Dr. Walk 0.1
mile up Kaʻelepulu Dr. to the trailhead.

ROUTE DESCRIPTION

Continue along Ka'elepulu Dr. on foot.

Before reaching the Bluestone entrance gate, turn left up a paved driveway past two bollards.

As the driveway curves left to house no. 269-275, bear right and up on an eroded trail between two chain-link fences.

Pass a utility pole.

Climb steeply up the side of Ka'iwa Ridge through scrub koa haole.

Reach the open ridgeline and the first of many viewpoints.

After a short level stretch, swing right and then left to avoid a rock scramble.

Work right to bypass a rock face and then left to regain the ridgeline.

On the left, pass a concrete observation post built during World War II. Look for a patch of night-blooming cereus after the building.

Continue climbing to a split-level bunker (map point B). Its flat roof makes a good rest spot and viewpoint.

Descend briefly and then climb to a knob. Bear left and down to bypass a rock outcrop at its top.

Ascend another knob in the ridge.

Reach a junction near the top of a broad hill. Keep left along the main ridge. (To the right, a trail leads down a side ridge to Keolu Hills subdivision.)

Shortly afterward, reach a rock platform, all that remains of a surveyors' triangulation station (elevation 603 feet) (map point C) (UTM 04 0632740E, 2364855N).

NOTES

This popular hike climbs scenic Ka'iwa Ridge above Lanikai on the windward side. The novice route is short and immediately rewarding, but the footing is treacherous. Much of the trail is over loose dirt and rock. Hike or sightsee, but don't do both at the same time! Be especially careful on the initial steep climb, which can be slippery when wet.

Ka'iwa Ridge provides an inspired setting at sunrise and a romantic evening for moonrise. For the evening outing, start just before sunset and hike to the second bunker. Enjoy a picnic on the roof and then watch the full moon rise over Kaiwi Channel. For the return trip, bring a flashlight, as night falls quickly in the tropics.

Ka'iwa is named after the frigate bird that sometimes soars over the ridge. Frigate birds are large, mostly black seabirds with slender wings and a forked tail. Early Hawaiians called them 'iwa, or thief, because they often forced other seabirds to drop their food, which the 'iwa would then catch in midair.

Along the ridge, look for the native shrub 'uhaloa, a woody, sprawling herb. Its gray-green leaves are oval, pointed, and covered with fine hairs. Small yellow flowers with five petals emerge from the angle between the stem and the leaf stalk. Early Hawaiians used 'uhaloa as a medicinal herb to relieve sore throats, congestion, chest pain, and asthma.

The view from the roof of the second bunker is breathtaking. *Makai* (seaward) from left to right are Kualoa (long back) Point, Kāne'ohe (bamboo husband) Bay, Mōkapu (taboo district) Point, Kailua (two seas) Bay, Waimānalo (potable water) Bay, and Makapu'u (bulging eye) Point. Directly offshore are two sea stacks, the Mokulua Islands. *Mauka* (inland) is Olomana (forked hill) with its three peaks, and in back are the fluted cliffs of the Ko'olau Range.

The second bunker also makes a good place to visualize the extent of the collapsed summit or caldera of the old Ko'olau volcano. The caldera was 8 miles long, stretching from Kāne'ohe to Waimānalo, and 4 miles wide from the Ko'olau cliffs to its eastern boundary between the Mokulua Islands and Ka'iwa Ridge. After volcanic activity ceased several million years ago, weathering and stream and wave erosion gradually removed the sides of the caldera and the soft lava beds inside. Olomana peak remained because of its complex of narrow, vertical dikes composed of hard, dense rock.

Past the second bunker is a large patch of night-blooming cereus, a climbing vine with fleshy, spiny, three-sided stems. The huge, showy flowers have greenish white petals and cream-colored stamens. They are short lived, however, opening only at night from June through October. Introduced from Mexico to Hawai'i about 1830, night-blooming cereus was first planted at Punahou School.

From the triangulation station, the trail continues *makai* along the ridge to Wailea, a prominent *pōhaku* (rock) surrounded by night-blooming cereus. Wailea was a fish god and a fish shrine that marked the best fishing grounds off Ka'ōhao (the early Hawaiian name for Lanikai). Do not descend the right side of the ridge into Bellows Air Force Station, a restricted military installation and recreation area.

30

Olomana

TYPE:	Ungraded ridge
LENGTH:	6-mile round-trip
ELEVATION GAIN:	1,600 feet
DANGER:	High
SUITABLE FOR:	Intermediate, Expert
LOCATION:	Olomana State Monument near Maunawili
TOPO MAP:	Mōkapu, Koko Head
ACCESS:	Open

HIGHLIGHTS

Olomana is the craggy, commanding mountain windward of Nuʻuanu Pali. The steep, narrow climb to its three peaks demands concentration, sure feet, and little fear of heights. From the summit is a panorama unsurpassed on Oʻahu.

TRAILHEAD DIRECTIONS

At Punchbowl St. get on Pali Hwy. (Rte. 61 north) heading up Nuʻuanu Valley.

Go under the Pali through the twin tunnels.

Pali Hwy. becomes Kalanianaʻole Hwy. at the first traffic light (Castle Junction).

At the third traffic light, turn right on Aʻuloa Rd.

For more convenient but less safe parking, immediately turn left on Luana Hills Rd. Leave your car on either side of

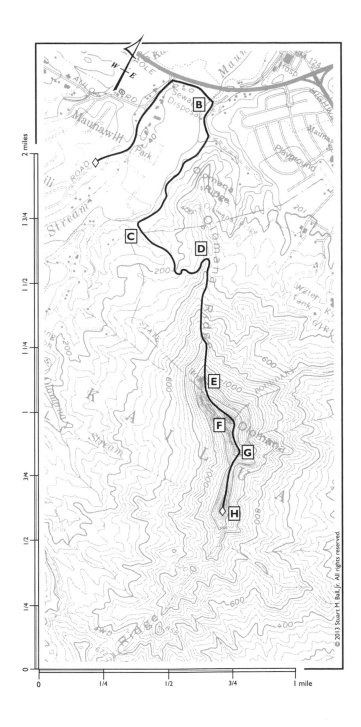

the road by a chain-link fence before reaching a bridge. Don't block any driveways.

Otherwise, continue driving along A'uloa Rd.

Shortly afterward, the road forks; keep left on Maunawili Rd.

Pass Maunawili Valley Neighborhood Park on the left. The park has restrooms and drinking water.

As the road widens, enter Maunawili subdivision.

Park on the street just past the intersection with Maunawili Lp. (elevation 80 feet) (map point A).

BUS: Routes 56, 57, 57A, 70, or 77 to Kalaniana'ole Hwy. and A'uloa Rd. Turn left on Luana Hills Rd. and pick up the description below. Route 77 runs only on weekdays.

ROUTE DESCRIPTION

Walk back toward Kalaniana'ole Hwy.

Just before reaching it, turn right on Luana Hills Rd., which parallels the highway.

After crossing Maunawili Stream on a bridge, turn right on the access road leading into Royal Hawaiian Golf Club (map point B).

As the road forks, keep right through a green gate and pass a security station on the left.

The golf club road ascends gradually past a white fence and then levels out.

As the road curves right and climbs, look for two thick yellow metal posts on the left.

Just past the second post, reach a signed junction (map point C). Turn left off the road, cross a narrow drainage ditch, and pick up the trail to Olomana. (Beyond the junction, the road is open only to club patrons.)

Ascend gradually along the right side of a gully.

Cross the gully near an abandoned pumping shack and keep left by a huge banyan tree.

Climb steadily up the side of Olomana Ridge through introduced forest. Lauaʻe ferns carpet the ground.

Gain the ridgeline at a small dip marked by a fencepost, a metal pipe, and a utility pole (map point D). Turn right, up the ridge.

Cross an eroded spot and enter an ironwood grove. Look for the native shrub ʻākia in the open sections.

Gradually ascend the flank of the mountain through a corridor of Christmas berry and lauaʻe. Watch out for a rusty barbed-wire fence on the right.

Begin climbing more steeply on a rocky trail (map point E).

Keep right up a long rock face partially covered by vegetation. A series of cables and ropes may provide some assistance.

Continue climbing very steeply. Underfoot are exposed rock dikes.

The angle of ascent decreases briefly through a hau grove (whew!).

Climb a short but nearly vertical rock face. A cable or rope may help in the ascent.

The ridgeline contracts to a thin rock dike.

Bear right off the ridge to avoid an especially narrow section.

Reach the summit of Olomana at a rocky outcrop (elevation 1,643 feet) (map point F) (UTM 04 0629539E, 2362630N). Admire the panoramic views of the windward coast and the Koʻolau cliffs.

Descend steeply to a saddle and then climb briefly to the second peak, known as Pākuʻi (map point G). Among the grass and Christmas berry are the sprawling ʻūlei and the lanky kokoʻolau, both native shrubs.

Just past the summit of the second peak, turn sharp right and down to continue along the main ridge.

Descend precipitously to a saddle between the second and third peaks. A series of cables and ropes may aid in the descent over loose dirt and rock.

Begin climbing the very thin ridge of the third peak.

Inch left around a large dike section with a hole in it. A cable may provide some security.

Scramble up a long, steep rock face.

Keep right around a large free-standing boulder.

Bear right off the ridgeline and climb the final rock face.

Reach the flat summit of the third peak, known as Ahiki (map point H).

NOTES

Olomana is Oʻahu's version of the Matterhorn. The main peak is a steep-sided pyramid that looks unclimbable from a distance. Closer inspection, however, reveals the classic route up the northwest ridge. Although thousands of hikers have taken that climb over the years, treat this alluring, dangerous mountain with respect.

Olomana (forked hill) has three distinct peaks. The elongated, razor-thin third peak is called Ahiki, and the second central peak is Pākuʻi. Both are named after *konohiki* (overseers) of the ancient fishponds of Kaʻelepulu (the moist blackness), now called Enchanted Lake, and Kawainui (the big water). The first and highest peak is named after the legendary giant Olomana.

Olomana was a fearsome, evil warrior, 12 yards high, who dominated the windward side. None dared challenge him, not even the chief of Oʻahu. One day the chief commanded Palila, a brash young soldier, to rid the island of the giant. Palila journeyed to Kaʻelepulu, where he surprised Olomana by jumping up on his shoulder. The giant haughtily asked the boy soldier what he was doing up there and where he was from. Palila replied that he came from a temple on Kauaʻi noted for great warriors with supernatural powers. On hearing that, Olomana became afraid and begged for his life. Palila deftly struck the giant, cutting him in two. One part flew *makai* (seaward) and became Mahinui (great champion) mountain along the coast. The other part remained as the present peak of Olomana.

Much of the route up the mountain is a scramble over loose rock and dirt. The climb to the first and second peaks is an intermediate hike with medium danger. You must negotiate a narrow rock dike and a nearly vertical rock face just below the first peak. The descent from the second peak and the ascent to the third are for experienced, acrobatic hikers only. The rock is rotten, and the ridge plunges straight down on both sides. Test any ropes or cables that you find before using them. Take your time and be extraordinarily careful. There is no shame in turning back if you don't like what you see.

On the hike, look for the native dryland shrub 'ākia in the open areas along Olomana Ridge. The shrub has dark branches jointed with white rings. Its leaves are bright green, oval, and pointed. Early Hawaiians pounded the leaves and bark and then dropped the mixture into tidal pools to poison the fish. The red-orange fruits were used in lei and as a poison for criminals.

From the top of the first peak is an awesome 360-degree view. *Makai* is the windward coast from Kualoa (long back) to Mōkapu (taboo district) to Makapu'u (bulging eye) points. On a clear day, you can see the islands of Moloka'i and Maui across Kaiwi (the bone) Channel. *Mauka* (inland) is Maunawili (twisted mountain) Valley and the sheer, fluted cliffs of the Ko'olau (windward) Range. The massive peak to the left of Nu'uanu Pali (cool height cliff) is Kōnāhuanui (large fat testicles), the highest point in the Ko'olau Range. Try picking out the other major peaks on the summit ridge. From left to right are Pu'u o Kona (hill of leeward), Lanipō (dense), and Olympus (Awāwaloa). Beyond Kōnāhuanui is Lanihuli (turning royal chief) and Pu'u Keahi a Kahoe (hill of Kahoe's fire). In the distance is the steep pyramid of Pu'u 'Ōhulehule (joining of the waves hill).

Between the first and second peaks is the sprawling native shrub 'ūlei. It has small, oblong leaves arranged in pairs; clusters of white, roselike flowers; and white fruit. Early Hawaiians ate the berries and used the tough wood for making digging sticks, fish spears, and 'ūkēkē (the musical bow).

From the second peak is a good view along the length of the mountain. Olomana is a remnant of the collapsed caldera of the old Ko'olau volcano. Filled with lava, the caldera stretched 8 miles from Waimānalo (potable water) to Kāne'ohe (bamboo husband). When the volcano became dormant, streams gradually eroded the softer lava, leaving intrusions of hard, dense rock known as dikes. Olomana remains because of its complex of narrow, vertical dikes, over which you carefully scramble.

While resting on the third peak, look for small white nodules of opal in the dark lava. Over millions of years, volcanic gases altered the composition of the rocks in the caldera. In the process, excess silica collected in small cavities to form the white spheres, called amygdules.

31

Maunawili Falls

TYPE:	Valley
LENGTH:	3-mile round-trip
ELEVATION GAIN:	400 feet
DANGER:	Low
SUITABLE FOR:	Novice
LOCATION:	Waimānalo Forest Reserve above Maunawili
TOPO MAP:	Koko Head, Honolulu
ACCESS:	Open

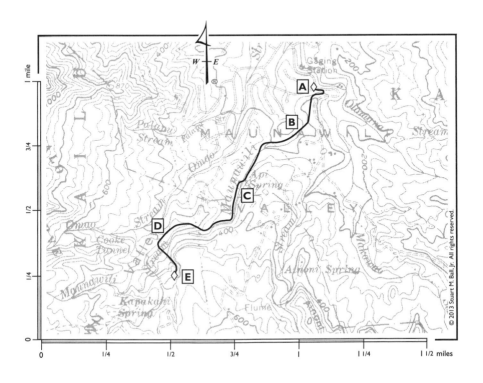

HIGHLIGHTS

This short hike winds along Maunawili Stream past remnant coffee groves and taro terraces. From a ridge lookout, you can see the Koʻolau Range and Kailua Bay. At the end is lovely Maunawili Falls, cascading into a deep swimming hole.

TRAILHEAD DIRECTIONS

At Punchbowl St. get on Pali Hwy. (Rte. 61 north) heading up Nuʻuanu Valley.

Go under the Pali through the twin tunnels.

At the first traffic light (Castle Junction), continue straight on Kalanianaʻole Hwy. (still Rte. 61).

At the third traffic light, turn right on Aʻuloa Rd.

Almost immediately, the road forks. Keep left on Maunawili Rd.

Drive through Maunawili subdivision.

The road narrows and winds through a forested area.

At the end of Maunawili Rd., turn right on Kelewina St.

Park on the street near that intersection (elevation 160 feet) (map point A).

BUS: Route 70 to Maunawili Rd. and Aloha ʻOhe Dr. Walk 0.3 mile along Maunawili Rd. to the trailhead.

ROUTE DESCRIPTION

Walk back to the intersection and bear right on a paved, private road with a yellow gate.

Just before the road swings right, reach a signed junction. Turn right on the access trail to Maunawili Falls. Nearby are three signs describing the agricultural history of the area.

Climb some steps through a hau tangle.

Parallel the private road above Makawao Stream.

Climb gradually and cross over a side ridge under some power lines.

Descend to Maunawili Stream and ford it by a rock painted with an orange "X" (map point B). Watch your footing while crossing. Ignore the wide, sloppy trail continuing along the left bank.

Go through a break in a stone wall and turn left upstream through a coffee grove.

Follow the stream under a canopy of mango and monkeypod trees. White ginger lines the trail.

Cross Maunawili Stream again and enter another coffee grove. Ignore the muddy trail along the left bank.

Shortly, turn right upstream, paralleling another stone wall.

Walk through a level section on a rock trail. Overhead are mango, coffee, and kukui trees; underfoot are kukui nuts.

Jump over a small stream channel coming from 'Api Spring on the left. Just before the spring are several ulu (breadfruit) trees on the left.

Ford Maunawili Stream for the third time.

Shortly afterward, reach the boundary of the Waimānalo Forest Reserve and the signed start of the official Maunawili Falls Trail (map point C).

Climb steadily above the stream. Because of heavy traffic, the trail has become wide and sloppy with slippery rocks, roots, and mud holes. Uphill sections are stabilized with gravel and plastic steps. Look for purple Philippine ground orchids.

Gain the top of a side ridge by some power lines (elevation 460 feet) and turn left uphill. *Mauka* (inland) are imposing views of the Ko'olau Range.

Ascend gradually along the ridge.

Just before an ironwood grove, reach a signed junction by a bench (map point D). Turn left off the ridge. (Straight ahead, the Maunawili Falls Trail climbs to a junction with the Maunawili Trail.)

Descend steeply on plastic steps. Kī (ti) plants anchor the eroding slope on the right.

Reach Maunawili Stream as it forks under a spreading mango tree. Cross the right fork.

Proceed up the right side of the left fork. Walk in the stream at first and then pick up a slippery rock trail along the right bank.

Reach Maunawili Falls and a large swimming hole (map point E) (UTM 04 0627292E, 2361221N).

NOTES

Volunteer crews under the direction of the Sierra Club, Hawai'i Chapter, completed this improved access to Maunawili (twisted mountain) Falls in October 1996. Since then, the hike has proven extremely popular, especially on sunny weekend afternoons. The route is short, pleasant, and leads to a superb swimming hole. To avoid the crowds, go on a weekday when school is in session or start early.

Before you begin hiking, several cautions are in order. The route initially follows a public right-of-way through private property; stay on the trail. In several places, hikers have rerouted the trail, not always for the better; the route described above is the original alignment. The treadway has deteriorated significantly from the heavy traffic over the years. Watch your footing constantly on the sloppy path with its exposed rocks, roots, and mud holes, and take care on the slippery stream crossings. As always, do not ford the stream if the water is much above your knees. Finally, don't feed the mosquitoes.

On the trail, look and listen for the white-rumped shama. It is black on top with a chestnut-colored breast and a long black and white tail. The shama has a variety of beautiful songs and often mimics other birds. A native of Malaysia, the shama has become widespread in introduced forests such as this one.

Along the stream are early Hawaiian *lo'i,* irrigated terraces for growing *kalo* (taro). Look for their remnant rock walls. After the first stream crossing are groves of Arabian coffee trees with glossy, dark green leaves and white flowers. Their fruit is red, drying to black or brown. Coffee was introduced to Hawai'i in the early 1800s and was widely cultivated in valleys along streams. Coffee is still commercially grown on the Big Island, where it is sold as Kona coffee.

Before reaching 'Api Spring, the trail is covered with fallen nuts from kukui trees. Their large, pale green leaves resemble those of the maple with several distinct lobes. Early Polynesian voyagers introduced kukui into Hawai'i. They used the wood to make gunwales and seats for their outrigger canoes. The flowers and sap became medicines to treat a variety of ailments. Early Hawaiians strung the nuts together to make *lei hua* (seed or nut garlands). The oily kernels became house candles and torches for night spearfishing.

From the short ridge section are impressive views. *Mauka* are the sheer, fluted cliffs of the Ko'olau (windward) Range. Kōnāhuanui (large fat testicles) (elevation 3,150 feet) is the massive peak above Nu'uanu (cool height) Pali. Along the summit ridge to the left are Mount Olympus (Awāwaloa) and Lanipō (dense). *Makai* (seaward) is triple-peaked Olomana (forked hill) and Kailua (two seas) Bay, ending at Mōkapu (taboo district) Point.

After the steep descent back to the stream, you soon reach Maunawili Falls. At its base is the large lower pool encircled by fern-covered cliffs. Up a slippery slope is a second smaller pool where the waterfall splits in two. Enjoy a refreshing swim in the cool mountain water. If you plan to jump into the lower pool from the cliffs, be sure to check its depth first!

For a longer hike, continue up the ridge on the falls trail to the junction with the Maunawili Trail. Turn left or right and go as far as you want.

32

Maunawili

TYPE:	Foothill
LENGTH:	9 miles one way
ELEVATION GAIN:	600 feet
DANGER:	Low
SUITABLE FOR:	Novice, Intermediate
LOCATION:	Waimānalo Forest Reserve above Maunawili
TOPO MAP:	Koko Head, Honolulu
ACCESS:	Open

HIGHLIGHTS

This popular hike snakes along the base of the sheer, fluted Koʻolau cliffs. Along the way are lush gulches, ridge lookouts, and a waterfall that smiles. The one-way route starts along Pali Hwy. and ends up in Waimānalo.

TRAILHEAD DIRECTIONS

At Punchbowl St. get on Pali Hwy. (Rte. 61 north) heading up Nuʻuanu Valley.

Go under the Pali through the twin tunnels.

At a sharp left curve called the hairpin turn, bear right on a short access road to a scenic viewpoint. Park in the narrow lot there by a rock wall (elevation 640 feet) (map point A).

BUS: Routes 56, 57, or 57A to Pali Hwy. and Kamehameha Hwy. (Castle Junction). Walk 0.8 mile back up Pali Hwy. to the viewpoint at the hairpin turn.

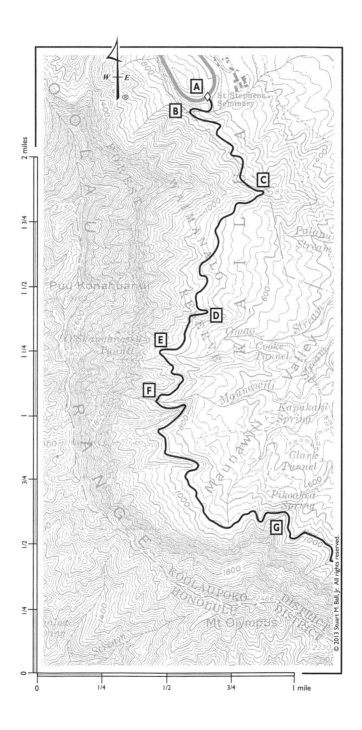

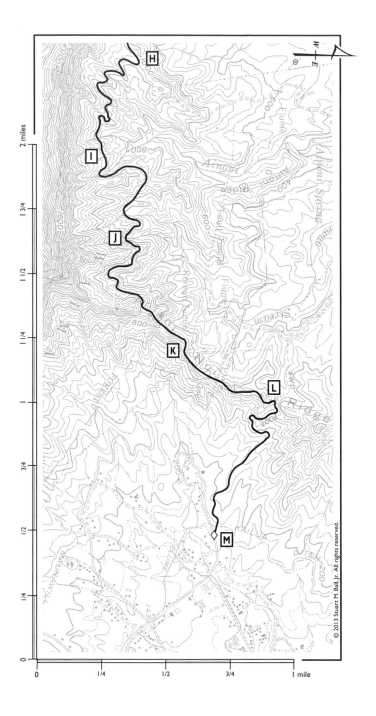

To get to the Waimānalo trailhead, continue along Pali Hwy. from the hairpin turn.

At the first traffic light (Castle Junction), Pali Hwy. becomes Kalanianaʻole Hwy. (still Rte. 61).

By Castle Memorial Hospital, turn right on Rte. 72 (still Kalanianaʻole Hwy.) to Waimānalo.

The highway narrows to two lanes by Olomana Golf Course.

Take the second right on Kumuhau St.

At the road's end, turn right on Waikupanaha St. and cross a bridge.

Pass the intersection with Mahiku Pl.

Shortly afterward, park in a small gravel area on the right by the signed trailhead (elevation 140 feet) (map point M). It's through a yellow gate just beyond a house on the left with a blue metal roof (no. 41-1020).

BUS: Route 57 or 77 to Kalanianaʻole Hwy. and Kumuhau St. Walk 1.2 miles to the trailhead. Route 77 runs only on weekdays.

ROUTE DESCRIPTION

Walk back up the access road.

Go through a gap in the guardrail on the left.

Just past a mango tree, turn left on a connector trail heading into the forest.

Cross a small culvert and pass a water tank below and on the left.

Switchback twice past several mango trees.

By some plastic steps, reach a signed junction with the Maunawili Trail (map point B). Turn left on it. (To the right, the trail climbs to Old Pali Rd. and Nuʻuanu Pali lookout.)

Pass a small water tank on the right.

Contour into and out of three gulches through guava (waiawī) trees.

Cross over a prominent side ridge known as Piliwale Ridge (map point C).

Break out into the open briefly through native uluhe ferns and scattered 'ōhi'a trees. *Mauka* (inland) are spectacular views of the Ko'olau cliffs.

Enter another ravine and then emerge into the open again.

Work into and out of a series of shallow gulches and then two larger ones with rocky streambeds. Look for kukui trees in the gulches and Chinese ground orchids along the trail in winter.

Cross over a broad side ridge with a stand of ironwood trees above and on the right.

Work into and out of another ravine and then cross over a narrow side ridge (map point D). In the cliffs ahead are four waterfall chutes.

Descend into a deep ravine on two switchbacks and then contour through a series of shallow gullies.

Enter a wide gulch with the four waterfall chutes in back.

Cross a pair of rocky streambeds that join just below the trail. At the first one, a faint side trail on the right leads to the bottom of a waterfall chute and the O'Shaughnessy Tunnel.

Cross intermittent 'Ōma'o Stream by some struggling bamboo (map point E). Another faint side trail leads upstream to Smiling Falls, named for the shape of the rock dike at its base.

Reach a signed junction (UTM 04 0626263E, 2361286N). Continue straight on the Maunawili Trail. (To the left, the Maunawili Falls Trail leads down a side ridge to the falls and out to Kelewina St.)

Contour through a small ravine and then cross over an open side ridge with several ironwoods on the right. Listen for the distinctive call of the Japanese bush warbler.

Descend into a large gulch on two switchbacks.

Cross Maunawili Stream in a grove of mountain apple trees

(map point F) and climb to the next side ridge and another good viewpoint.

Work into and out of two more gulches.

Wind through a long stretch of shallow ravines, some choked with hau trees. Along the trail are a few native naupaka kuahiwi shrubs.

Cross over a side ridge with a lone ironwood and several native koa trees (map point G).

Climb gradually through two narrow gulches.

Cross over a prominent side ridge with a power-line tower on top (map point H).

Work into and out of a long series of deep gulches. Look for 'ōhi'a in the open sections and native māmaki trees in the ravines. In the last two gulches are bird's-nest ferns.

Climb gradually to cross over another prominent side ridge with a small knob on the left.

Wind through four more gulches, which form the watershed of 'Ainoni Stream (map point I). The third one may have a tiny waterfall. After the fourth gulch are a few native lama trees.

Descend along the side of 'Ainoni Ridge and then resume contouring in a paperbark grove.

Pass two waterfall chutes side by side in a deep ravine with kī (ti) plants. On the next side ridge are several native alahe'e trees.

Work into and out of a large double gulch with a line of ironwoods and a small pool and waterfall (map point J). The trickle of water is a branch of Makawao Stream.

Descend gradually through three small gulches, two with weeping walls.

Reach a junction under some power lines (map point K). Continue straight through the clearing. (The dirt road to the left leads to Old Government Rd.)

Contour below Anianinui Ridge.

Gain the ridgeline and walk along its crest. To the right are views of Waimānalo town and the Ko'olau cliffs.

Descend gradually along the right side of the ridge.

By a large mango tree, reach a junction with Old Government Rd. (map point L). Turn right on the road. (To the left, some boulders block vehicle access.)

Descend gradually on two switchbacks.

Reach a signed junction. Continue straight on the road. (To the left is the Maunawili Ditch Trail.)

Go around a yellow gate and reach paved Waikupanaha St. (map point M) (UTM 04 0630442E, 2360608N).

NOTES

Maunawili is the showpiece of the O'ahu trail system. Richard H. Davis of the Hawaiian Trail and Mountain Club scouted and flagged the proposed route. Volunteer crews under the direction of the Sierra Club, Hawai'i Chapter, constructed 7 miles of trail during the summer and fall of 1991 through 1993. The remaining 2 miles were completed in 1993 by the Boy Scouts, U.S. Marines, and prisoners from O'ahu Correctional Facility. Starting from Pali Hwy., the trail winds for 9 miles along the base of the Ko'olau cliffs to Waimānalo.

With its well-groomed and graded treadway, the Maunawili Trail is popular with hikers, runners, and mountain bikers. To avoid the crowds, start early or go during the week. Better yet, try the hike right after a heavy rainstorm when waterfalls suddenly appear out of every notch in the cliffs. Watch your footing in the slippery stream crossings, though.

Lining the gulches along the trail are kukui trees. Their large, pale green leaves resemble those of the maple with several distinct lobes. Early Polynesian voyagers introduced kukui into Hawai'i. They used the wood to make gunwales and seats for their outrigger canoes. The flowers and sap became medicines to treat a variety of ailments. Early Hawaiians strung the nuts together to make *lei hua* (seed or nut garlands). The oily kernels became house candles and torches for night spearfishing.

The views from the open side ridges are breathtaking. *Makai* (seaward) are Kailua (two seas) and Waimānalo (potable water) Bays with triple-peaked Olomana (forked hill) in front. *Mauka* (inland) loom the sheer, fluted Koʻolau (windward) cliffs from Makapuʻu (bulging eye) Point to Kōnāhuanui (large fat testicles), the highest peak in the range. The aspect of the cliffs and Olomana constantly changes as you work around the Maunawili (twisted mountain) drainage.

Near the Maunawili Falls Trail junction listen for the Japanese bush warbler (uguisu), a bird often heard, but rarely seen. Its distinctive cry starts with a long whistle and then winds down in a series of notes. The bush warbler is olive brown on top with a white breast and a long tail.

After crossing Maunawili Stream, the trail enters a series of shallow ravines choked with tangled hau trees. They have large, heart-shaped leaves and bright yellow flowers with a dark red center, resembling those of a hibiscus. Early Hawaiians used the wood for kites and canoe outriggers, the bark for sandals, and the sap as a laxative. In the same area is the native shrub naupaka kuahiwi. It has light green, toothed leaves and white half-flowers.

After crossing the side ridge with a power-line tower, look for māmaki, a small native tree. It has leathery, light green leaves with toothed margins and prominent veins. Along the stems are the white, fleshy fruits. Early Hawaiians used the bark and sap in making *kapa* (bark cloth). They also steeped the leaves to prepare a tea as a tonic.

In the ʻAinoni drainage are a few native lama trees. Their oblong, pointed leaves are dark green and leathery. The fruits are green, then yellow, and finally bright red when fully ripe. Lama was sacred to Laka, goddess of the hula. Early Hawaiians used the hard, light-colored wood in temple construction and in hula performances.

On the final descent along Anianinui Ridge are the sprawling native shrubs ʻūlei and ʻilima. ʻŪlei has small, oblong leaves arranged in pairs; clusters of white, roselike flowers; and white fruit. Early Hawaiians ate the berries and used the tough wood for making digging sticks, fish spears, and ʻūkēkē (the musical bow). ʻIlima has oblong, serrated leaves, about 1 inch long. The yellow-orange flowers strung together have been used to make regal lei in both ancient and modern Hawaiʻi.

There are numerous variations to the one-way route as described. You can, of course, take the complete hike in the opposite direction. Most people, however, start from Pali Hwy., go as far as they want, and then turn around. You can also access the Maunawili hike from two other trailheads. From the Nuʻuanu Pali (cool height cliff) lookout, follow the route description of the Likeke hike and then pick up the Maunawili Trail at the horseshoe curve of the Old Pali Rd. From the Maunawili subdivision, follow the route description of the Maunawili Falls hike and then continue up the falls trail to its junction with the Maunawili Trail. Both of those trailheads offer safer parking than the official ones. For a similar but less crowded hike, try Likeke, which follows the foot of the Koʻolau cliffs toward Kāneʻohe (bamboo husband).

33

Likeke

(VIA OLD PALI ROAD)

TYPE:	Foothill
LENGTH:	7-mile round-trip
ELEVATION GAIN:	600 feet
DANGER:	Low
SUITABLE FOR:	Novice, Intermediate
LOCATION:	Kāneʻohe Forest Reserve below Nuʻuanu Pali
TOPO MAP:	Honolulu, Kāneʻohe
ACCESS:	Open

HIGHLIGHTS

This hike follows the old road down from Nuʻuanu Pali to a waterfall nestled below the Pali lookout. The path then winds along the base of the Koʻolau cliffs to a pleasant windward overlook. In the lush, dark gulches en route are delicious mountain apples and guava.

TRAILHEAD DIRECTIONS

At Punchbowl St. get on Pali Hwy. (Rte. 61 north) heading up Nuʻuanu Valley.

Just before the tunnels, turn right to the Pali lookout.

Enter Nuʻuanu Pali State Park.

Park in the lot (elevation 1,186 feet) (map point A). Non-residents must a pay a parking fee.

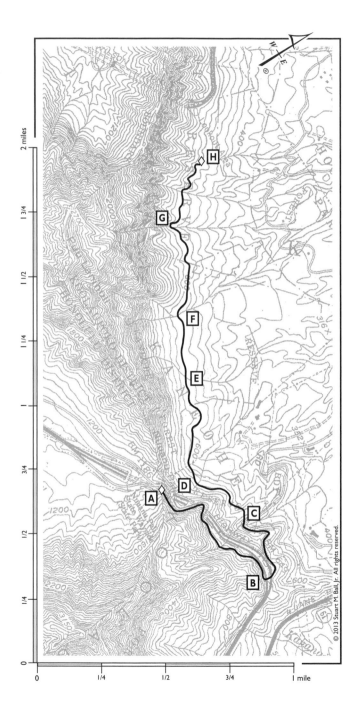

BUS: Routes 56, 57, or 57A to Pali Hwy. and Kamehameha
Hwy. (Castle Junction). Walk 0.8 mile back up Pali Hwy. to the
viewpoint at the hairpin turn and follow the route narrative
for the Maunawili hike to the first signed junction. Turn right
there and climb to the horseshoe curve on the Old Pali Road.
Pick up the route description below at the curve.

ROUTE DESCRIPTION

Walk to the Pali lookout.
   Turn right down the ramp to Old Pali Rd.
   Go through a gate by a Road Closed sign.
   Descend gradually along the paved road, which is lined
with yellow ginger. Encroaching vegetation and small landslides narrow the road to one lane or to a path in several
spots.
   After passing a rockfall on the right, reach a junction (map
point B). Swing left and down, following the horseshoe curve
of the road through grass. (Straight ahead is the signed start of
the Maunawili Trail.)
   Almost immediately, drop down below the Pali Hwy. on
some rickety wooden stairs.
   Squeeze through a narrow passageway underneath the
Kailua-bound lanes.
   Go under the Honolulu-bound lanes on a much wider
walkway.
   Pick up Old Pali Rd again, partially overgrown with grass.
   Descend gradually, working back toward Nuʻuanu Pali.
Look and listen for the white-rumped shama.
   Walk by several supports for the Honolulu-bound lanes of
the highway.
   The grass ends and the pavement of the old road reappears.
Look up for a view of two notches cut into the ridge above
Nuʻuanu Pali by early Hawaiians.

Reach a junction with Aʻuloa Rd and bear left on it.

Almost immediately, look for a short concrete wall on the left before the road curves right.

Just past the wall and by a metal post, turn left up some stone steps, partially hidden by vegetation (map point C).

The steps become the Likeke Trail, leading up the right side of a small gulch.

Climb the right side of the gulch on five short switchbacks.

Reach a four-way junction at the top of a side ridge. Continue straight across the ridge and then bear left down its other side.

Contour along the side of the ridge on a sometimes narrow trail. In the gulch on the right are some kukui trees.

Descend gradually through a grove of white-barked paraserianthes (albizia).

The trail widens to become the previous Old Pali Rd. with stone pavement.

Reach an unmarked junction by a large paraserianthes with initials carved into its trunk. Turn left off the road onto a trail. (The road leads down to Kīʻonaʻole St. and the Koʻolau golf course.)

Descend gradually and then climb briefly through a series of hau groves.

Pass a wet fern grotto and a low concrete structure on the left.

Cross a small stream and turn left upstream.

Almost immediately, reach a lovely waterfall with a shallow pool at its base (elevation 680 feet) (map point D).

Descend beside a small gully filled with hau tangles.

Break out into the open through grass. Look *mauka* (inland) and up for a view of the Pali lookout.

Pass two groves of magnificent mango trees on the right. Near the second grove is a stand of mountain apple trees.

Cross a small, steep gulch lined with coffee trees and kī (ti) plants.

Cross a larger gulch, dark with guava (waiawī) trees (map point E).

By a mango tree, descend into a deep gulch (map point F). Work up the gulch briefly and then climb out on one switchback.

By another mango tree, descend into a narrow gulch and cross the streambed. Walk down the gulch for a short distance through ʻawapuhi (shampoo ginger) and then climb out.

Work into and out of a gulch with a tiny pool and a kukui grove.

Descend into a large gulch on one switchback and cross the streambed. Walk down the gulch briefly and then climb out between two mango trees (map point G).

Enter a hala grove and then traverse an open section with good views *makai* (seaward). Look for remnant native ʻōhiʻa trees and naupaka kuahiwi shrubs with their white half-flowers.

Cross a small gulch with hau tangles.

Contour through an open mixed forest. Purple Philippine ground and bamboo orchids line the trail.

Descend into a large gulch on one switchback through ʻawapuhi and then climb out.

Cross a wide rocky streambed in a grove of mountain apple.

Cross a small streambed near a stand of bamboo and then turn left uphill through ʻawapuhi.

Descend gradually into a deep gulch filled with mountain apple trees. Work up the gulch, first on one side of the streambed and then on the other.

Go through two more gulches, a stretch of hala trees, and then break out into the open through uluhe ferns.

Just after a gulch filled with rose apple trees, reach a pleasant overlook under a shady hala and a mango tree (map point H) (UTM 04 0623432E, 2364470N). After the overlook, the Likeke Trail crosses one more gulch and then climbs to a closed-off parking lot on Likelike Hwy. near the Wilson Tunnel.

NOTES

The Likeke hike comes in two parts. The novice segment follows the Old Pali Road and a short section of the Likeke Trail to a small waterfall. More experienced hikers can then continue along the base of the Koʻolau (windward) cliffs to the hala lookout. The trail was built singlehandedly by Richard H. Davis in the early 1960s at the request of the Boy Scouts. Davis was a member of the Hawaiian Trail and Mountain Club, which named the trail Likeke, Richard in Hawaiian, in appreciation for all his hard work.

The view at the Nuʻuanu Pali (cool height cliff) lookout is world renowned. The windward coast stretches from Kāneʻohe (bamboo husband) to Kailua (two seas) bays. In the distance to the right is triple-peaked Olomana (forked hill). From the old road, look back along the summit ridge to see the peak of Lanihuli (turning royal chief). Towering above you and frequently in the clouds is Kōnāhuanui (large fat testicles) (elevation 3,150 feet), the highest peak in the Koʻolau Range.

The Old Pali Road was constructed in 1897 and opened to vehicle traffic a year later. It maintains a grade of 8 percent along its 1.7-mile length. The road switchbacks once through a tight bend known as the horseshoe curve. Imagine what an adventure it was to drive a small car on this narrow, windy, winding road!

Past the horseshoe curve, keep your eye out for the white-rumped shama. It is black on top with a chestnut-colored breast and a long black and white tail. The shama has a variety of beautiful songs and often mimics other birds. A native of Malaysia, the shama has become widespread in introduced forests such as this one.

After walking under the supports for the Pali Highway, look for two notches in the flat ridge above and to the left of the Pali lookout. They are early Hawaiian observation posts carved out of natural depressions. Nearby are windbreaks and throwing stones.

In the side gulches along the trail to the waterfall are kukui trees. Their large, pale green leaves resemble those of the maple with several distinct lobes. Early Polynesian voyagers introduced kukui into Hawai'i. They used the wood to make gunwales and seats for their outrigger canoes. The flowers and sap became medicines to treat a variety of ailments. Early Hawaiians strung the nuts together to make *lei hua* (seed or nut garlands). The oily kernels became house candles and torches for night spearfishing.

Stop for a break by the small, delightful cascade below Nu'uanu Pali. The fall began flowing in 1959, when workers building the two Pali tunnels inadvertently tapped into water-bearing dike rock above. The sound of the water splashing on the rocks and into the shallow pool is very soothing. Framing the idyllic scene are sun-dappled kukui and hau trees. Just down the trail you can gaze straight up at the Pali lookout.

Past the waterfall, the Likeke Trail is occasionally hard to follow. Remember that it contours along the base of the Ko'olau cliffs at roughly the same elevation. The trail some-times goes up or down a gulch or ridge, but not for long. Do not be diverted by side trails heading *mauka* (inland) or *makai* (seaward).

Along the trail are several stands of mountain apple trees ('ōhi'a 'ai). They have dark, oblong, shiny leaves. In spring their purple flowers carpet the trail. The delicious pink or red fruit usually ripens in late July or early August. If none are in reach, shake the tree and try to catch the apples as they come down. The species is native to Malaysia and was brought over by early Hawaiians.

Before reaching the final overlook, look for a grove of hala trees. They have distinctive prop roots that help support the heavy clusters of leaves and fruit on the ends of the branches. Early Hawaiians braided the long, pointed leaves, called *lau hala,* into baskets, fans, floor mats, and sails.

The hike ends at an overlook under a shady hala tree. From there you can see Kāne'ohe Bay from Mōkapu (taboo district) to Kualoa (long back) points. Hoʻomaluhia Botanical Garden lies *makai* of the H-3 Freeway. *Mauka* are the nearly vertical cliffs of the Koʻolau Range.

For a similar, more popular hike, take the Maunawili Trail that starts at the horseshoe curve on the Old Pali Road. The Maunawili Trail contours along the base of the Koʻolau cliffs in the opposite direction toward Waimānalo (potable water).

34

ʻĀhuimanu

TYPE:	Valley
LENGTH:	1-mile round-trip
ELEVATION GAIN:	200 feet
DANGER:	Low
SUITABLE FOR:	Novice
LOCATION:	Waiāhole Forest Reserve above ʻĀhuimanu
TOPO MAP:	Kāneʻohe
ACCESS:	Open

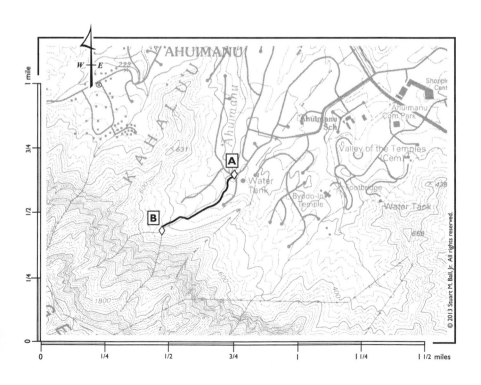

HIGHLIGHTS

This short hike visits an early Hawaiian agricultural site for growing taro. At the end is an impressive rock dike across the back of the gulch.

TRAILHEAD DIRECTIONS

At Punchbowl St. get on Lunalilo Fwy. (H-1) heading ʻEwa (west).

Take Likelike Hwy. (exit 20A, Rte. 63 north) up Kalihi Valley through the Wilson Tunnel.

As the highway forks, keep right for Kahekili Hwy. (Rte. 83 west).

Kahekili narrows to two lanes past Haʻikū Rd.

On the left, pass the entrance to Valley of the Temples Memorial Park.

At the next traffic light, turn left on W. Hui ʻIwa St.

Continue straight at the stop sign.

Take the second left onto Hui Kēlū St.

Park on Hui Kēlū just after its intersection with Lile Pl. (elev. 220 ft) (map point A).

BUS: Route 65 to Hui ʻIwa and Hui Kēlū St. Walk 0.3 mile along Hui Kēlū to the trailhead.

ROUTE DESCRIPTION

Continue briefly down Hui Kēlū St. on foot.

Before crossing ʻĀhuimanu Stream and passing a yellow fire hydrant, turn left onto a makeshift trail into the forest. Look and listen for the white-rumped shama.

Shortly, cross a section of pavement and a line of metal posts. On the right toward the stream is a sign explaining the ʻĀhuimanu *loʻi* complex, consisting of over a hundred irrigated terraces for growing *kalo* (taro).

Cross several *lo'i*. Use the short metal ladders provided to avoid damaging the rock walls of the terraces. Above are tangled hau branches.

On the right, pass a second interpretive sign by the stream.

Climb briefly to a third sign and then follow an *'auwai* (irrigation ditch). Walk in the ditch briefly.

Bear right, leaving the *'auwai* behind, and parallel the stream.

Cross and recross a dry stream channel.

Reach the main stream and turn left along it.

Presently, ford the stream by some rock walls on the left.

Climb along the right bank of the stream on a rough, rooty trail. Look for hala trees with their prop roots.

Turn left at a T-junction. Memorize that junction for the return trip.

Cross a dry channel and then the main stream by a large kukui tree.

Follow a water pipe upstream to a massive rock dike across the gulch (elevation 400 feet) (map point B) (UTM 04 0620027E, 2370056N). At the base of the dike, a spring gushes water.

Turn right along the dike through coffee trees. 'Āhuimanu Stream pours through a break in the dike. Just upstream are a waterfall chute and a tiny pool.

NOTES

The 'Āhuimanu hike explores one of the most extensive and best preserved early Hawaiian agricultural sites on O'ahu. The complex consists of over a hundred *lo'i*, rock-walled terraces for growing wetland *kalo* (taro). *'Auwai* or ditches diverted water from the stream to the descending terraces to irrigate and fertilize the thirsty *kalo*. The three interpretive signs provide details about the site and how important *kalo* was, and still is, to the Hawaiian people.

The trail through the complex to the dike is mostly unimproved, with several rough, rooty sections. Watch your footing at the slippery stream crossings. As always, do not ford the stream if the water gets much above your knees. Also, don't spend a lot of time at the base of the dike, as it is obviously shedding rock. Finally, watch for marauding mosquitoes.

In the forest, look and listen for the white-rumped shama. It is black on top with a chestnut-colored breast and a long black and white tail. The shama has a variety of beautiful songs and often mimics other birds. A native of Malaysia, the shama has become widespread in introduced forests such as this one.

While crossing the *lo'i,* the trail winds under tangled hau trees with large, heart-shaped leaves. Their flowers are bright yellow with a dark red center and resemble those of a hibiscus. Early Hawaiians used the wood for kites and canoe outriggers, the bark for sandals, and the sap as a laxative.

After crossing the stream, watch for hala trees on the right. They have distinctive prop roots that help support the heavy clusters of leaves and fruit on the ends of the branches. Early Hawaiians braided the long, pointed leaves, called *lau hala,* into baskets, fans, floor mats, and sails.

Above the water pipe is a towering kukui tree. Its large, pale green leaves resemble those of the maple with several distinct lobes. Early Polynesian voyagers introduced kukui into Hawai'i. They used the wood to make gunwales and seats for their outrigger canoes. The flowers and sap became medicines to treat a variety of ailments. Early Hawaiians strung the nuts together to make *lei hua* (seed or nut garlands). The oily kernels became house candles and torches for night spearfishing.

The hike ends at a massive lava dike, which blocks much of the gulch. The rock is part of a dike complex in the northwest rift zone of the old Ko'olau (windward) volcano. Rift zones are areas of structural weakness extending from the summit of a shield volcano. Rising molten rock or magma worked its way into cracks in the rift zone and solidified. The resulting dikes are sheetlike, vertical intrusions of hard, dense rock. Over the years 'Āhuimanu Stream has managed to carve a narrow channel through the dike.

35

Pu'u Manamana

TYPE:	Ungraded ridge
LENGTH:	4-mile loop
ELEVATION GAIN:	2,100 feet
DANGER:	High
SUITABLE FOR:	Expert
LOCATION:	Ahupua'a 'O Kahana State Park
TOPO MAP:	Kahana
ACCESS:	Open

HIGHLIGHTS

This challenging hike loops around the steep, knife-edge ridges above Kahana Valley. The dangerous route demands sure feet, agile hands, and a cool head. In between the narrow spots are stunning views, a good variety of native plants, and several early Hawaiian sites.

TRAILHEAD DIRECTIONS

At Punchbowl St. get on Lunalilo Fwy. (H-1) heading 'Ewa (west).

Take Likelike Hwy. (exit 20A, Rte. 63 north) up Kalihi Valley through the Wilson Tunnel.

As the highway forks, keep right for Kahekili Hwy. (Rte. 83 west).

Kahekili becomes Kamehameha Hwy. (still Rte. 83), which continues up the windward coast.

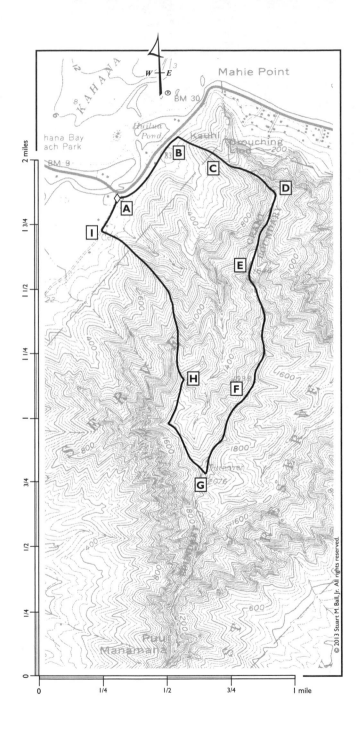

Drive through the villages of Kahalu'u and Waiāhole to Ka'a'awa.

Pass Swanzy Beach Park on the right and Crouching Lion Inn on the left. The park has restrooms and drinking water.

The road curves left to go around Kahana Bay.

Park on the right shoulder just before the road swings right and crosses Kahana Stream (map point A). The spot is near a bus stop and a rock with a missing plaque.

BUS: Route 55 to the trailhead.

ROUTE DESCRIPTION

Walk back along Kamehameha Hwy. toward the Crouching Lion Inn.

Pass a short guardrail on your right with a Rte. 83 sign near it.

Just beyond the first utility pole past the guardrail, turn right into the forest on a makeshift trail (map point B). Across the road is a line of ironwood trees and Huilua Fishpond.

Climb straight up the slope through kī (ti) plants.

Before the slope levels off, jog left and then right through tangled Christmas berry trees.

Ascend gradually through another patch of ti plants. Ignore a pig trail to the left. Nearby on the right are the scant remnants of Pu'u Makāne Heiau (a religious site).

Go through a second Christmas berry tangle.

Work left and break out into the open. Look for the low-lying native shrub 'ūlei.

Switchback right and then left across a rocky outcrop.

Swing right and begin climbing straight up the ridge.

The ridge levels off briefly by the site of a fish lookout (map point C). The rock formation to the left is Kauhi'īmaka-okalani, better known as the Crouching Lion.

Resume serious climbing up Puʻu o Māhie Ridge. Along the trail are the native shrubs ʻākia and akoko.

Cross a narrow, rocky neck.

Ascend very steeply past several rock faces. Cables may provide some assistance.

Reach the main ridgeline and a stunning view of Kahana Bay and the windward coast (map point D). Turn right up the ridge heading *mauka* (inland).

Enter a small Christmas berry grove and then cross two eroded spots.

Climb steadily, mostly over rock, to a pointed peak. The worst spot may have a cable.

After a level section, go right around a rock face, perhaps with the aid of another cable.

Descend a steep rock face with the possible help of a cable.

Ascend steadily, first over rock and then through native lama trees.

Pass a small overlook on the right with views into Kahana Valley (map point E).

Descend steeply and then negotiate another rock face, perhaps with the assistance of a cable.

The ridge levels off somewhat and then resumes steep climbing. Don't let your guard down in this section. The vegetation provides some security, but the ridge is still very narrow, and the trail is rocky and rooty. The tricky spots may have cables.

As the ridge finally widens, enter native forest dominated by ʻōhiʻa trees, woody ʻieʻie vines, and scratchy uluhe ferns.

Climb briefly to a knob on the ridge.

Descend and then climb steeply to a second knob.

Reach a junction at the top of a third knob (map point F). (To the left, a steep trail descends a side ridge into Makaua or Hidden Valley.)

Descend briefly and then climb moderately to a broad knob. Watch for native manono and kōpiko trees.

Descend and then climb to a smaller knob.

Traverse a muddy level section. The ridge is quite broad

here, and the trail works from side to side following the easiest route. Look for native pū'ahanui (kanawao) shrubs.

Pass a small open space with a nice updraft from the back of Makaua Valley.

Climb moderately toward a broad knob called Turnover.

Along its top, reach a junction (map point G). Continue straight along the main ridge. (The trail to the right and down is the return portion of the loop.)

Shortly afterward, reach a small clearing with a benchmark and the remains of a triangulation marker (elevation 2,076 feet) (UTM 04 0617499E, 2382130N). Nearby is a native 'ōhi'a tree with yellow blossoms.

From the clearing, backtrack to the junction and turn left down the side ridge.

Descend, steeply at first and then more gradually along the ridge. Keep to its left side.

Cross a wet level section interspersed with several muddy dips.

Climb briefly to a small knob (map point H).

Resume the descent as the ridge begins to narrow.

Cross a short level section.

Descend very steeply on the ever-narrowing ridge under lama trees. Watch your footing on the rocky, rooty trail.

The ridge becomes razor thin. Short stretches are carpeted with moss.

The ridge finally widens through uluhe ferns, but the descent remains steep.

Descend a narrow rocky section. Look for the native herb ko'oko'olau and the shrub pūkiawe.

Go left around a rock outcrop, perhaps with the help of a cable.

Descend steeply through a hala grove.

Follow the main path down through a small graveyard and by a grass plot, the site of an old Mormon chapel.

Reach Trout Farm Rd. by a speed bump (map point I). Turn right on the paved road.

Reach Kamehameha Hwy. directly across from the bus stop (map point A).

NOTES

Mountain man Richard H. (Dick) Davis of the Hawaiian Trail and Mountain Club scouted the exciting and dangerous Puʻu Manamana route in 1953. The hike that he developed is for experienced hikers only, as it becomes difficult right away and then gets worse. Start early, as this short loop takes longer than you think. Frequently the clouds roll in from the ocean and blanket the ridge in swirling mist and rain, making the going slow and slippery.

The rock faces and narrow sections along the *makai* (seaward) portion of the main ridge are legendary. Watch your footing constantly on the bare roots, loose dirt, and crumbly rock. Test any cables before using them. There is no shame in turning back if you don't like what you see.

The return route down a wooded side ridge is just as narrow and steep. The precipitous trail drops 2,000 feet in a little over a mile. Hang on to tree trunks and exposed roots to control your descent. Before and after the Turnover clearing, the hike route may be overgrown with *Clidemia* shrubs and scratchy uluhe ferns.

Before starting the climb, take a quick look at Huilua (twice joined), a fishpond fed by natural springs as well as the ocean. In earlier times, the brackish water was perfect for raising ʻamaʻama (mullet) and awa (milkfish). According to legend, the pond was built by the Menehune, an elusive race of small people who worked only at night. Above the pond along the trail is the site of Puʻu Makāne Heiau, a small temple devoted to fishing and farming.

Along Puʻu o Māhie (hill of pleasure) Ridge above the *heiau* is the rock formation Kauhiʻīmakaokalani (the watchtower of heaven). According to legend, the malihini (newcomer) demigod Kauhi was stationed permanently in the cliff above Kahana Bay. One day he spied Hi'iaka, the beautiful sister of Pele, goddess of fire. The bored Kauhi longed to join Hi'iaka on her travels around the island chain. However, she had no time for Kauhi and told him to stay put. With all his might, he heaved his body into a crouching position on all fours, but that was the limit of his strength and so Kauhi remains there to this day. The rock formation is more recently and widely known as the Crouching Lion.

Past the lion, look for the native shrubs 'ākia and 'akoko. 'Ākia has oval, pointed, bright green leaves. Its dark branches are jointed with white rings. Early Hawaiians pounded the leaves and bark and then dropped the mixture into tidal pools to poison the fish. The red-orange fruits were used in lei and as a poison for criminals. 'Akoko has oval, darker green leaves with rounded ends. At the tips of the jointed branches are red seed capsules. Early Hawaiians used the milky sap as a stain for their canoe hulls.

Along the drier *makai* portion of the main ridge are native lama trees. Their oblong, pointed leaves are dark green and leathery. The fruits are green, then yellow, and finally bright red when fully ripe. Lama was sacred to Laka, goddess of the hula. Early Hawaiians used the hard, light-colored wood in temple construction and in hula performances.

Look for native manono and kōpiko trees in the wet *mauka* section of the ridge. Manono has thick, glossy, oblong leaves with purple stems, small yellow-green flowers shaped like anchors, and purple-black fruits. A native member of the coffee family, kōpiko has leathery, oblong leaves with a light green midrib. Turn the leaf over to see a row of tiny holes (*piko* or navel) on either side of the midrib. The kōpiko produces clusters of little white flowers and fleshy, orange fruits.

All along the main ridge are magnificent views. *Makai* the windward coast stretches from Lā'ie to Mōkapu (taboo district) to Makapu'u (bulging eye) points. The massive peak across Kahana (cutting) Valley is Pu'u Piei. From the Turnover clearing, you can see Ka'a'awa Valley on the left and Punalu'u (coral dived for) Valley on the right. Ahead along the ridge are Pu'u Manamana and Pu'u 'Ōhulehule (joining of waves hill). In back of Kahana Valley is the long Ko'olau (windward) summit ridge.

Before reaching Turnover, keep your eye out for the native shrub pū'ahanui (kanawao), a relative of hydrangea. It has large, serrated, deeply creased leaves and clusters of delicate pink flowers. Early Hawaiians used the plants for medicinal purposes.

After the hair-raising descent, the small graveyard in the valley is always a welcome sight. Several people buried there fell victim to a huge tsunami (literally, "harbor wave," a wave produced by submarine seismic activity) that swept inland from the bay on April 1, 1946. Just beyond the graveyard is the site of an old Mormon chapel.

36

Kahana Valley

TYPE:	Valley
LENGTH:	6-mile double loop
ELEVATION GAIN:	400 feet
DANGER:	Low
SUITABLE FOR:	Novice, Intermediate
LOCATION:	Ahupua'a 'O Kahana State Park
TOPO MAP:	Kahana, Hau'ula
ACCESS:	Open

HIGHLIGHTS

This double-loop hike meanders around a vast, undeveloped windward valley. The intricate route has numerous junctions and stream crossings. Along the stream are deep, inviting pools and groves of mountain apple.

TRAILHEAD DIRECTIONS

At Punchbowl St. get on Lunalilo Fwy. (H-1) heading 'Ewa (west).

Take Likelike Hwy. (exit 20A, Rte. 63 north) up Kalihi Valley through the Wilson Tunnel.

As the highway forks, keep right for Kahekili Hwy. (Rte. 83 west).

Kahekili becomes Kamehameha Hwy. (still Rte. 83), which continues up the windward coast.

Drive through the villages of Kahaluʻu and Waiāhole to Kaʻaʻawa.

Pass Crouching Lion Inn on the left.

The road curves left to go around Kahana Bay.

Cross Kahana Stream on two bridges.

By a large palm grove, turn left into Ahupuaʻa ʻO Kahana State Park.

Pass the front parking lot on the right and the visitor center on the left. A shelf by the front door contains park brochures and trail maps.

Just beyond the center are restrooms and drinking water in a green building on the right.

Drive another 0.5 mile into the valley on the paved road.

Park in the grassy area just before a locked gate with a stop sign (elevation 20 feet) (map point A).

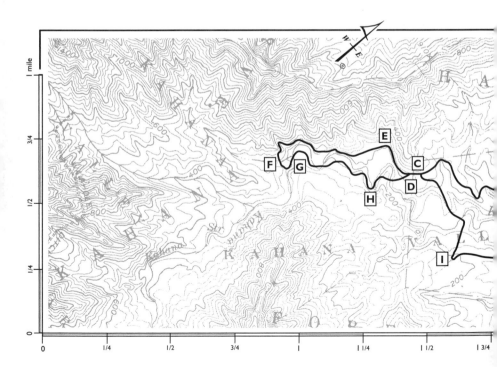

BUS: Route 55 to the entrance of Ahupuaʻa ʻO Kahana State Park. Walk 0.6 mile along the park access road to the locked gate.

ROUTE DESCRIPTION

Continue along the paved access road on foot.

Pass houses on both sides of the road.

Go around a second locked gate. The road narrows to one lane.

Climb steadily through introduced forest.

On the left, pass two grass parking lots. The second one has a picnic table and a dirt road leading down to some *kalo* (taro) *loʻi* (terraces) by Kahana Stream.

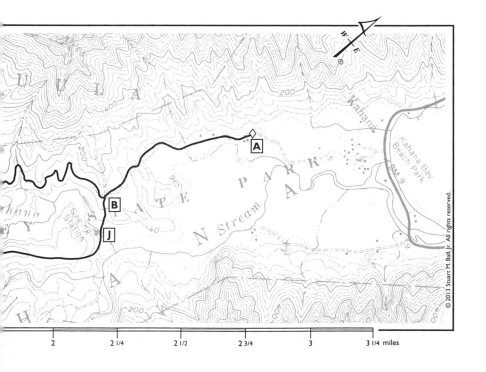

Shortly afterward, reach a junction marked by hunting area and interpretive signs (map point B). After signing in at the hunter/hiker check-in mailbox, turn left and down on a dirt road. (The paved road curves right and up through a locked gate.)

Almost immediately, reach a signed junction. Turn right onto the Nakoa Trail. (The dirt road descends to Kahawainui Stream and is the return portion of the hike.)

Contour along the side of the valley through hala groves and hau tangles. Look for hāpuʻu tree fern and mountain apple trees in this long section. In the openings, you can see Puʻu Manamana and Puʻu ʻŌhulehule on the ridge to the left.

Descend into a gully and turn right alongside it.

Bear left out of the gully and resume contouring through hala and kī (ti) plants.

Work into and out of a side gulch with a stream.

Go through a series of dense hau groves.

Descend briefly on a switchback and ford a small stream in a second gulch.

Descend into a third gulch on one switchback and cross another stream.

On the right, pass a rusted triangular tank trap left over from World War II army training.

Shortly afterward, reach a signed four-way junction in a clearing surrounded by hala trees (map point C) (UTM 04 0614846E, 2381757N). Continue straight across. (To the left, the Nakoa Trail descends to Kahawainui Stream and is the return portion of the hike. To the right, a trail leads to a water tank and the paved access road.)

Pass several observation bunkers partially hidden in the trees on the left.

Shortly afterward, reach a fork by a bamboo grove (map point D). Take the right fork. (The left fork leads down to Kahawainui Stream and is the return portion of the hike.)

Contour above Kahawainui Stream under magnificent paraserianthes (albizia) and kukui trees.

Cross a side stream just after a grove of mountain apples.

Cross a second side stream by two mango trees.

Reach an obscure junction in a flat area surrounded by hala (map point E). Continue straight on the trail into the valley. (To the left, a trail provides a shortcut to Kahawainui Stream.)

Cross several side streams in groves of mountain apple. The narrow trail hugs a cliff above the stream.

Swing left and down to reach another obscure junction by a large side stream (elevation 360 feet) (map point F) (UTM 04 0614080E, 2381115N). (To the right is the overgrown upper trail, which crosses the side stream and continues to the back of the valley.)

Parallel the side stream briefly, cross to its right bank, and then leave it behind.

Reach Kahawainui Stream and turn left downstream.

Cross the side stream again where it enters the main stream (map point G). Continue along the left bank of Kahawainui Stream.

Cross to the right bank of the main stream by two huge paraserianthes trees with white-flecked trunks.

On the left, pass a sign marking nearby *lo‘i.*

Ford the stream to the left bank at the tip of an island splitting the stream in two.

Cross the stream to the right bank by two large paraserianthes trees.

On the right, pass a sign marking Pu‘ulena (yellow hill), a swampy area where *kalo* was planted in mounds.

On the opposite bank of the stream are a large mango tree with exposed roots and a breadfruit tree.

Ford the stream to the left bank just before it turns sharp left (map point H). Nearby is a large mango tree and a deep, inviting pool with emerald green water.

Continue downstream briefly and reach an obscure junction. Turn right and cross Kahawainui Stream to the right bank. (To the left, a short trail leads back to map point E on the contour trail.)

The stream splits briefly. Traverse the island in between and then return to the right side.

Reach a large mango tree and a lovely pool.

Ford the stream there to the left bank and enter a bamboo grove.

Ascend through the grove, leaving the stream behind.

Work left and then straight up the slope on a narrow, rutted trail.

Reach the familiar junction with the contour trail (map point D) and turn right on it.

Reach the four-way junction again (map point C). This time, turn right downhill on the continuation of the Nakoa Trail.

Descend steadily through hala on an army road built of crushed coral.

Enter a hau grove.

Shortly afterward, ford Kahawainui Stream past two concrete bridge piers and turn right upstream.

Ascend steadily on a bench just below the ridgeline.

Reach a signed junction at the ridgeline (map point I). Turn sharp left down the ridge on another army road.

Descend gradually down the flat ridge through hala. Lining the trail are Chinese ground orchids, which bloom in winter.

Break out into the open briefly. The peak on the ridge to the left is Puʻu Piei.

Veer right, off the ridgeline onto a bench.

The trail curves left to reach Kahawainui Stream by a gaging station (map point J).

Ford the stream for the last time on a small dam. Watch your footing on the slippery concrete. At the dam is a large swimming hole popular with valley residents.

Climb gradually on an eroded gravel road.

A sign on the left marks an *ʻauwai* (ditch) for irrigating *loʻi*.

Reach the familiar junction by the hunting area sign (map point B). Turn right on the paved access road to reach your car.

NOTES

This hike is an intriguing double loop in a largely undeveloped valley on the windward side. The initial stretch leaves something to be desired, but the stream loop is perhaps the most beautiful valley walk on the island. The water rushing by is cool and clear, and the pools are deep and inviting. There are few things better in life than spending a sunny afternoon by Kahawainui Stream.

Ahupuaʻa ʻO Kahana (cutting) is a unique state park, established to foster and spread native Hawaiian culture. About thirty families live in the lower section of the valley. They are helping to restore some of the ancient sites, such as Huilua (twice joined) Fishpond and *loʻi* (irrigated terraces for growing *kalo* [taro]). Years ago, the *ahupuaʻa* (land division) of Kahana supported a thriving community based on ocean fishing, taro farming, and fish raising.

During World War II, the U.S. Army established the Unit Jungle Training Center to better prepare its soldiers for combat in the Pacific Islands. The center had three layouts or courses of instruction: red and blue in Kahana Valley and green in nearby Punaluʻu Valley. Soldiers learned to identify edible plants, build rope bridges across streams, and attack a mock-up Japanese village with pop-up targets. Look for remnant tank traps and bunkers near the four-way junction.

The trails in this wet valley are invariably muddy, sometimes overgrown, and occasionally obscure. Watch your footing while crossing the stream. If possible, change to tabis (Japanese reef walkers) or other water footwear for better traction on the slippery rocks. As always, do not ford the stream if the water is much above your knees.

Unfortunately, this magnificent valley harbors a large mosquito population. Local mosquitoes are usually laid back, but not so in Kahana. Bring insect repellant or cover up or keep moving. For lunch, pick a sunny pool with a breeze, and you won't be constantly bothered.

On the first section of the Nakoa Trail are groves of tangled hau trees with large, heart-shaped leaves. Their flowers are bright yellow with a dark red center and resemble those of a hibiscus. Early Hawaiians used the wood for kites and canoe outriggers, the bark for sandals, and the sap as a laxative.

Also common in the valley is the hala tree. It has distinctive prop roots that help support the heavy clusters of leaves and fruit on the ends of the branches. Early Hawaiians braided the long, pointed leaves, called *lau hala,* into baskets, fans, floor mats, and sails.

The wet side gulches are lined with kukui trees. Their large, pale green leaves resemble those of the maple with several distinct lobes. Early Polynesian voyagers introduced kukui into Hawai'i. They used the wood to make gunwales and seats for their outrigger canoes. The flowers and sap became medicines to treat a variety of ailments. Early Hawaiians strung the nuts together to make *lei hua* (seed or nut garlands). The oily kernels became house candles and torches for night spearfishing.

On the second loop, look for mountain apple trees ('ōhi'a 'ai) along the contour trail. They have dark, oblong, shiny leaves. In spring their purple flowers carpet the trail. The delicious pink or red fruit usually ripens in late July or early August. If none are in reach, shake the tree gently and try to catch the apples as they come down. The species is native to Malaysia and was brought over by early Hawaiians.

The walk along the stream is very pleasant, but the trail there may be obscure in spots. Follow the directions closely. Various colors of surveyor's ribbon may mark the correct route, but don't count on it. If you do lose the trail, continue walking downstream until you pick it up again. Watch for the bamboo grove on the left bank where the trail leaves the stream for good.

On the return portion of the first loop, look for the Chinese ground or nun's orchid in winter. Its lovely flowers have tapered petals that are white on the outside and reddish brown within. The lowest petal is a cream-colored tube with purple marking.

There are several variations to the route as described. You can, of course, do one or both loops in the opposite direction. However, the hike is complicated enough without having to read the narrative in reverse. For a short novice outing, walk only the first loop, on the Nakoa Trail. Be sure to visit the lovely pool near the bamboo by keeping left and down at the junction with the contour trail (map point D). Total distance for the first loop is about 5 miles. To shorten the second loop, turn left off the contour trail at map point E to reach the deep pool by the mango tree near map point H.

For a more difficult hike in the valley, explore the overgrown upper trail that leaves from the second loop and ends at the intake of Waiāhole Ditch. Across the intake is the start (end) of the Waiāhole Ditch Trail, which contours around the back of Kahana, Waikāne, and Waiāhole Valleys. Mountain man Richard H. (Dick) Davis of the Hawaiian Trail and Mountain Club reopened the upper trail in 1981–1982.

37

Pu'u Piei

(VIA KAPA'ELE'ELE KO'A FISHING SHRINE)

TYPE:	Ungraded ridge
LENGTH:	3-mile round-trip
ELEVATION GAIN:	1,700 feet
DANGER:	Medium
SUITABLE FOR:	Novice, Intermediate, Expert
LOCATION:	Ahupua'a 'O Kahana State Park
TOPO MAP:	Kahana
ACCESS:	Open

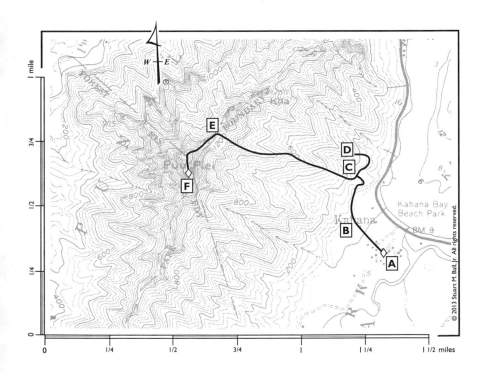

HIGHLIGHTS

Pu'u Piei is the broad peak overlooking Kahana Bay and Valley. This rugged climb to its summit is short but very steep. A brief side trip leads to an early Hawaiian fishing shrine and lookout.

TRAILHEAD DIRECTIONS

At Punchbowl St. get on Lunalilo Fwy. (H-1) heading 'Ewa (west).

Take Likelike Hwy. (exit 20A, Rte. 63 north) up Kalihi Valley through the Wilson Tunnel.

As the highway forks, keep right for Kahekili Hwy. (Rte. 83 west).

Kahekili becomes Kamehameha Hwy. (still Rte. 83), which continues up the windward coast.

Drive through the villages of Kahalu'u and Waiāhole to Ka'a'awa.

Pass Crouching Lion Inn on the left.

The road curves left to go around Kahana Bay.

Cross Kahana Stream on two bridges.

By a large palm grove, turn left into Ahupua'a 'O Kahana State Park.

Pass the front parking lot on the right and the visitor center on the left. A shelf by the front door contains park brochures and trail maps.

On the right, park in a small lot in front of a green building, which has restrooms and drinking water (map point A).

BUS: Route 55 to the entrance of Ahupua'a 'O Kahana State Park. Walk 0.1 mile along the park access road to the trailhead.

ROUTE DESCRIPTION

Take the gravel road on the right just before the restrooms.

Go over a chain across the road.

Ignore driveways on both sides of the road.

The road becomes dirt and parallels a utility line.

Just past utility pole no. 3, reach a signed junction. Turn left on the Kapaʻeleʻele Koʻa and Keaniani Kilo Trail (map point B). (The road continues straight and becomes overgrown.)

The trail gradually angles away from the road through tangled hau groves.

Bear left and climb the side of a ridge on the rooty trail.

Reach a bench with a view of the bay and Huilua Fishpond. Look for ʻūlei, a low-lying native shrub.

The trail swings left and descends into a gully.

At a rocky streambed, reach a junction (map point C). For now, keep right and cross the streambed. (The wide path on the left is the route to Puʻu Piei.)

Climb briefly through hala and octopus trees. Look for purple Philippine ground orchids.

Reach Kapaʻeleʻele Koʻa, an ancient fishing shrine.

After contouring for a short distance, reach another junction. Turn left upslope. (The trail to the right leads down to Kamehameha Hwy.) At the junction are several native ʻākia shrubs.

By a stand of ironwoods reach Keaniani Kilo, a fish lookout (map point D).

Retrace your steps past the fishing shrine to the junction by the streambed (map point C). Now continue straight on the wide but less traveled path uphill.

Shortly afterward, the trail turns right and ascends gradually along the left edge of the ridge.

At an eroded spot, reach a magnificent overlook of Kahana Valley and the surrounding peaks (map point D) (UTM 04 0616181E, 2384390N). Novice hikers should turn around here.

Turn right toward the Piei cliffs and begin serious climbing.

Almost immediately, the ridge narrows briefly by another eroded section.

Climb steadily through grass and scattered octopus trees. Generally keep to the right side of the broad ridge.

Pass another eroded section on the right.

Cross a small, bare patch backed by hala trees.

As the ridge narrows, climb steeply through hau and hala trees and ʻākia shrubs.

Go around to the left of a rock outcrop.

The angle of ascent decreases briefly in a hala grove (phew!). Take a break.

As the top nears, the climbing becomes very steep and rocky. Roots and tree trunks provide some security.

Ascend several especially steep sections, perhaps with the aid of cables.

Reach the top of the Piei ridge with its magnificent view of Kahana Valley (map point E). While catching your breath, look for the native herb koʻokoʻolau.

Turn left along the very narrow ridge.

Climb over a small hump. The worst sections may have cables.

Reach the broad summit of Puʻu Piei (elev. 1,740 feet) (map point F). Vegetation blocks most of the views there.

NOTES

Puʻu Piei is for hikers who love to scramble. The route ascends 1,700 feet in a little over a mile. Now, that's serious climbing! On the way up or down, be sure to visit the early Hawaiian fishing shrine and lookout.

This hike is made up of two very different trails. The improved route to the fish lookout is suitable for novices, as it is well graded and groomed. The trail up the ridge, however, is steep, unimproved, and may be overgrown. Watch your footing on the loose rock and dirt. Be very careful on the narrow and often slippery stretch just below the ridgetop. Test any cables before using them.

The hike initially follows the route of the Ko'olau Railway, built in the early 1900s. Its steam engines hauled sugarcane grown in Kahana Valley to a mill up the coast at Kahuku (the projection). Kahana was the southern terminus of the line and had a one-engine roundhouse. Step lively through this section to escape the hordes of mosquitoes.

On the trail, watch for the sprawling native shrub 'ūlei in the sunny sections. It has small, oblong leaves arranged in pairs; clusters of white, roselike flowers; and white fruit. Early Hawaiians ate the berries and used the tough wood for making digging sticks, fish spears, and 'ūkēkē (the musical bow).

At the fishing shrine, Kapa'ele'ele (black bark cloth) Ko'a, early Hawaiians made offerings to ensure a good catch of akule (bigeye scad) in the bay below. The rectangular *ko'a* was enclosed on three sides by large stones. The *makai* side facing the bay was left open. Stay on the trail to avoid disturbing the already deteriorated site.

At the junction to the fish lookout are several native 'ākia shrubs with oval, pointed, bright green leaves. Their dark branches are jointed with white rings. Early Hawaiians pounded the leaves and bark and then dropped the mixture into tidal pools to poison the fish. The red-orange fruits were used in lei and as a poison for criminals.

Keaniani (the mirror) Kilo lookout offers an unobstructed view of Kahana Bay. In earlier times, a *kilo i'a* (fish watcher) at the lookout would spot a school of akule and quickly hoist a flag of white *kapa* to signal fishermen waiting on the beach. They would then encircle the fish with nets and pull the catch to shore.

From the eroded overlook are breathtaking views into largely undeveloped Kahana (cutting) Valley. Along the far ridge are Pu'u Manamana and the prominent peak of Pu'u 'Ōhulehule (joining of waves hill). In the back of the valley are the sheer, fluted flanks of the Ko'olau (windward) Range. Along the near ridge is rugged Pu'u Piei.

From the valley overlook, a rough, unimproved trail leads to Pu'u Piei. The steep route to its summit is for experienced scramblers only, as it has several narrow sections with drop-offs on both sides. The larger view from the ridgetop is well worth the climb. You can see into Punalu'u Valley and up the windward coast to Lā'ie Point.

Along the ridge is the native herb ko'oko'olau, related to the daisy and sunflower families. It has pointed, serrated leaves and flower heads with yellow petals. Early Hawaiians steeped the leaves to make a tea used as a tonic.

38

Hau'ula-Papali

TYPE:	Foothill
LENGTH:	7-mile double loop
ELEVATION GAIN:	700 feet (Hau'ula), 800 feet (Papali)
DANGER:	Low
SUITABLE FOR:	Novice, Intermediate
LOCATION:	Hau'ula Forest Reserve above Hau'ula
TOPO MAP:	Hau'ula
ACCESS:	Open

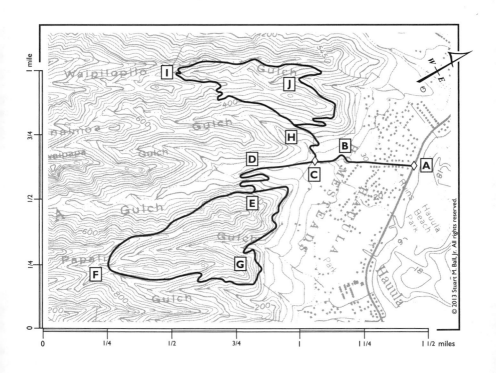

HIGHLIGHTS

This intricate double loop traverses the foothills of the windward Ko'olau Range. From secluded viewpoints, you look down into deep, narrow gulches. Along the way are groves of stately Cook pines and some remnant native vegetation.

TRAILHEAD DIRECTIONS

At Punchbowl St. get on Lunalilo Fwy. (H-1) heading 'Ewa (west).

Take Likelike Hwy. (exit 20A, Rte. 63 north) up Kalihi Valley through the Wilson Tunnel.

As the highway forks, keep right for Kahekili Hwy. (Rte. 83 west).

Kahekili becomes Kamehameha Hwy. (still Rte. 83), which continues up the windward coast.

Drive through the villages of Ka'a'awa and Punalu'u to Hau'ula.

Pass a fire station on the left and cross a bridge.

Look for Hau'ula Beach Park on the right. At the park are restrooms and drinking water.

Park on Kamehameha Hwy. at the far end of the beach park near the intersection with Hau'ula Homestead Rd. Nearby are Hau'ula Congregational Church and the Hau'ula Base Yard (map point A).

BUS: Route 55 to Kamehameha Hwy. and Hau'ula Homestead Rd.

ROUTE DESCRIPTION

Proceed *mauka* (inland) along Hau'ula Homestead Rd.

As the road curves left, continue straight on Ma'akua Rd.

Go around a yellow gate and pass a private driveway on the left.

The road forks by a utility pole (map point B). Take the left fork and go around another yellow gate.

Cross Hānaimoa Stream and swing right to reach a signed junction (map point C). Keep left on the paved road. (To the right is the Hau'ula Loop Trail, which is described later on.) Register at the nearby hunter/hiker check-in mailbox.

The road straightens out briefly by a concrete retaining wall.

Before the road curves right, reach a second signed junction (map point D). Bear left and down off the road onto the Ma'akua Ridge Trail. (To the right, the road leads to the Ma'akua Gulch Trail, which is closed because of rockfall danger.)

Cross Ma'akua Stream presently and climb the embankment on the far side.

Work right and then left through a tangled hau grove.

Climb gradually up the side of Ma'akua Gulch on eight switchbacks. At the sixth one is a good view of Hau'ula town and the ocean. After the seventh, a short trail leads left to a covered picnic table.

At the eighth switchback by a bench, the trail splits to become a loop (map point E). Turn sharp right and start the Papali loop in a counterclockwise direction.

Switchback four more times and then steadily ascend *mauka* up the side of the ridge through mixed introduced forest. You can look deep into Ma'akua Gulch through breaks in the trees. Watch for hala trees with their prop roots.

Reach the ridgeline and stroll along it under shady Formosa koa trees.

By a large, yellow strawberry guava tree, reach a junction (elevation 800 feet). Bear left off the ridge and descend gradually into Papali Gulch. (A rough, makeshift route continues up the ridge.)

Cross the stream by a stand of kī (ti) shrubs and turn left downstream. Watch for native pāpala kēpau trees with their large, leathery leaves.

Climb gradually out of the gulch, which is lined with kukui trees.

Gain the narrow ridgeline briefly near a tall Cook pine and a mango tree (map point F) (UTM 04 0612142E, 2388404N).

Switch to the right side of the ridge and descend along the side of Punaiki Gulch on a series of twin switchbacks.

Break out into the open through ʻūlei, a sprawling native shrub.

Contour around the front of the ridge under arching Christmas berry trees.

Descend once again into Papali Gulch to the stream and turn right.

Follow the rocky streambed briefly and then angle left onto the trail (map point G).

Climb out of the gulch on four switchbacks.

Contour along the front of the next ridge. A dark rock cliff overhangs the trail on the left.

Reach the end of the loop (map point E). Bear right and down.

Retrace your steps to the paved road and its junction with the Hauʻula Loop Trail (map point C).

Turn left off the road onto the trail to start the second loop.

Briefly parallel Hānaimoa Stream on your right and then cross it.

Ascend through ironwood trees on two long switchbacks. After the second switchback, look for noni, a small tree with large, shiny leaves and warty fruit.

The trail splits, becoming a loop (map point H). This time, keep left and start the loop in a clockwise direction.

Climb gradually up the side of Hānaimoa Gulch heading *mauka*. Switchback three times through an ironwood grove. At the first and third switchbacks are several sandalwood trees.

By a paperbark tree, reach the ridgeline and cross over it to the left.

Descend gradually into Waipilopilo Gulch.

Cross the stream between two small waterfalls and climb out of the gulch on two short switchbacks.

Reach the ridgeline (elevation 680 feet) (map point I) (UTM 04 0611290E, 2389502N) and turn right heading *makai* (seaward). Below on the left are the sheer walls of Kaipapa‘u Gulch. Look for a few native ‘ōhi‘a trees and pūkiawe shrubs along the trail.

Descend steadily along the ridge. Steps are provided at steep, eroded sections.

Bear right off the ridgeline through a grove of ironwoods and then Cook pines. The ground near the trail is covered with lau‘ae ferns.

Switchback to the right and descend into Waipilopilo Gulch (map point J). Ignore a narrow trail continuing straight at the switchback.

Cross the stream again and climb out of the gulch.

Contour around the front of the ridge through Cook pines and ironwoods. Through gaps in the trees, you can see up the windward coast to Lā‘ie Point and down the coast to Māhie Point on the far side of Kahana Bay.

Descend on two switchbacks through grass on rougher trail.

Reach the end of the loop (map point H) and turn left.

Retrace your steps back to the paved road (map point C).

Turn left on it to return to the highway (map point A).

NOTES

Hau‘ula-Papali is the perfect hike for beginners. The two loops are short, mostly shady, and surprisingly scenic. Along the trail are some easily identified native and introduced plants. Although in the same general area, each loop is different, so try them both. An inexpensive interpretive pamphlet, *Hau‘ula Loop Trail: Field Site Guide,* is available from Moanalua Gardens Foundation, whose address is listed in the appendix.

The route narrative describes the Papali (small cliff) loop first in a counterclockwise direction and then the Hau'ula (red hau tree) loop in a clockwise direction. You can, of course, do just one or both loops in either order or direction. The Hau'ula loop is somewhat easier and more popular than Papali. Neither loop is crowded, however, probably because of their distance from Honolulu.

Territorial Forestry built the two loops in the early 1930s to provide access to the Hau'ula Forest Reserve for tree planters, pig hunters, and fence builders. Trail crews finished the Papali loop first in December 1932 and the Hau'ula loop in April 1933. Civilian Conservation Corps workers regraded and cleared both loops in 1935. Even today, the trails remain wide, well graded, and easy to follow for the most part. Watch you step, however, while crossing the rocky streambeds in the gulches. The Papali loop may be overgrown in spots with introduced shrubs.

On the trail, look and listen for the white-rumped shama. It is black on top with a chestnut-colored breast and a long black and white tail. The shama has a variety of beautiful songs and often mimics other birds. A native of Malaysia, the shama has become widespread in introduced forests such as this one.

Look for native pāpala kēpau trees in Papali Gulch. They have large, leathery, oval leaves and clusters of small, white flowers. Early Hawaiians smeared glue from the sticky, ripe fruit on poles to catch native birds for their feathers. Craftsmen then fashioned capes and religious objects from the bright red and yellow feathers.

On the return portion of the Papali loop, watch for the sprawling native shrub 'ūlei in the sunny sections. It has small, oblong leaves arranged in pairs; clusters of white, roselike flowers; and white fruit. Early Hawaiians ate the berries and used the tough wood for making digging sticks, fish spears, and 'ūkēkē (the musical bow).

Above Kaipapa'u (shallow sea) Gulch on the Hau'ula loop are a few pūkiawe shrubs and 'ōhi'a trees. Pūkiawe has tiny, rigid leaves and small white, pink, or red berries. 'Ōhi'a has oval leaves and clusters of delicate red flowers. Early Hawaiians used the flowers in lei and the wood in outrigger canoes. The hard, durable wood was also carved into god images for *heiau* (religious sites).

On the return leg of the Hau'ula loop is a forest of tall Cook pines planted by Territorial Forestry in 1933. They have overlapping, scalelike leaves about ¼ inch long rather than true needles. Named after Captain James Cook, they are native to New Caledonia's Isle of Pines in the South Pacific, between Fiji and Australia.

39

Koloa Gulch

TYPE:	Valley
LENGTH:	8-mile round-trip
ELEVATION GAIN:	1,300 feet
DANGER:	Medium
SUITABLE FOR:	Intermediate
LOCATION:	Kahuku Forest Reserve above Lāʻie
TOPO MAP:	Kahuku, Hauʻula
ACCESS:	Conditional; open to individuals with an annual permit. Contact Hawaii Reserves, Inc., 55-510 Kamehameha Hwy., Laie, HI 96762 (phone 293-9201).

HIGHLIGHTS

This deceptive hike starts purposefully up a hot, open ridge and then descends lazily into a cool, narrow gulch. The meandering path has abundant stream crossings and mountain apple groves. Awaiting you at the end is an inviting pool with a split-level waterfall.

TRAILHEAD DIRECTIONS

At Punchbowl St. get on Lunalilo Fwy. (H-1) heading ʻEwa (west).

Take Likelike Hwy. (exit 20A, Rte. 63 north) up Kalihi Valley through the Wilson Tunnel.

As the highway forks, keep right for Kahekili Hwy. (Rte. 83 west).

Kahekili Hwy. becomes Kamehameha Hwy. (still Rte. 83), which continues up the windward coast.

Drive through Ka'a'awa and Punalu'u to Hau'ula.

Pass Hau'ula Beach Park on the right and Hau'ula Shopping Center on the left.

On the right, look for Kokololio Beach Park with its long rock wall. Turn right into the lot there and park at its far end (map point A). The beach park has restrooms and drinking water.

BUS: Route 55 to Kokololio Beach Park.

ROUTE DESCRIPTION

Walk through an opening in the rock wall by a false kamani tree and turn right on Kamehameha Hwy.

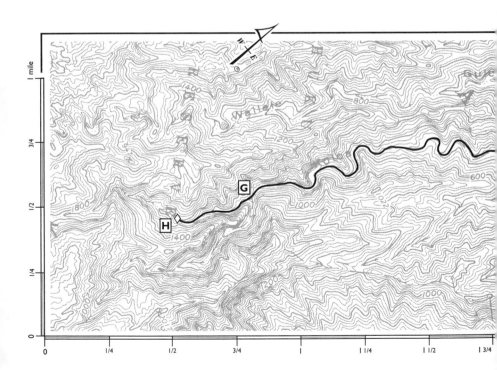

Cross Kokololio Stream on a bridge with a guardrail.

Pass a bus stop and cross a small culvert.

Almost immediately, turn left on a semipaved road across from house number 55-147 (map point B). Lining the road are ironwood trees.

Ignore a dirt road coming in on the right through a gate.

As the road curves left to a house, continue straight on a grassy road with a chain across it.

On the right, pass a stone monument honoring a Boy Scout killed in a flash flood in 1994.

Go through a gate in a barbed-wire fence.

Ascend gradually beside a gully through scrub koa haole trees and then grass.

The road swings right, between two rows of ironwoods (map point C). (An obscure trail on the left enters ʻAʻakakiʻi Gulch.)

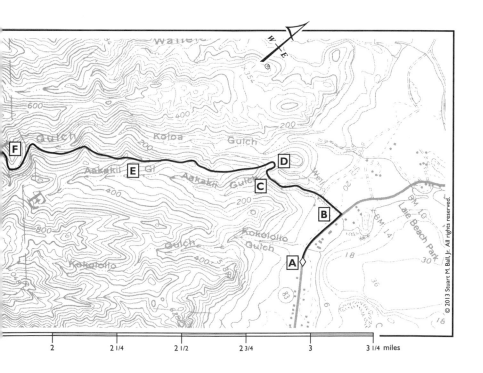

Keep left along the edge of a grassy field.

As the road curves right, reach a junction by the remains of a collapsed shack. Turn left upslope on a trail through a grove of ironwoods (map point D).

Climb steeply to the ridgeline and bear left up it. Ignore several side trails on the right leading into Koloa Gulch.

Ascend steadily through scattered ironwoods. Enjoy the breeze sighing through their branches. Along the ridge are native 'ūlei and 'ākia shrubs.

Pass a huge white-barked paraserianthes (albizia) tree on the right.

Reach a large eroded spot. Look back for views of the Polynesian Cultural Center and Lāʻie Point.

Keep left around a bare knob.

Just after a level, grassy section, reach a junction (map point E). Bear right off the ridge through a tunnel of guava (waiawī). (The less used trail to the left continues up the ridge.)

Descend into Koloa Gulch, gradually at first, and then more steeply. Watch for native lama trees among the introduced vegetation.

Reach Koloa Stream (map point F) and ford it. Memorize that crossing for the return trip.

On the far bank, bear left and head upstream on a makeshift trail that is often rocky, rooty, and muddy.

Ford the stream twenty-two more times. Watch your footing on the sometimes slippery rocks. Look for hīhīwai, a native freshwater snail.

After the fourth crossing is a stand of yellow ginger.

After the fifth are some coffee trees.

After the seventh is a grove of hala trees.

After the eighth are an old house site under huge mango trees and a mountain apple grove.

At the ninth crossing, look for the remains of a concrete dam.

At the fifteenth are twin streambeds with a tiny island in between.

After the seventeenth and eighteenth are kukui trees and more mountain apples.

After the twenty-second, look for bird's-nest ferns.

After the twenty-third crossing, work around to the right of some fallen trunks and huge boulders in the stream. Nestled among them is a small pool with a miniature waterfall.

Inch around a huge boulder to reach the twenty-fourth crossing.

The trail becomes rough and obscure. Walk in the streambed as necessary.

Pass several lone loulu palms. Watch for native māmaki trees.

The stream briefly splits and then rejoins. Keep to the right. Pass a small pool and a large boulder on the right.

Edge around a massive rock dike that juts into the stream on the right.

Just past another dike forming a cliff on the left, reach a major fork in the stream (map point G). Again, keep to the right.

As the gulch narrows significantly, pass two waterfall chutes.

Reach a circular, limpid pool backed by vertical cliffs and a small waterfall, which blocks further progress (elevation 1,120 feet) (map point H) (UTM 04 0609225E, 2388581N). Above and to the right is a larger waterfall.

NOTES

Koloa Gulch penetrates deep into the heart of the windward Koʻolau Range. The hike starts up an open ridge and ends in a deep, narrow ravine. In the process, you ford Koloa (native duck) Stream over twenty-four times. The reward for all that rock hopping is a lovely pool and waterfall nestled near the back of the gulch.

July and early August are the best months to take this hike. The mountain apples are in season then, and the midday sun is high enough to reach the pool at the end of the hike. Without the sun, the back of the gulch is a damp and chilly spot.

Before you start the hike, a few cautions are in order. Watch your footing on the slippery rocks in the streambed. Don't hesitate to get your boots wet if the rock hopping becomes dicey. Around the twenty-fourth crossing, switch to tabis (Japanese reef walkers) or other water footwear that can grip wet surfaces.

The trail along the stream is usually rocky and rooty, sometimes muddy, and occasionally obscure. Each bank at a stream crossing may be marked with surveyor's ribbon of various colors, but don't count on it. If you lose the trail, keep walking upstream until you find the route again. The lower portion of the gulch is the home of some very persistent mosquitoes.

The stone monument at the start of the hike is a stark reminder of the major hazard in the gulch: flash flooding. During a very heavy rainstorm, Koloa Stream can rise suddenly with little warning. If that happens, head for the nearest high ground and wait there for the stream to go down. It is far better to be stranded for half a day than to get swept away.

A secondary hazard is rock falling from the cliffs above with little or no warning. The danger becomes greater as the gulch narrows because the walls are steeper, and there is less room to maneuver. If caught in a rockfall, protect your head with your arms and pack and hope for the best.

On the ridge portion of the hike, look for the native dryland shrub 'ākia. It has dark branches jointed with white rings. Its leaves are bright green, oval, and pointed. Early Hawaiians pounded the leaves and bark and then dropped the mixture into tidal pools to poison fish. The red-orange fruits were used in lei and as a poison for criminals.

While crossing the stream, look for hīhīwai, a native snail with a black, knobby shell. The snail eats freshwater algae from the stream rocks. Early Hawaiians ate hīhīwai when other more palatable food was scarce.

After the seventh stream crossing is a grove of hala trees. They have distinctive prop roots that help support the heavy clusters of leaves and fruit on the ends of the branches. Early Hawaiians braided the long, pointed leaves, called *lau hala,* into baskets, fans, floor mats, and sails.

After the eighth ford is an old Hawaiian house site with *lo'i* (terraces) for growing *kalo* (taro) nearby. Beyond the site is a dense stand of mountain apple ('ōhi'a 'ai) trees with dark, oblong, shiny leaves. In spring their purple flowers carpet the trail. The delicious pink or red fruit usually ripens in late July or early August. If none are in reach, shake the tree gently and try to catch the apples as they come down. The species is native to Malaysia and was brought over by early Hawaiians.

After the twenty-fourth crossing, the stream trail winds around steep, narrow side ridges jutting into the gulch. Look at the exposed rock where the ridge meets the stream. The rock is part of a dike complex in the northwest rift zone of the old Ko'olau (windward) volcano. Rift zones are areas of structural weakness extending from the summit of a shield volcano. Rising molten rock or magma worked its way into cracks in the rift zone and solidified. The resulting dikes are sheetlike, vertical intrusions of hard, dense rock. Over the years, the stream has eroded the softer surrounding material, leaving the parallel dikes exposed.

Toward the back of the gulch are native māmaki trees. They have leathery, light green leaves with toothed margins and prominent veins. Along the stems are the white, fleshy fruits. Early Hawaiians used the bark and sap in making *kapa* (bark cloth). They also steeped the leaves to prepare a tea as a tonic.

The hike ends at a small but inviting pool backed by a waterfall. Take a cool, refreshing dip; you've earned it after all that rock hopping. From the pool, look around the corner to see a larger waterfall, one level up.

For a slightly longer outing, go left where the stream splits near the end of the hike. Like the right fork, the left also leads to a pool and a waterfall.

40

Lā'ie

TYPE:	Graded ridge
LENGTH:	12-mile round-trip
ELEVATION GAIN:	2,200 feet
DANGER:	Low
SUITABLE FOR:	Intermediate, Expert
LOCATION:	Kahuku Forest Reserve above Lā'ie
TOPO MAP:	Kahuku, Hau'ula
ACCESS:	Conditional; open to individuals with an annual permit. Contact Hawaii Reserves, Inc., 55-510 Kamehameha Hwy., Laie, HI 96762 (phone 293-9201).

HIGHLIGHTS

This long hike follows a hot dirt road and then a rugged ridge trail to the Ko'olau summit. On the way up is a cool swimming hole with waterfalls above and below. At the top are superb views of both sides of the island.

TRAILHEAD DIRECTIONS

At Punchbowl St. get on Lunalilo Fwy. (H-1) heading 'Ewa (west).

Take Likelike Hwy. (exit 20A, Rte. 63 north) up Kalihi Valley through the Wilson Tunnel.

As the highway forks, keep right for Kahekili Hwy. (Rte. 83 west).

Kahekili Hwy. becomes Kamehameha Hwy. (still Rte. 83), which continues up the windward coast.

Drive through the villages of Ka'a'awa, Punalu'u, and Hau'ula to Lā'ie.

Pass the Polynesian Cultural Center and Lā'ie Village Shopping Center on the left.

Turn left on Naniloa Loop, which is the fourth left after the entrance road to the Mormon Temple. The loop has a grass median strip and a green Lā'ie town sign.

Enter a small traffic circle and exit at the second right on Po'ohaili St.

On your left, look for Lā'ie Park, a baseball field, and park on the grass along the road at the far end of the field (map point A).

BUS: Route 55 to Kamehameha Hwy. and Naniloa Loop. Walk 0.2 mile along Naniloa Loop and Po'ohaili St. to Lā'ie Park.

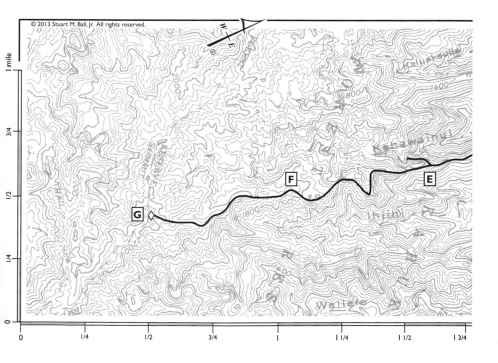

ROUTE DESCRIPTION

Continue along Po'ohaili St. on foot.

After passing the last house, go through a yellow gate.

Cross the grassy, abandoned railbed of the Ko'olau Railway and pass Lā'ie Cricket Field on your right.

As the paved road curves left, reach a junction. Bear right through a gate onto a dirt/gravel road paralleling a utility line. An opening on the left provides access if the gate is closed (map point B).

Ignore driveways leading to fields on both sides of the road.

Pass a green pump shack on the right.

Cross a small stream on a short concrete bridge.

Shortly afterward, reach a signed junction (map point C). Turn left and up on a side road through a faded yellow gate.

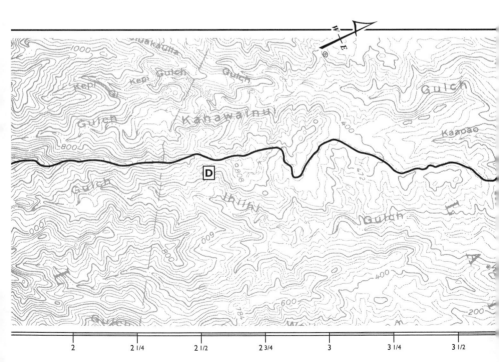

(The main road swings right and leads to the Mālaekahana Falls hike.)

Reach a second signed junction. Bear left uphill. (The right fork leads to a dirt area, informally known as Scrambling Hills.)

Climb steadily along the broad ridge for a long stretch. Ironwoods and other introduced trees provide some shade. Ignore several side roads and dirt bike trails.

Pass a wooden gatepost attached to a barbed-wire fence on the right. The badly eroded road curves right to follow the fence line and then curves left away from it. A trail on the right bypasses the worst section of the road.

Shortly afterward, reach another junction. Take the right fork.

In an open, flat area, an overgrown side road comes in on the left. Keep right uphill on the main road.

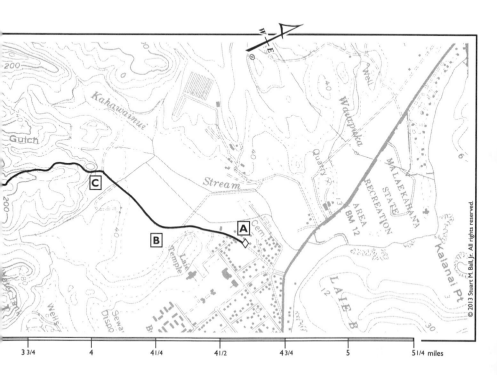

The road narrows to a trail and is flanked by uluhe ferns and strawberry guava trees.

Reach a grove of Cook pines and the start of the Lāʻie Trail (map point D). Look *makai* (seaward) for a good view of Lāʻie Point and the town.

Walk through the pine grove and then descend briefly.

Climb gradually along the left side of the ridge through a long corridor of strawberry guavas.

After the trailside vegetation switches to uluhe ferns and purple Philippine ground orchids, reach a signed junction (map point E). Keep left toward the summit on the Lāʻie Trail. (To the right and up a low embankment is a short side trail that descends steeply to a small pool and two waterfalls along Kahawainui Stream.)

Ascend gradually in and out of small side gulches. The trail becomes rough and narrow in spots. Native ʻōhiʻa, lama, and kōpiko trees gradually replace the strawberry guavas.

Walk through a section recovering from a fire in 2008.

Pass an open stretch with a steep cliff on the right and sharp drop-off on the left. Watch out for a deep trench on the right.

Continue the gradual ascent along the left side of the ridge. Downslope on the left are native loulu palms and lapalapa trees with their fluttering leaves. Look for introduced bamboo orchids along the trail.

Reach the ridgeline at a small saddle and cross over to the right side of the ridge (map point F). A small clearing there ringed by bamboo orchids makes a good rest stop before the final push to the summit. Watch for deep trenches along the trail before and after the crossover.

Work up the side of Kahawainui Gulch toward its end at the summit ridge. Along the usually muddy trail are native ʻōlapa trees, more loulu palms, and naupaka kuahiwi shrubs. Listen for the Japanese bush warbler.

Reach a signed junction with the Koʻolau Summit Trail. Turn left on the Summit Trail briefly and then climb the small mound on the right. At the top is a foxhole with a view of both sides of the island (elevation 2,240 feet) (map point G) (UTM 04 0607899E, 2388500N). Behind the viewpoint are native alani shrubs and ōlapa trees.

NOTES

Lāʻie (ʻieʻie leaf) is three hikes in one. First comes a hot climb on a dry dirt road. Next follows a pleasant stroll in a cool corridor of Cook pines and strawberry guava trees. Last is a rough, wet slog through native forest to reach the Koʻolau (windward) summit.

Start early to avoid the hot sun on the approach road. The road and the trail to the pool junction are usually in good condition. Although still graded, the trail above the pool has some rough sections because of erosion and landslides. The treadway may also be overgrown with bristly uluhe ferns and *Clidemia* shrubs. Watch your footing constantly; expect to slip a few times and get muddy and wet. The trail was built by the Wahiawa Camp of the Civilian Conservation Corps in 1934–1935.

At the start of the Lāʻie Trail is a shady grove of Cook pines planted by Territorial Forestry in 1929. Take a break there and admire the grand view of the windward coast. Behind Lāʻie town, a small peninsula called Laniloa (tall majesty) juts into the ocean. According to legend, the peninsula was a *moʻo*, or giant lizard, in ancient times. The *moʻo* often reared up and killed Hawaiian people passing by. One day the demigod Kana and his brother Nīheu set out to destroy the lizard. After a long, drawn-out battle, the two succeeded in slaying the monster. Kana cut the head of the *moʻo* into five pieces and threw them in the ocean. The pieces became five small islands, which you can still see today. Kīhewamoku islet is offshore of Kahuku town. *Makai* (seaward) of Mālaekahana are Mokuʻauia (island to one side), better known as Goat Island, and Pulemoku (broken prayer). Close to Laniloa are Kukuihoʻolua (oven-baked candlenut) and Mokuālai (island standing in the way). All five islands are now state seabird sanctuaries.

Beyond the pines, strawberry guava trees (waiawī ʻulaʻula) line the trail. They have glossy, dark green leaves and smooth brown bark. Their dark red fruit is delicious, with a taste reminiscent of strawberries. The guavas usually ripen in August and September. The strawberry guava is a native of Brazil but was introduced to Hawaiʻi from England in the 1800s.

The swimming hole along Kahawainui Stream is small but refreshing after the hot climb. Intermediate hikers can make the pool their goal. Summit hikers can stop there on the way back. The makeshift trail down to the pool is steep, narrow, and slippery, but the initial section has been improved with plastic steps.

Between the burned section and the crossover, look for native loulu palms and lapalapa trees. The palms have rigid, fan-shaped fronds in a cluster at the top of a ringed trunk. Early Hawaiians used the fronds for thatch and plaited the blades of young fronds into fans and baskets. Lapalapa has roundish leaves that are arranged in groups of three and flutter in the slightest wind. Early Hawaiians used the bark, leaves, and purple fruit to make a blue-black dye to decorate their *kapa* (bark cloth). The leaves also make a distinctive lei.

Just before and after the crossover, watch for deep trenches along the trail. The U.S. Army dug the twin pits during World War II to deny use of the trail to an attacking Japanese force. If an invasion had occurred, soldiers would have filled the trenches with explosives and blown out the trail at this key point. A third trench is located farther down the route where the trail narrows past a vertical cliff.

On the final slog to the Koʻolau summit, listen for the Japanese bush warbler (uguisu), a bird often heard but rarely seen. Its distinctive cry starts with a long whistle and then winds down in a series of notes. The bush warbler is olive brown on top with a white breast and a long tail.

From the foxhole lookout at the top you can see Kahuku (the projection) and Lāʻie towns to windward. To leeward are the Wahiawā (place of noise) plain and the Waiʻanae (mullet water) Range. Along its crest, from left to right, are Puʻu Kaua (war hill), Kolekole (raw) Pass, flat-topped Kaʻala (the fragrance), and Kaʻena (the heat) Point. All around is the convoluted topography of the northern Koʻolau Range.

On the leeward side of the overlook is the native tree ʻōlapa. Its leaves are opposite and oblong, and flutter in the slightest wind. In a special hula stance named after the tree, dancers mimic the exquisite movements of the leaves. Like lapalapa, early Hawaiians used the bark, leaves, and purple fruit to make a blue-black dye to decorate their *kapa* (bark cloth).

Below the overlook is the junction with the Summit Trail, an 18.5-mile footpath along the top of the Koʻolau Range. As you face the overlook, turn right to reach Pūpūkea Road. See the Pūpūkea Summit hike for a partial description of that segment. Turn left to get to the Poamoho and Schofield-Waikāne Trails. The Summit Trail is for experienced hikers only, as it is overgrown, obscure, and frequently socked in.

The Mālaekahana Falls hike starts from the same trailhead. That route follows a nearby ridge to several pools and waterfalls along Mālaekahana Stream.

41

Mālaekahana Falls

TYPE:	Ungraded ridge
LENGTH:	8-mile round-trip
ELEVATION GAIN:	1,500 feet
DANGER:	Low
SUITABLE FOR:	Intermediate, Expert
LOCATION:	Kahuku Forest Reserve above Lāʻie
TOPO MAP:	Kahuku
ACCESS:	Conditional; open to individuals with an annual permit. Contact Hawaii Reserves, Inc., 55–510 Kamehameha Hwy., Laie, HI 96762 (phone 293-9201).

HIGHLIGHTS

This hike follows farm roads and then an open, scenic ridge toward the Koʻolau summit. The reward is a series of idyllic waterfalls and swimming holes along Mālaekahana Stream.

TRAILHEAD DIRECTIONS

At Punchbowl St. get on Lunalilo Fwy. (H-1) heading ʻEwa (west).

Take Likelike Hwy. (exit 20A, Rte. 63 north) up Kalihi Valley through the Wilson Tunnel.

As the highway forks, keep right for Kahekili Hwy. (Rte. 83 west).

Kahekili Hwy. becomes Kamehameha Hwy. (still Rte. 83), which continues up the windward coast.

Drive through the villages of Ka'a'awa, Punalu'u, and Hau'ula to Lā'ie.

Pass the Polynesian Cultural Center and Lā'ie Village Shopping Center on the left.

Turn left on Naniloa Loop, which is the fourth left after the entrance road to the Mormon Temple. The loop has a grass median strip and a green Lā'ie town sign.

Enter a small traffic circle and exit at the second right on Po'ohaili St.

On your left, look for Lā'ie Park, a baseball field, and park on the grass along the road at the far end of the field (map point A).

BUS: Route 55 to Kamehameha Hwy. and Naniloa Loop. Walk 0.2 mile along Naniloa Loop and Po'ohaili St. to Lā'ie Park.

ROUTE DESCRIPTION

Continue along Po'ohaili St. on foot.

After passing the last house, go through a yellow gate.

Cross the grassy, abandoned railbed of the Ko'olau Railway and pass Lā'ie Cricket Field on your right.

As the paved road curves left, reach a junction. Bear right through a gate onto a dirt/gravel road paralleling a utility line. An opening on the left provides access if the gate is closed (map point B).

Ignore driveways leading to fields on both sides of the road.

Pass a green pump shack on the right.

Cross an intermittent stream channel on a short concrete bridge.

Shortly afterward, reach a signed junction (map point C). Keep right on the main dirt road. (The road on the left leads through a yellow gate to the Lā'ie Trail.)

A dirt road comes in on the left. Continue straight.

As the road splits, take the left fork marked by a wooden sign to Mālaekahana Falls.

Keep right on the main road by a fence post and white water pipe.

Ford Kahawainui Stream. Immediately turn left onto a less traveled dirt road following the stream.

Presently, bear left as the road splits. (The right fork parallels a field.)

At the next fork, keep right by another wooden sign. (The left fork goes into a field.)

Reach a junction by an old metal gate and a fence post (map point D). Turn left on a narrow dirt road. (Along the main road to the right is a blue No Trespassing sign.)

Climb gradually up ʻŌmao Gulch between an intermittent stream on the left and a barbed-wire fence on the right.

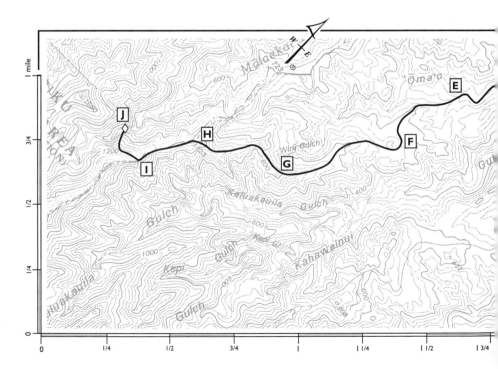

Cross the streambed twice, once over a pipe and once by fording.

Reach an obscure junction by a fence post (map point E). Bear left and up.

Climb the side of a ridge on the rutted road past Formosa koa trees.

Gain the broad ridgeline and bear right uphill.

On the left, pass two wooden fence posts in a stand of iron-wood trees (map point F). A narrow dirt road comes in on the left.

Climb steadily up the right side of the ridge through grass and scattered guava interspersed with groves of ironwood. On the right is a barbed-wire fence.

Work to the left side of the ridge across a gentle, grassy slope. Look for the native shrub ʻākia among the stunted strawberry guava trees.

A line of fence posts comes in on the left.

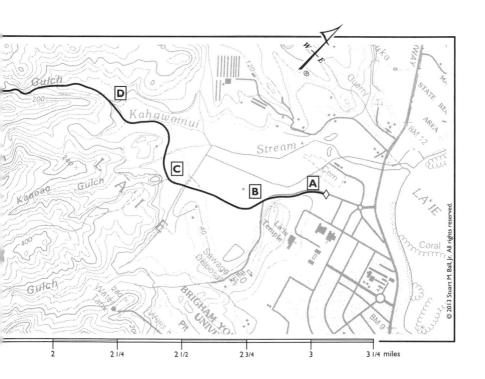

After ascending steeply up an eroded slope, reach a flat, open lookout with good views *makai* of Lāʻie Point and the town (map point G). Across Kahawainui Gulch on the left, you can see the Cook pines at the start of the Lāʻie Trail.

The ridge curves right and descends briefly through native koa trees and strawberry guava. Watch for the native shrub pūkiawe as the road ends.

Resume climbing over a rounded knob covered with dense strawberry guava.

Ascend steeply through guava and uluhe ferns to a second knob with a large native ʻōhiʻa tree (map point H). The abandoned original route of the Mālaekahana Trail comes in on the side ridge to the right.

Cross an open, relatively level stretch through uluhe.

Ascend and descend a smaller knob through a tunnel of guava.

After crossing a short level section with strawberry guava on the left and uluhe on the right, reach an obscure junction (map point I) (UTM 04 0607396E, 2391566N). Turn right and down on a narrow trail. (To the left and up, the Mālaekahana Trail continues to the Koʻolau summit.)

Angle down the side of the ridge, gradually at first and then more steeply through guava.

Bear right straight downhill, paralleling a shallow gully.

Swing right, across the slope, leaving the gully behind.

Reach a larger gully and descend it briefly, perhaps with the aid of a rope.

Angle right, out of the gully and across the slope.

As you approach the stream, go straight downhill through scattered kī (ti) plants.

Reach a junction at Mālaekahana Stream (map point J). For now, ford the stream. (To the left, a trail continues upstream to a small waterfall and pool.)

Follow the stream and cross it above a waterfall. A steep trail then leads to a pool at the base of the falls. Below is a second waterfall and pool.

Backtrack to the junction across the stream. Turn right, heading upstream. (The trail to the left is the way you came in.) Walk in the stream briefly around some large boulders and pick up a faint trail on the right bank. Note the rock dike crossing the streambed.

Pick up a faint trail on the right bank.

Inch around a large boulder above a small pool and waterfall.

Reach a larger pool with a double waterfall.

NOTES

The initial portion of the hike tracks dirt roads with several crucial junctions, some marked and some not. Follow the narrative closely to avoid wandering into the adjacent farm fields. Bring poles or pick up a stout stick along the way to ward off the occasional loose dog.

Look for the native dryland shrubs 'ākia and pūkiawe along the dirt road that climbs the ridge. 'Ākia has dark branches jointed with white rings. Its leaves are bright green, oval, and pointed. Early Hawaiians pounded the leaves and bark and then dropped the mixture into tidal pools to poison the fish. The red-orange fruits were used in lei and as a poison for criminals. Pūkiawe has tiny, rigid leaves and small white, pink, or red berries.

Soon after the dirt road ends, the old Mālaekahana Trail comes in on a side ridge to the right. A Territorial Forestry crew began construction of the partially graded route in March 1931 to provide access for pig hunters. When completed several months later, the trail stretched 2.7 miles to the Ko'olau summit. Near the top, the crew built a small cabin in a grove of native loulu palms.

Watch your step on the rough, steep route into the gulch. At Mālaekahana Stream, the trail splits. Head downstream first to a double waterfall with two cool, refreshing swimming holes.

Upstream is a single pool with twin cascades above. Tread gingerly on the slippery rocks in the streambed and around the pools and waterfalls.

In the gulch are scattered kī (ti) plants. They have shiny leaves 1–2 feet long that are arranged spirally in a cluster at the tip of a slender stem. Early Polynesian voyagers introduced ti to Hawaiʻi. They used the leaves for house thatch, skirts, sandals, and raincoats. Food to be cooked in the *imu* (underground oven) was first wrapped in ti leaves. A popular sport with the commoners was *hoʻoheʻe kī,* or ti-leaf sledding. The sap from ti plants stained canoes and surfboards.

For a longer hike, continue along the ridge on the Mālaekahana Trail instead of visiting the pools. The route to the Koʻolau summit is long and rough and may be overgrown with scratchy uluhe ferns and *Clidemia* shrubs. Look for traces of the original graded sections of the old trail.

The Lāʻie hike starts from the same trailhead. That route climbs a nearby ridge to a pool, waterfall, and the Koʻolau summit.

NORTH SHORE

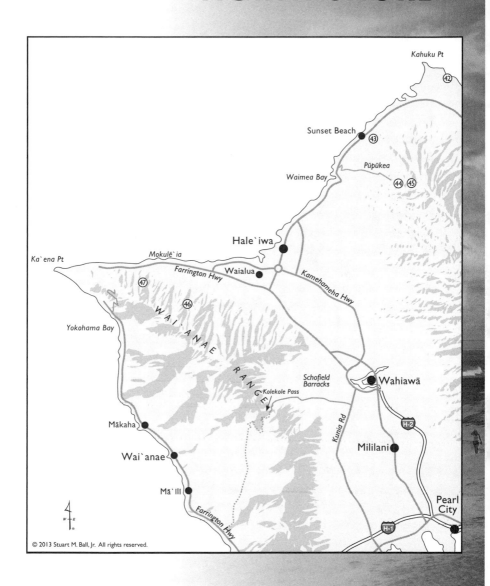

42

Kahuku Shoreline

TYPE:	Shoreline
LENGTH:	6 miles one way
ELEVATION GAIN:	Minimal
DANGER:	Low
SUITABLE FOR:	Novice, Intermediate
LOCATION:	Shoreline between Kahuku Golf Course and Turtle Bay Resort
TOPO MAP:	Kahuku
ACCESS:	Open

HIGHLIGHTS

This beach walk follows the wild, windswept, mostly undeveloped coast of north Oʻahu. Along the way you may see humpback whales, migratory shorebirds, and endangered monk seals.

TRAILHEAD DIRECTIONS

At Punchbowl St. get on Lunalilo Fwy. (H-1) heading ʻEwa (west).

Take Likelike Hwy. (exit 20A, Rte. 63 north) up Kalihi Valley through the Wilson Tunnel.

As the highway forks, keep right for Kahekili Hwy. (Rte. 83 west).

Kahekili Hwy. becomes Kamehameha Hwy. (still Rte. 83), which continues up the windward coast.

Drive through the villages of Kaʻaʻawa, Punaluʻu, and Hauʻula to Lāʻie.

Pass the Polynesian Cultural Center and Lāʻie Village Shopping Center on the left.

Pass Mālaekahana State Recreation Area on the right.

Enter Kahuku town.

At the lone traffic light, turn right on Puʻuluana St. On the left are Kahuku High and Intermediate Schools.

The road ends at a small parking lot overlooking Kahuku Golf Course. Turn left and park in the lot near the clubhouse (elevation 40 feet) (map point A). If that lot is full, as it sometimes is on weekends, park in the overflow lot at the road's end. The clubhouse has restrooms and drinking water.

BUS: Route 55 to Kamehameha Hwy. and Puʻuluana St. Walk 0.2 mile along Puʻuluana to the trailhead.

To get to the Turtle Bay trailhead, continue along Kamehameha Hwy.

Turn right into Turtle Bay Resort.

After passing the entrance station, take the second right, marked Shoreline Public Access and Parking. Park at the far end of the large lot near the electric car charging stations. The public beach has restrooms, drinking water, and an outdoor shower.

BUS: Route 55 to Turtle Bay Resort. The covered bus stop is in the *mauka* (inland) corner of the large parking lot under a banyan tree.

ROUTE DESCRIPTION

Go around a locked yellow gate at the far end of the clubhouse parking lot and take the paved road heading along the perimeter of the golf course.

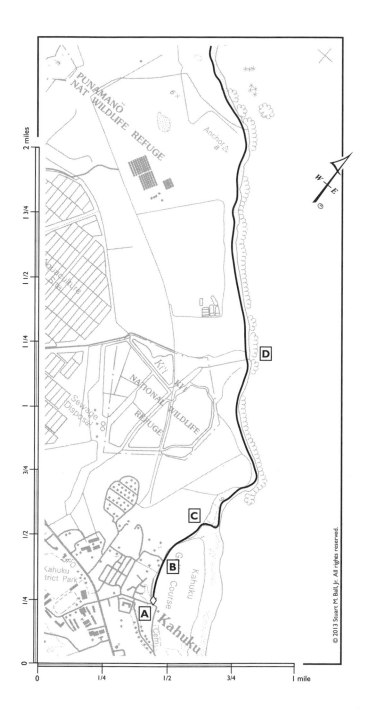

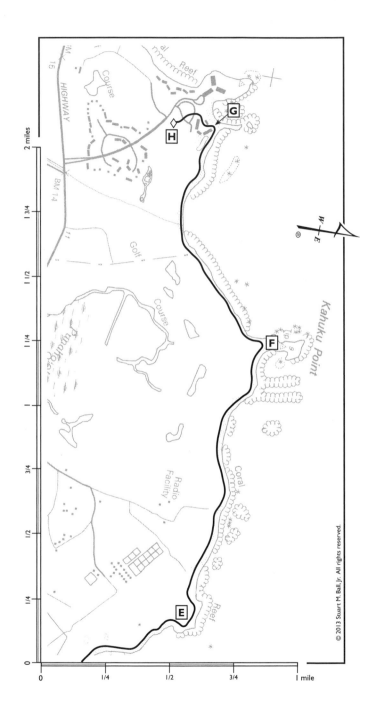

After the pavement ends, reach a fork (map point B). Keep right, across the golf course. Allow golfers to complete their shots before walking quickly across the two fairways.

The road splits twice. Bear right the first time and left the second.

On the left, pass a nesting area of 'ua'u kani, the wedge-tailed shearwater.

Reach a vehicle turnaround (map point C) (UTM 04 0609134E, 2398199N). Descend to windswept Kahuku Beach through naupaka kahakai shrubs and turn left toward Turtle Bay. A wooden fence on the left marks the end of the golf course and the beginning of a long stretch of private and federal government property. Stay below the vegetation line or the debris line to avoid trespassing.

After the fence line is a small Japanese plantation cemetery and a pasture of the Kahuku Kai Horse Ranch.

Past the ranch, the coast straightens out somewhat, and an eroded limestone shelf frequently fronts the beach. Look for small flocks of 'akekeke (ruddy turnstone) skittering along the shoreline in the winter.

Mauka (inland) is the James Campbell National Wildlife Refuge. Watch for kioea (bristle-thighed curlew) among the sand dunes.

Cross a stream coming out of the refuge wetlands (map point D).

Pass a small concrete structure with a pipe leading into the ocean. Just beyond is a shady beach heliotrope tree.

Next along the coast is the site of a nudist camp popular in the 1970s. Instead of naked, sunburned bodies, look for 'ulili (wandering tattler) along the shoreline.

Pass signs in the sand dunes marking the boundary of the wildlife refuge.

Reach a short rocky section of coastline called Kaleuila (map point E) (UTM 04 0605082E, 2401196N). Keep to the rocks rather than following the sandy road, which is on private property.

Cross lovely Hanakaʻīlio Beach. Watch for monk seals resting on the sand and give them a wide berth. *Mauka* is the abandoned Kahuku Airfield and an abandoned Marconi wireless transmitting station.

Reach flat Kalaeokaunaʻoa, better known as Kahuku Point, the northernmost spot on Oʻahu (map point F). In the distance is the main building of Turtle Bay Resort.

Pass a small cove frequented by monk seals.

Walk along Kaihalulu Beach, backed by ironwood trees.

Pass several low-rise resort buildings.

Across from a rocky spit called Kalaeokamanu, turn left onto a sandy path through naupaka kahakai (map point G).

Bear right by a snack hut and parallel the crowded public beach.

Turn left up a paved walkway past restrooms to the parking lot.

Find your car or head across the lot to the bus stop under a shady banyan tree near the entrance road (map point H) (UTM 04 0603791E, 2400326N).

NOTES

Kahuku Shoreline is a walk into the past through a less developed, less crowded part of Oʻahu. The coast is wild and windswept, with tide pools, rocky points, and crescent beaches. Hike in a small group—two is best—and take your time.

Take this hike during winter (November–April), as the temperature is cooler then and the sun less intense. You also have a chance of seeing humpback whales, migratory shorebirds, and large waves. Take this hike at low tide, so you have a wide beach to walk without trespassing on private property. Check the tides online for Lāʻie Bay or get the Hawaiʻi Marine Tide calendar. For complete solitude, go during the week or on Super Bowl Sunday.

The narrative describes the route from south to north. You

can, of course, do the hike in reverse; however, the sun will be in your face most of the way. If you have only one car, start at either trailhead, go as far as you want, and then turn around. Better yet, do the whole hike and take the bus back to your car.

Kahuku (the projection) Shoreline is a beach hike, not a beach stroll, and several suggestions and cautions are in order. Bring water, sunscreen, and binoculars to check out the birds and whales. Wear sturdy footwear, as the route crosses a stream and traverses uneven and sometimes sharp rocky sections along the shore. Stay on the beach below the vegetation line or the debris line marking the highest reach of the waves. Inland is private or federal government property, and the landowners will not hesitate to challenge you if you stray *mauka*. Although the ocean looks inviting, do not go swimming, except at the public beach at Turtle Bay. Limestone ledges frequently block access to the water, and this stretch of coast is well known for its rip currents heading out to sea. Finally, remember the old saying: never turn your back on the ocean.

On the beach, watch for 'akekeke or ruddy turnstone, a common winter visitor to the islands. 'Akekeke are brown above and white below with red-orange legs. They often travel in small flocks, feeding on insects and crustaceans along the shoreline. Note their odd-shaped bill, which they use to over-turn stones in search of prey.

Often marking the vegetation line are small beach helio-trope trees and the native low-lying shrub naupaka kahakai. The latter has bright green, fleshy leaves and half-formed white flowers with purple streaks. Its round white fruits float in the ocean, helping to spread the species to remote areas.

Past the ranch is the James Campbell National Wildlife Refuge, established in 1976 to provide habitat for endangered native waterbirds and migratory shorebirds. Managed by the U.S. Fish and Wildlife Service, the 1,100-acre refuge incorpo-rates the last remaining intact coastal dunes on O'ahu. *Mauka* are sugarcane settling ponds, now managed as emergent marsh, and natural spring-fed wetlands. Do not enter the refuge from the beach. Instead, take a guided tour, which is offered twice a week from October through February, when the birds are not breeding.

Look for kioea, or bristle-thighed curlew, in the sand dunes of the refuge. Kioea are large brown shorebirds with a long, slightly curved bill. They arrive from Alaska in late summer and spend the winter along undisturbed shorelines such as this one.

Near the site of the nudist camp, watch for 'ulili, or wandering tattler, another winter bird from Alaska. 'Ulili are dark gray above and light gray below, with yellow legs. They are usually found alone, probing for mollusks and other invertebrates in the sand and under rocks.

Mauka of Hanaka'ilio Beach is an abandoned Marconi wireless transmitting station. When completed in 1914, it was the most powerful wireless station in the world, sending radio telegraphic messages all the way to California and Japan. A second station below Koko Crater received messages from east and west. The two stations were important links in an international wireless network developed by radio pioneer Guglielmo Marconi.

Look for the endangered Hawaiian monk seal at Hanaka'ilio Beach and the small cove past Kahuku Point. Also known as 'ilio holo i ka uaua (dog that runs in rough water), it has a silvery gray back and creamy underside. Folds of skin on its head resemble a monk's hood, thus the name. The seal spends much of its time in the water, hunting for fish and invertebrate sea creatures. However, the seal does haul out on the beach regularly to rest, molt, and breed. Give it a wide berth, at least 150 feet, and don't feed or otherwise interact with it. In both locations mentioned above, you have room *mauka* to circle around a resting seal.

While not an entirely welcome sight, Turtle Bay Resort does mark the end of this sublime shoreline walk and a return to civilization. You can swim at the public beach there, take an outdoor shower, or get something to eat. Enjoy the short ride back to your car on the Route 55 bus, marked Honolulu.

43

'Ehukai

TYPE:	Foothill
LENGTH:	3-mile loop
ELEVATION GAIN:	600 feet
DANGER:	Low
SUITABLE FOR:	Novice
LOCATION:	Pūpūkea Paumalū State Park Reserve above Sunset Beach
TOPO MAP:	Waimea
ACCESS:	Open

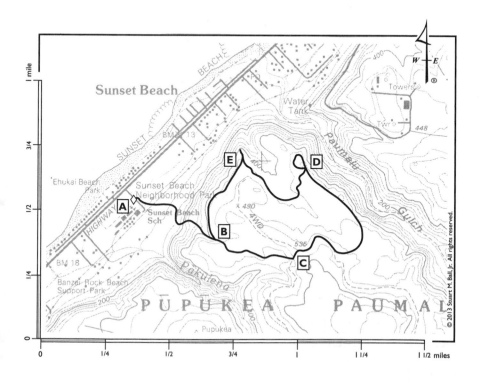

HIGHLIGHTS

This short loop meanders around the upland above Sunset Beach. From a bunker lookout, you can look for whales or watch the swells at several famous surfing spots.

TRAILHEAD DIRECTIONS

At Punchbowl St. get on Lunalilo Fwy. (H-1) heading 'Ewa (west).

Near Middle St., keep left on Moanalua Fwy. (H-201) to 'Aiea.

By Aloha Stadium, bear right to rejoin H-1 to Pearl City.

Take Veterans Memorial Hwy. (H-2) (exit 8A) to Wahiawā.

As the freeway ends, continue on Rte. 99 north (Wilikina Dr.), bypassing Wahiawā.

Pass Schofield Barracks on the left.

The road narrows to two lanes, dips, and then forks at a traffic light. Take the right fork to Hale'iwa and the north shore (Kamananui Rd., but still Rte. 99 north).

At the road's end, turn left on Kamehameha Hwy.

Pass Dole and Helemano Plantations on the right.

Before entering Hale'iwa, reach an intersection with a traffic light. Keep right on Joseph P. Leong Hwy., better known as the Hale'iwa bypass (Rte. 83). (To the left, Kamehameha Hwy. continues into Hale'iwa town.)

At the next traffic light, the bypass becomes Kamehameha Hwy. (still Rte. 83).

Go around lovely Waimea Bay and pass Foodland Supermarket on the right.

Look for the ball field and tennis courts of Sunset Beach Neighborhood Park on the right.

At the far end of the park, turn right by the sign for Sunset Beach Elementary School. On the left is 'Ehukai Beach Park.

Park in the stalls on the right by the restrooms and bas-ketball courts (elevation 20 feet) (map point A). Do not leave your car in the school lot.

BUS: Route 55 to the trailhead.

ROUTE DESCRIPTION

Walk *mauka* (inland) toward the school entrance, marked by a gate and a large sign.

Just before reaching the gate, turn left onto a trail through a stand of koa haole trees.

The trail curves right, paralleling the edge of the school parking lot.

Ascend gradually and then more steeply up the *pali* (cliff) past several banyan trees. Ropes may provide assistance in the slippery sections.

Swing left past a small cave on the right.

Ignore a narrow trail coming in on the left.

Reach a junction by a large ironwood tree (map point B) (UTM 04 0598868E, 2395782N). Bear right on the Pākūlena Komohana Trail to begin the loop in a counterclockwise direc-tion. (The contour trail on the left is the return portion of the loop.)

Cross a small gully and resume climbing through ironwoods.

Reach the top of a ridge and another junction. Keep left on the Pākūlena Komohana Trail. (To the right, a marked side trail leads to a view point.)

Meander across the broad ridge to another junction. Turn left and down on the Lean-to Trail. (The Secret Trail contin-ues straight, to Pākūlena Gulch and a junction with the Jungle Trail.)

Pass a makeshift lean-to on the right.

At the next junction, continue straight and climb steadily. (The abandoned road on the right leads to the gulch and the Jungle Trail.)

Reach a junction with a wide dirt road. Turn left on it and begin to contour.

Reach a four-way junction with another dirt road in a bare, eroded area. Continue straight across the intersection.

A marked side trail on the right leads to Pu'u Waihu'ena. Stay on the road.

Reach a junction (elevation 560 feet) (map point C) (UTM 04 0599667E, 2395610N). Turn left onto a trail marked by red and white blazes and informally known as Kalahiki. (The road bears right under a huge fallen tree.)

Descend gradually through ironwoods. Keep right along the edge of Paumalū Gulch, marked by a barbed-wire fence.

Reach a T-junction (map point D). For now, turn right. (The trail to the left marked Kahikilani is the continuation of the loop.)

In an open area, the trail splits. Take the side trail on the right for a good view toward the ocean and across the gulch to the Inmarsat Satellite Access Station. Look for the native shrubs 'ūlei and 'uhaloa.

The side trail rejoins the main trail. Turn left and return to the Kahikilani junction (map point D). This time continue straight.

Pass a dilapidated corral on the left.

Turn right at the next intersection and contour through groves of ironwoods.

The trail ends at a dirt road. Turn right on it.

Reach a concrete observation post with a view of the north shore (map point E) (UTM 04 0598986E, 2395610N). Watch for humpback whales in season.

Backtrack *mauka* (inland) on the road.

Almost immediately, reach a junction. Turn right onto a trail marked Ka'ena Kai. (The dirt road continues uphill.)

Contour above the *pali*.

At the next junction, keep left on the upper contour trail.

Reach the familiar junction (map point B), which ends the loop. Turn right and backtrack to the neighborhood park (map point A).

NOTES

This short loop above the north shore is exceedingly pleasant. However, the route has many twists and turns, so follow the narrative closely to stay on course. The North Shore Trail Association has marked some of the junctions with small, narrow signs attached to the trees. On Sunday mornings, you may have to park along the highway, as churchgoers often fill up the lot.

The 'Ehukai hike lies entirely within the newly established Pūpūkea Paumalū State Park Reserve. In August 2007, the Trust for Public Land transferred the title of the 1,104-acre property to the state. The trust had earlier purchased the land from Obayashi Corporation, which had planned to turn the area into a residential subdivision. The north shore community played a large role in the proceedings and was instrumental in preserving the site as open space.

Much of the loop travels though stands of ironwood, or casuarina. They are native to Australia and nearby islands and were introduced to Hawai'i around 1882. The trees resemble pines, but the "needles" occur singly along the twigs, rather than in bundles as in true pines. Take a break on the soft, fallen needles and enjoy the sound of the ironwoods sighing in the wind.

Watch for two native shrubs in the open sections. Sprawling 'ūlei has small, oblong leaves arranged in pairs; clusters of white, roselike flowers; and white fruit. Early Hawaiians ate the berries and used the tough wood for making digging sticks, fish spears, and 'ūkēkē (the musical bow). 'Uhaloa has toothed, hairy, gray-green leaves and tiny yellow flowers between the stem and the leaf stalk. Hawaiians pounded the stems, leaves, or bark to make a gargle to relieve sore throats.

From the observation post is good view along the north shore. To the left in the distance is Ka'ena Point. Below are the swells of the Pipeline and Sunset Beach, two renowned surfing spots. Scan the ocean farther out for humpback whales. They migrate from the North Pacific to the Hawaiian Islands, arriving in October and leaving in May. The whales congregate off the leeward coast of Maui and occupy themselves calving, nursing, breeding, and generally horsing around.

44

Kaunala

TYPE:	Foothill
LENGTH:	6-mile loop
ELEVATION GAIN:	500 feet
DANGER:	Low
SUITABLE FOR:	Novice, Intermediate
LOCATION:	Pūpūkea Paumalū Forest Reserve above Pūpūkea
TOPO MAP:	Waimea, Kahuku
ACCESS:	Conditional; open on weekends and federal and state holidays only.

HIGHLIGHTS

This meandering loop hike winds through the lush gulches of the Koʻolau foothills above Pūpūkea. On the return leg are some beautiful views of the north shore.

TRAILHEAD DIRECTIONS

At Punchbowl St. get on Lunalilo Fwy. (H-1) heading ʻEwa (west).

Near Middle St., keep left on Moanalua Fwy. (H-201) to ʻAiea.

By Aloha Stadium, bear right to rejoin H-1 to Pearl City.

Take Veterans Memorial Hwy. (H-2) (exit 8A) to Wahiawā.

As the freeway ends, continue on Rte. 99 north (Wilikina Dr.), bypassing Wahiawā.

Pass Schofield Barracks on the left.

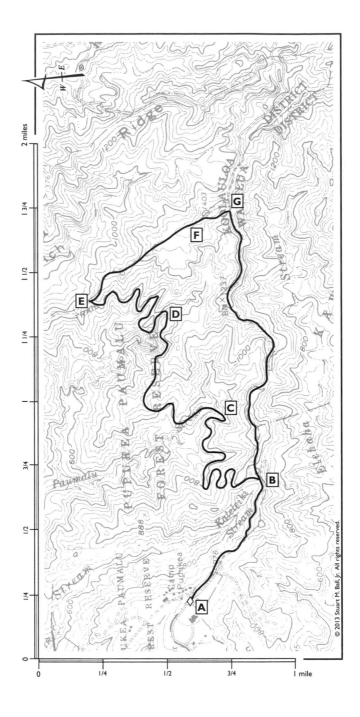

The road narrows to two lanes, dips, and then forks at a traffic light. Take the right fork to Haleʻiwa and the north shore (Kamananui Rd., but still Rte. 99 north).

At the road's end, turn left on Kamehameha Hwy.

Pass Dole and Helemano Plantations on the right.

Before entering Haleʻiwa, reach an intersection with a traffic light. Keep right on Joseph P. Leong Hwy., better known as the Haleʻiwa bypass (Rte. 83). (To the left, Kamehameha Hwy. continues into Haleʻiwa town.)

At the next traffic light, the bypass becomes Kamehameha Hwy. (still Rte. 83).

Go around Waimea Bay, passing the entrance to Waimea Valley on the right.

At the first traffic light after the bay, turn right on Pūpūkea Rd. by Foodland Supermarket.

Switchback once up a small *pali* (cliff).

Drive to the end of the paved road at Camp Pūpūkea (elevation 960 feet) (map point A). Park off the road near the entrance to the Boy Scout camp. Leave plenty of room for vehicles exiting the camp and the farm across the street.

BUS: None within reasonable walking distance of the trailhead.

ROUTE DESCRIPTION

Proceed along the dirt road past the Boy Scout camp, following the route of the old Pūpūkea-Kahuku Trail.

Go through a locked yellow gate and enter Kahuku Range, an army training area. Sign in at the hunter-hiker check-in mailbox on the left.

On the right, pass the remains of a cattle loading ramp in a stand of ironwoods.

Reach a junction. Keep left on the main road, which has become paved. (The road to the right through the locked yellow gate is Paʻalaʻa Uka Pūpūkea Rd.)

Shortly afterward, reach a signed junction at the edge of a grove of paperbark trees (map point B). Turn left on the wide Kaunala Trail. (The paved road curves to the right and is the return portion of the loop.)

The path splits immediately. Take the left fork. (The right fork goes up a hill.)

Contour around the hill, which is covered with paperbark trees.

Descend gradually on four switchbacks through a eucalyptus forest. Ignore trails going straight down the side ridges. On the left, watch for hala pepe, a small native tree with its slender leaves in bunches.

Cross over a side ridge and begin to contour into and out of several gulches. Look and listen for the white-rumped shama.

The first gulch is long and narrow.

Descend into the second gulch on two short switchbacks (map point C). At the bottom are kukui trees, kī (ti) plants, and tiny Paumalū Stream.

Contour around a broad gulch with no stream.

Cross over a side ridge in a paperbark grove. Watch for two large ʻiliahi (sandalwood) trees near a grassy section.

Descend gradually through several small gulches past hāpuʻu, the native tree fern.

Work into and out of a large gulch with a stream (map point D).

After crossing a small stream in the next gulch, climb gradually to an open area covered with uluhe ferns. In front are the rolling ridges of Paumalū. Listen for the distinctive call of the Japanese bush warbler.

Ascend the right side of a side ridge through native koa and ʻiliahi trees.

Contour briefly and then switchback once.

Reach a signed junction with a gravel road in a grove of paperbark trees (map point E) (UTM 04 0602738E, 2394122N). Turn right on the road. (To the left, it leads down to Camp Paumalū, a Girl Scout camp. Kaunala Trail extended continues across the road.)

Climb steadily on top of a wide ridge past native ʻōhiʻa and koa trees. Keep to the main road.

Reach a flat, cleared area (elevation 1,403 feet) (map point F). From there is a good view of the Waiʻanae Range and the north shore.

Descend steeply but briefly and then go through a locked gate.

Presently, reach a junction with the original paved road near a stand of Cook pines (map point G). Turn right on it. (To the left, the road is the route of the Pūpūkea Summit hike.)

Descend gradually along an up-and-down ridge, passing a covered picnic table on your right.

Reach the familiar junction with the Kaunala Trail at the far edge of the paperbark grove (map point B).

Retrace your steps to the Boy Scout Camp (map point A).

NOTES

Kaunala (the plaiting) is a pleasant valley-ridge combination above Pūpūkea (white shell) along the north shore. The trail section contours in and out of lush gulches through mostly introduced forest. The return portion follows a paved ridgetop road through the Kahuku training area of the U.S. Army.

Territorial Forestry built the Kaunala Trail in 1933 to provide access to the Pūpūkea section of the Paumalū Forest Reserve for reforestation efforts. In February, trail crews started work at Owl Flat near a newly planted section of paperbark seedlings. After the crew finished the trail in May, Territorial Forester Charles S. Judd erected hand-painted wooden signs identifying twenty-three native trees and shrubs along the route. Unfortunately, most of the native plants are gone, but the trail remains generally wide and well graded, with gradual elevation changes. However, expect mud and mosquitoes in the gulches and watch out for mountain bikers on the dirt roads.

On the trail, look and listen for the white-rumped shama. It is black on top with a chestnut-colored breast and a long black and white tail. The shama has a variety of beautiful songs and often mimics other birds. A native of Malaysia, the shama has become widespread in introduced forests such as this one.

On the initial switchbacks and in the gulches, watch for hala pepe, a tall, slender native tree. The narrow leaves hang in bunches from the branch tips. The tree produces clusters of yellowish blossoms and then red berries. Early Hawaiians used the flowers in making lei.

Lining the many small gulches are kī (ti) plants. They have shiny leaves 1–2 feet long that are arranged spirally in a cluster at the tip of a slender stem. Early Polynesian voyagers introduced ti to Hawai'i. They used the leaves for house thatch, skirts, sandals, and raincoats. Food to be cooked in the *imu* (underground oven) was first wrapped in ti leaves. A popular sport with the commoners was *ho'ohe'e kī* or ti-leaf sledding. The sap from ti plants stained canoes and surfboards.

After crossing the stream in the large gulch, listen for the Japanese bush warbler (uguisu), a bird often heard but rarely seen. Its distinctive cry starts with a long whistle and then winds down in a series of notes. The bush warbler is olive brown on top with a white breast and a long tail.

Beyond the clearing on the last side ridge are a few native 'iliahi (sandalwood) trees. Their small leaves are dull green and appear wilted. 'Iliahi is a partially parasitic, with outgrowths on its roots that steal nutrients from nearby plants. Early Hawaiians ground the fragrant heartwood into a powder to perfume their *kapa*. Beginning in the late 1700s, sandalwood was indiscriminately cut down and exported to China to make incense and furniture. The trade ended around 1840, when the forests were depleted of 'iliahi.

On the return, look for native koa and 'ōhi'a trees along the dirt road. Koa has sickle-shaped foliage and pale yellow flower clusters. Early Hawaiians made surfboards and outrigger canoe hulls out of the beautiful red-brown wood. Today it is made into fine furniture. 'Ōhi'a has oval leaves and clusters of delicate red flowers. Early Hawaiians used the flowers in lei and the wood in outrigger canoes. The hard, durable wood was also carved into god images for *heiau* (religious sites).

From the cleared area along the road are fine views of the north shore, Ka'ena (the heat) Point, and the Wai'anae (mullet water) Range. Its main peaks are Pu'u Kaua (war hill), Hāpapa (rock stratum), Kalena (the lazy one), and flat-topped Ka'ala (the fragrance) from left to right. Kolekole (raw) Pass separates Hāpapa and Kalena.

For a longer hike, take the rough Kaunala extension, which starts across the road at the end of the official Kaunala Trail. After contouring through more gulches, the extension eventually reaches the main paved road. Turn right to return to the Boy Scout camp. The first left on the way back is the start of the Ko'olau (windward) Summit Trail, which is described in the Pūpūkea Summit hike. Access to Kaunala extended or the Summit Trail requires permission from the U.S. Army. See the Pūpūkea Summit hike for the address.

45

Pūpūkea Summit

TYPE:	Graded ridge
LENGTH:	9-mile round-trip
ELEVATION GAIN:	900 feet
DANGER:	Low
SUITABLE FOR:	Novice, Intermediate
LOCATION:	Pūpūkea Paumalū and Kahuku Forest Reserves above Pūpūkea
TOPO MAP:	Waimea, Kahuku
ACCESS:	Conditional; open to individuals and outdoor organizations with permission. Write Directorate of Public Works, Real Estate Branch, 947 Wright Ave, Wheeler Army Airfield, Schofield Barracks, HI 96857-5000.

HIGHLIGHTS

This hike follows a short, tame section of the wild and woolly Koʻolau Summit Trail. Along the way are intriguing native plants and convoluted topography. Our destination is a remote, secluded lookout over the windward coast.

TRAILHEAD DIRECTIONS

At Punchbowl St. get on Lunalilo Fwy. (H-1) heading ʻEwa (west).

Near Middle St., keep left on Moanalua Fwy. (H-201) to ʻAiea.

By Aloha Stadium, bear right to rejoin H-1 to Pearl City.

Take Veterans Memorial Hwy. (H-2) (exit 8A) to Wahiawā.

As the freeway ends, continue on Rte. 99 north (Wilikina Dr.), bypassing Wahiawā.

Pass Schofield Barracks on your left.

The road narrows to two lanes, dips, and then forks at a traffic light. Take the right fork to Haleʻiwa and the north shore (Kamananui Rd., but still Rte. 99 north).

At the road's end, turn left on Kamehameha Hwy.

Pass Dole and Helemano Plantations on the right.

Before entering Haleʻiwa, reach an intersection with a traffic light. Keep right on Joseph P. Leong Hwy., better known as the Haleʻiwa bypass (Rte. 83). (To the left, Kamehameha Hwy. continues into Haleʻiwa town.)

At the next traffic light, the bypass becomes Kamehameha Hwy. (still Rte. 83).

Go around Waimea Bay, passing the entrance to Waimea Valley on your right.

At the first traffic light after the bay, turn right on Pūpūkea Rd. by Foodland Supermarket.

Switchback once up a small *pali* (cliff).

Drive to the end of the paved road at Camp Pūpūkea (elevation 960 feet) (map point A). Park off the road near the entrance to the Boy Scout camp. Leave plenty of room for vehicles exiting the camp and the farm across the street.

BUS: None within reasonable walking distance of the trailhead.

ROUTE DESCRIPTION

Proceed along the dirt road past the Boy Scout camp, following the route of the old Pūpūkea-Kahuku Trail.

Go through a locked yellow gate and enter Kahuku Range, an army training area. Sign in at the hunter-hiker check-in mailbox on the left.

On the right, pass the remains of a cattle loading ramp in a stand of ironwoods.

Reach a junction. Keep left on the main road, which has become paved. (The road to the right through the locked yellow gate is Paʻalaʻa Uka Pūpūkea Rd.)

Shortly afterward, reach a signed junction at the edge of a grove of paperbark trees (map point B). Continue straight on the paved road. (To the left, the Kaunala Trail contours below the ridge.)

Climb along the up-and-down ridge through mostly introduced forest. Look for an occasional kukui or native koa tree downslope.

Pass a covered picnic table on the left.

Reach another junction by some Cook pines (map point C). Continue straight on the main road. (The dirt road to the left is the return portion of the Kaunala loop.)

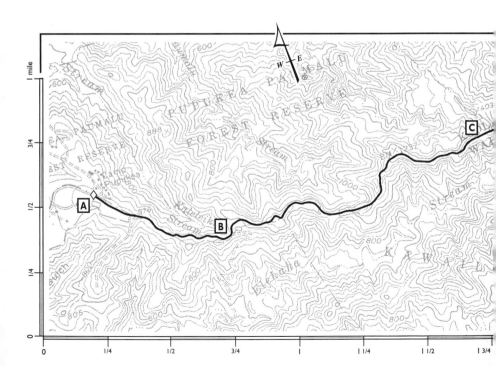

Just after that junction, walk around a locked gate and descend briefly.

Resume the gradual climb along the ridge, now lined with white-barked paraserianthes (albizia) and ironwood trees.

The road descends gradually, curves left, and begins to climb.

Just before a guardrail on the right, reach a junction with an overgrown dirt road in a grove of paraserianthes trees (map point D). Turn right onto the side road, a remnant of the Pūpūkea-Kahuku Trail. The dirt road soon deteriorates and then narrows to a trail past a small clearing ringed by uluhe ferns.

Climb gradually along the right side of the ridge below its top. On the hillside to the right are some native loulu palms.

Cross the ridgeline and contour along the left (windward) side of the ridge. Along the trail are native 'ōhi'a and kōpiko trees and maile shrubs.

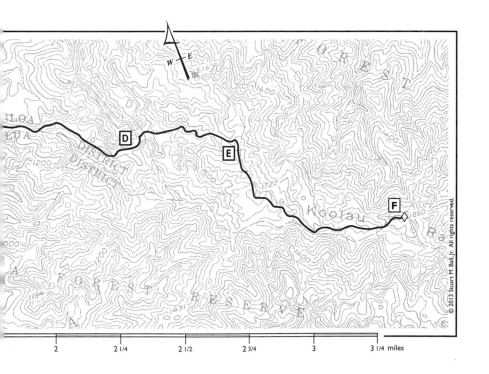

Reach signed Black Junction (map point E). For now, keep left on the Pūpūkea-Kahuku Trail, which leads shortly to a scenic windward lookout. (The Koʻolau Summit Trail starts to the right.)

From the lookout, backtrack to Black Junction and turn left on the Summit Trail.

Keep left in a grove of paperbark trees.

Switch to the right (leeward) side of the ridge. In the distance are the Waiʻanae Range and Kaʻena Point.

Walk through an open section with views to windward and leeward.

Switch to the left side of the ridge through strawberry guava trees.

On the left, pass an intermittent stream in a dense stand of denuded rose apple trees.

Cross a flat, grassy, marshy area. Keep left to avoid the wettest sections.

Ascend steadily on the right side of the ridge around a large hill.

Reach an obscure junction on the leeward side of the hill. Turn left and up on a rough side trail. (To the right, the Koʻolau Summit Trail contours around the hill.)

Climb steeply up the side of the hill through native vegetation. Look for hāpuʻu tree ferns and kōpiko trees.

Reach the top of the hill at a small lookout with a benchmark (elevation 1,860 feet) (map point F) (UTM 04 0605581E, 2391938N).

NOTES

The Pūpūkea (white shell) Summit hike follows the remnants of two old trails: the Pūpūkea-Kahuku and the Koʻolau Summit. The latter is the most rugged and least used footpath on Oʻahu. The U.S. Army built the Pūpūkea-Kahuku Trail in 1924, widened the initial section to a dirt road during

World War II, and paved it in 2009. Between 1934 and 1936, the Civilian Conservation Corps (CCC) constructed the Koʻolau Summit Trail from Black Junction to the end of the Kīpapa (placed prone) Trail above Mililani (beloved place of chiefs), a distance of 18.5 miles.

Unfortunately, the Summit Trail has received minimal maintenance since its initial construction. Although still graded, the treadway is often uneven because of slippage and erosion through the years. Sections of the trail may be overgrown with strawberry guava (waiawī ulaʻula) and scratchy uluhe ferns. Watch your footing constantly. Try not to fall into one of the legendary mud holes!

After the long walk on the paved approach road, the Summit Trail is actually a welcome sight. The graded route gradually winds upward through the convoluted topography of the northern Koʻolau Range. The scrub forest along the way consists mostly of native ʻōhiʻa trees, which have oval leaves and clusters of delicate red flowers. Early Hawaiians used the flowers in lei and the wood in outrigger canoes. The hard, durable wood was also carved into god images for *heiau* (religious sites).

Among the ʻōhiʻa are a few native loulu palms. They have rigid, fan-shaped fronds in a cluster at the top of a ringed trunk. Early Hawaiians used the fronds for thatch and plaited the blades of young fronds into fans and baskets.

Also along the initial trail section is kōpiko, a native member of the coffee family. It has leathery, oblong leaves with a light green midrib. Turn the leaf over to see a row of tiny holes (*piko* or navel) on either side of the midrib. The kōpiko produces clusters of little white flowers and fleshy, orange fruits.

At Black Junction, take the short side trip down to the lovely windward lookout. The grassy, windswept area has some old landing mats and foxholes once used by the army in training. From the lookout, you can see Kahuku (the projection) and Lāʻie (the ʻieʻie leaf), backed by Lāʻie Point. Offshore, between the two towns, is Mokuʻauia (island to one side), better known as Goat Island, a state seabird sanctuary.

From the lookout, retrace your steps to the main trail and continue the gradual ascent toward a prominent hill on the summit ridge. At the base of the hill, leave the Summit Trail once again and climb steadily to a second lookout, which has a benchmark and more windward views. From there the side trail proceeds along the top of the hill, passes an obscure junction with the abandoned Kahuku Trail, and then descends to rejoin the main summit route. It continues along the Koʻolau crest to the junction with the Lāʻie Trail. That segment is heavily overgrown with strawberry guavas and uluhe ferns.

For a shorter outing, try the Kaunala (the plaiting) loop that starts from the same trailhead. Unlike Pūpūkea Summit, Kaunala does not require permission from the army.

46

Mākua Rim

TYPE:	Graded ridge
LENGTH:	11-mile round-trip
ELEVATION GAIN:	2,350 feet
DANGER:	Low
SUITABLE FOR:	Novice, Intermediate, Expert
LOCATION:	Mokulēʻia Forest Reserve and Pahole Natural Area Reserve above Mokulēʻia
TOPO MAP:	Kaʻena
ACCESS:	Open for groups of ten or less; for larger groups, obtain a special-use permit. See the appendix for more information.

HIGHLIGHTS

A long, uphill road walk leads to expansive and rewarding views of the north shore, the Waiʻanae Range, and Mākua Valley. The upper section of the route passes through Pahole Natural Area Reserve, established to protect remnants of native lowland forest.

TRAILHEAD DIRECTIONS

At Punchbowl St. get on Lunalilo Fwy. (H-1) heading ʻEwa (west).

Near Middle St., keep left on Moanalua Fwy. (H-201) to ʻAiea.

By Aloha Stadium, bear right to rejoin H-1 to Pearl City. Take H-2 Freeway north (exit 8A) to Wahiawā.

As the freeway ends, continue on Rte. 99 north (Wilikina Dr.), bypassing Wahiawā.

Pass Schofield Barracks on your left.

The road narrows to two lanes, dips, and then forks at a traffic light. Take the left fork toward Waialua (still Wilikina Dr., but now Rte. 803).

Wilikina Dr. becomes Kaukonahua Rd. (still Rte. 803).

At Thomson Corner (flashing yellow light), continue straight on Farrington Hwy. (Rte. 930).

At the small traffic circle, bear left under the overpass to Mokulēʻia. Reset your trip odometer (0.0).

Pass Waialua Intermediate and High School on your left (0.1 mile).

Mahinaʻai St. intersects Farrington Hwy. from the right (2.3 miles).

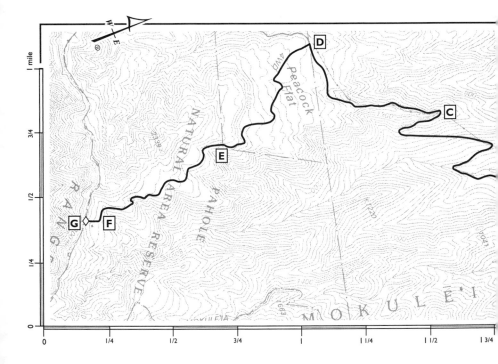

Park on the highway near its intersection with Mokulēʻia Forest Reserve Access Rd., which is on the left just before a large coconut grove (2.6 miles) (elevation 10 feet) (map point A).

BUS: None within reasonable walking distance of the trailhead.

ROUTE DESCRIPTION

On foot, proceed up the paved access road through two green gates.

Walk through or go around two more green gates. On the right are ranch buildings and overgrown pasture with scattered monkeypod trees.

The road begins to climb into a gulch and narrows to one lane after a fifth green gate.

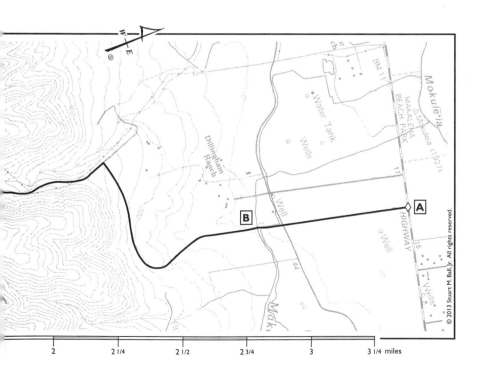

After crossing a wide streambed (map point B), swing right and then switchback left past a small green building.

Switchback right and then cross over a ridge by another green building (map point C).

Ascend gradually along the right side of the ridge.

After going through a sixth green gate, reach a signed junction at the Mokulēʻia Forest Reserve boundary (map point D). Turn left on the Mokulēʻia Trail, a dirt road leading into Peacock Flat. (The paved road continues straight to an abandoned Nike missile site now used as a nursery to propagate native plants.)

Pass the Earl Pan campground under stately Cook pines. Each campground has a pit toilet but no water.

Ascend gradually through a mixed introduced forest of Cook pines, eucalyptus, silk oak, and Christmas berry.

On the left, pass a small water catchment tank for wildlife.

The road narrows to a trail at the boundary of Pahole Natural Area Reserve (map point E). Clean your boots of weed seeds with the brushes provided. Look for the native tree alaheʻe with its shiny leaves.

Ascend steadily under arching Christmas berry. Watch for native ʻōhʻia and pāpala kēpau trees.

Go through a gate in a fence erected to keep feral pigs out of a section of the reserve. The fence line periodically parallels the trail on the right.

By a bench, reach an overlook of the north shore and flat Kaʻala, the highest peak on Oʻahu. On the skyline to the right are the twin Piko pines.

Reach a signed junction by a dilapidated shelter (map point F). Bear right on a makeshift trail, keeping the shelter on your left. (Straight ahead, the wide Mokulēʻia Trail descends to the forest reserve boundary.)

Climb briefly to the Waiʻanae summit ridge and turn left along a fence line.

Ascend steeply to an overlook of Mākua Valley with two benches (elevation 2,360 feet) (map point G) (UTM 04 0584851E, 2381212N).

NOTES

The Mākua Rim outing combines a long road walk with a short but superb trail hike. The paved access road climbs steadily through pastureland and open country to the Peacock Flat campground. The walk is usually hot and sweaty, so take a break occasionally, turn around, and admire the unfolding view of the beautiful north shore. From the campground, the route follows the shady Mokulēʻia (isle of abundance) Trail through Pahole Natural Area Reserve to the Waiʻanae summit and a scenic overlook of Mākua Valley.

The Civilian Conservation Corps (CCC) constructed the Mokulēʻia Trail in six months during 1934. The 5.2-mile project was one of the easiest trails to build because of the relatively dry and gentle terrain in this portion of the Waiʻanae (mullet water) Range. Much of the original route has been replaced by a dirt road, but a short section in the reserve remains as a trail.

Pahole Natural Area Reserve protects native plants and animals living in a lowland forest habitat. The State Forestry and Wildlife Division manages the 658-acre preserve, which was established in 1981. Workers and volunteers there control invasive weeds and plant native species suited to the area. They also build protective fences around native tree snail colonies and especially rare plants. For more information about the reserve, check the Division of Forestry and Wildlife Web site, whose address is listed in the appendix. Remember to clean your boots of weed seeds at the station by the entrance sign.

In the reserve, watch for native alaheʻe trees, which have oblong leaves that are shiny and dark green. Their fragrant white flowers grow in clusters at the branch tips. Early Hawaiians fashioned the hard wood into farming tools and hooks and spears for fishing.

Look also for native pāpala kēpau trees, which are abundant in the reserve. They have large, leathery, oval leaves and clusters of small, white flowers. Early Hawaiians smeared glue from the sticky, ripe fruit on poles to catch native birds for their feathers. Craftsmen then fashioned capes and religious objects from the bright red and yellow feathers.

The rim lookout at the end of the hike makes an awesome lunch spot. A thousand feet below lies the green expanse of Mākua (parents) Valley leading to the ocean. To the left are the dark, sheer walls of ʻŌhikilolo (scooped out brains) Ridge. Spend some time watching the interplay of sun and clouds on ocean, ridge, and valley. Who says Oʻahu isn't as beautiful as the Neighbor Islands?

If your energy level is still high after lunch, take two short side trips, one historical and one botanical. From the lookout, backtrack to the junction with the trail down to the shelter. Continue straight along the rim and fence line for about five minutes to reach two tall Cook pines. On October 30, 1932, Major General Briant H. Wells and his wife Mary each planted a pine seedling there during an outing of the Piko Club, an association of forestry rangers and army officers. Also along that Sunday was Territorial Forester Charles S. Judd, who, with Wells, determined much of Oʻahu's trail network during the CCC era several years later. The pines mark the end of the Piko Trail, an old forestry route coming up from Mākua Valley. No evidence of the trail remains, as it was abandoned after World War II, when the valley became an army firing range.

For the botanical side trip, return to the shelter and turn right on the wide Mokuleʻia Trail. Descend gradually on two switchbacks to a small gulch with an intermittent stream. Along the way, you will find a variety of native shrubs and trees, including ʻōhiʻa, koʻokoʻolau, hōʻawa, maile, lama, kōpiko, and kokio keʻokeʻo. If the ʻōhiʻa trees are in bloom, you may catch a glimpse of the native ʻapapane in the forest canopy. It has a red breast and head, black wings and tail, and a slightly curved black bill. In flight, the ʻapapane makes a whirring sound as it darts from tree to tree searching for nectar and insects.

Just across the stream is a fenced enclosure protecting the hāhā, a rare native lobeliad. The small tree resembles a palm, with elongated leaves bunched at the top. When in bloom, clusters of white tubular flowers droop from the central stalk below the leaves. From the enclosure, the Mokulēʻia Trail descends another 1.5 miles to the forest reserve boundary, marked by a fence with a wooden gate. Beyond is private pastureland closed to the public.

47

Keālia

TYPE:	Graded ridge
LENGTH:	7-mile round-trip
ELEVATION GAIN:	2,000 feet
DANGER:	Low
SUITABLE FOR:	Intermediate
LOCATION:	Kuaokalā and Mokulēʻia Forest Reserves above Mokulēʻia
TOPO MAP:	Kaʻena
ACCESS:	Open

HIGHLIGHTS

This hot, dry hike ascends a steep *pali* (cliff) en route to the summit of the Waiʻanae Range. While climbing, you may see fixed-wing gliders soaring above the north shore of Oʻahu. At the end is a scenic overlook of an undeveloped leeward valley.

TRAILHEAD DIRECTIONS

At Punchbowl St. get on Lunalilo Fwy. (H-1) heading ʻEwa (west).

Near Middle St., keep left on Moanalua Fwy. (H-201) to ʻAiea.

By Aloha Stadium, bear right to rejoin H-1 to Pearl City.

Take H-2 Freeway north (exit 8A) to Wahiawā.

As the freeway ends, continue on Rte. 99 north (Wilikina Dr.), bypassing Wahiawā.

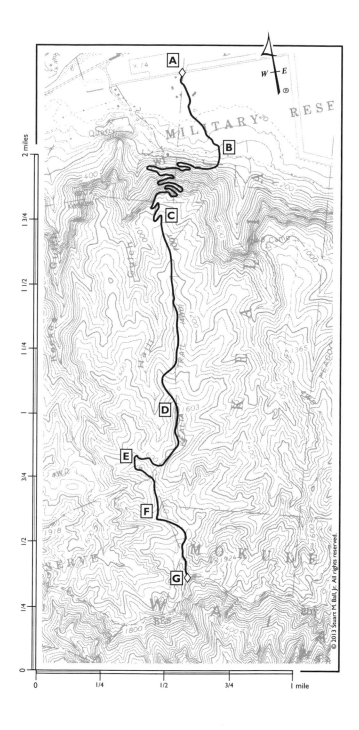

Pass Schofield Barracks on the left.

The road narrows to two lanes, dips, and then forks at a traffic light. Take the left fork toward Waialua (still Wilikina Dr., but now Rte. 803).

Wilikina Dr. becomes Kaukonahua Rd. (still Rte. 803).

At Thomson Corner with its flashing yellow light, continue straight on Farrington Hwy. (Rte. 930).

At the small traffic circle, bear left under the overpass to Mokulēʻia and Dillingham Airfield.

Pass Waialua Intermediate and High School on the left.

Drive through Mokulēʻia.

On the left, pass Dillingham Airfield and Glider Port, surrounded by a green fence.

At the far end of the airfield, turn left through the West Gate by a Low-Flying Aircraft warning sign. The gate is open from 7 a.m. to 6 p.m. daily.

Go around the end of the runway and head back along the other side.

Pass a low concrete building and a house on the left.

Turn left into the paved lot in front of the airfield control tower and park there (elevation 20 feet) (map point A).

BUS: None within reasonable walking distance of the trail-head.

ROUTE DESCRIPTION

From the lot, walk back across the access road and proceed along a wide, partially paved road heading *mauka* (inland).

By a trail sign, go around a chain across the road.

Bear left immediately, keeping a large concrete building on your right.

The road narrows to a gravel track through koa haole trees.

The track splits twice. Keep right at the first fork and left at the second one.

Go through an opening in a low green fence by a yellow warning sign (map point B) and immediately bear left on the Keālia Trail.

Work toward the base of the cliffs through grass and koa haole.

Pass a utility pole on the right.

Ascend the *pali* (cliff) gradually on nineteen switchbacks. Watch your footing on the loose rock.

After the second zigzag, look for native lonomea trees with dark green leaves.

At the third is a lone noni shrub.

After the fourth, views of the north shore begin to open up.

After the eighth, note the alternating layers of rough *'a'ā* and smooth *pāhoehoe* lava along the trail.

After the eleventh, watch for an inscription carved into the rock by a member of the CCC trail crew in 1934.

On the upper switchbacks are large native alahe'e and wiliwili trees.

At the top of the cliff, reach a covered picnic table in an ironwood grove (map point C).

Pick up a dirt road at the far end of the grove.

Ascend gradually up the wide ridge through an introduced forest of silk oak, black wattle, and Christmas berry. Look for the native shrub 'a'ali'i along the roadside.

Reach a junction by an old fence line. Turn right on the main road through two weathered wooden gateposts. (To the left, a less traveled dirt road heads downhill.)

Continue climbing through introduced ironwoods and pines.

Pass a rusted water tank on the left.

Enter Kuaokalā Public Hunting Area marked by a sign (map point D).

The road levels, dips briefly, and then resumes climbing around a hump in the ridge. Listen for the cackling cry of the Erckel's Francolin.

As the road curves left in a eucalyptus grove, reach a

junction (map point E). Continue left on the main road. (To the right, another dirt road heads downhill.)

Ascend steeply up the side of the hump and then descend just as steeply to a saddle on the ridge.

Climb steadily until the road ends at a signed T-junction (map point F). Turn left on Kuaokalā Access Rd. toward Mākua Valley. (To the right, the access road leads to Kaʻena Point Satellite Tracking Station.)

On the right, pass a small water catchment tank for wildlife.

Reach a signed junction. Bear slightly right and up on the Kuaokalā Trail, the less traveled dirt road. (Kuaokalā Access Rd. veers left and leads to an abandoned Nike missile site and the Mākua Rim Trail.)

Reach the road's end at an overlook of Mākua Valley (elevation 1,960 feet) (map point G) (UTM 04 0581528E, 2383274N).

NOTES

Keālia means salt encrustation in English. The name probably refers to sea salt along the coast, but it is also an apt description of your shirt after you finish the hike. Keālia is a hot, dry, unrelenting climb to the summit ridge of the Waiʻanae Range. Switchbacks on the *pali* (cliff) and a dirt road to the top ease the gradient some. Magnificent views and a variety of native plants and introduced birds make the effort worthwhile.

The best time to take this hike is from February to April. The weather is cooler then, and you will miss the bird hunting season. Whenever you go, drink plenty of water and use lots of sunscreen.

The switchback section is usually clear, wide, and well graded. However, don't sightsee and walk at the same time because of the nearby drop and the loose rock that sometimes litters the trail. On the road, watch out for the occasional four-wheel-drive vehicle. At the lookout, don't even think of descending into Mākua Valley, as it is a military range once used for live-fire exercises.

On the initial zigzags, look for native lonomea trees. They have dark green leaves with a prominent yellow midrib. Early Hawaiians strung the black seeds into *lei hua* (seed or nut garlands). The wood was used to make spears and in house construction.

Above the fourth switchback are superb views of the beautiful north shore of Oʻahu. Along the coast are the towns of Waialua and Haleʻiwa (house of the frigate bird). Beyond are Waimea (reddish water) Bay and Sunset Beach. In the distance is the Koʻolau (windward) Range. Directly below lies Dillingham Airfield. The large pond nearby was once a quarry used to mine rock for the airstrip and other construction projects. In the brackish water are farmed tilapia destined for Honolulu restaurants. Above the cliff and ocean, look for fixed-wing gliders and sky divers with their colorful parachutes.

After the eleventh zigzag, watch for some historical graffiti left by a member of the crew building the trail in 1934. He carved his initials, the date, and "C. C. C." for Civilian Conservation Corps. The Wahiawā Unit of the corps began construction of the Keālia Trail in March and finally finished it in September. Whole sections of the route had to be blasted out of the lava rock. The holes near the inscription, however, are not left over from CCC blasting but were drilled more recently by geologists studying changes in the earth's magnetic field.

Along the upper switchbacks are native wiliwili and alaheʻe trees. Alaheʻe has small, oblong leaves that are shiny and dark green. Its fragrant white flowers grow in clusters at the branch tips. Early Hawaiians fashioned the hard wood into farming tools and hooks and spears for fishing.

Wiliwili has heart-shaped, leathery leaflets in groups of three. Flowers appear in the spring and are yellow-orange. Early Hawaiians used the soft, light wood for surfboards, canoe outriggers, and fishnet floats. The red seeds were strung together to form *lei hua* (seed or nut garlands).

Along the switchbacks and the road, look for a variety of introduced birds. Much in evidence is the white-rumped shama, a Malaysian songbird with a chestnut-colored breast. Watch for the red northern cardinal from the mainland and the red-crested cardinal from South America. Listen for the cackling cry of the Erckel's Francolin, a brown game bird introduced from Africa. Look and listen for the iridescent peacock with its wailing call.

On the first road section, look for native 'a'ali'i shrubs. They have shiny, narrow leaves and red seed capsules. Early Hawaiians used the leaves and capsules in making lei. When crushed or boiled, the capsules produced a red dye for decorating *kapa* (bark cloth).

After the uphill road walk, the summit lookout is a welcome sight. A thousand feet below lies the green expanse of Mākua (parents) Valley leading to the ocean. In back are the dark, sheer walls of 'Ōhikilolo (scooped out brains) Ridge. To the left, the Wai'anae (mullet water) summit ridge gradually rises to flat-topped Ka'ala (the fragrance), the highest peak on the island.

For a longer hike, continue along the Kuaokalā (back of the sun) Trail to the right until turnaround time. The trail hugs the rim of Mākua Valley and then follows the coastal cliffs to Ka'ena (the heat) Point Satellite Tracking Station. See the Kuaokalā hike for a description of the route.

LEEWARD SIDE

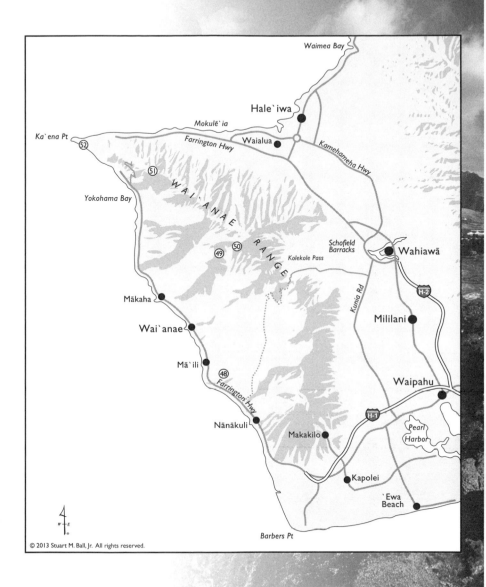

48

Puʻu o Hulu

TYPE:	Ungraded ridge
LENGTH:	2-mile round-trip
ELEVATION GAIN:	800 feet
DANGER:	Medium
SUITABLE FOR:	Intermediate
LOCATION:	Leeward Waiʻanae Range above Māʻili
TOPO MAP:	Waiʻanae
ACCESS:	Open

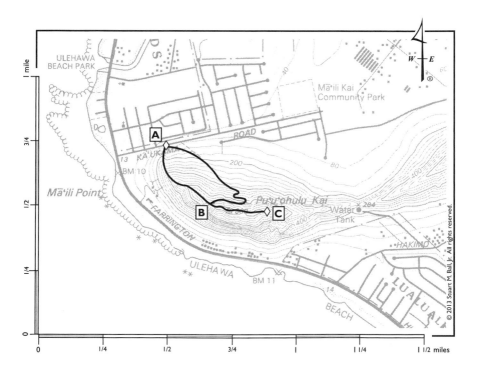

HIGHLIGHTS

A short but steep climb leads to a spectacular leeward lookout. At the top are abandoned fire control stations for army coastal artillery batteries.

TRAILHEAD DIRECTIONS

At Punchbowl St. get on Lunalilo Fwy. (H-1) heading 'Ewa (west).

Near Middle St., keep left on Moanalua Fwy. (H-201) to 'Aiea.

By Aloha Stadium, bear right to rejoin H-1 to Pearl City and on toward Wai'anae.

As the freeway ends near Campbell Industrial Park, continue along the leeward coast on Farrington Hwy. (Rte. 93).

Pass Ko Olina resort on the left and Kahe Point power plant on the right.

Pass the entrance to Naval Station Pearl Harbor Lualualei Annex on the right.

Pass the intersection with Hakimo Rd.

At the next stoplight, turn right on Kaukama Rd., after going by Pu'u o Hulu. Immediately start counting streetlight poles on the right.

Park by the eighth pole near the top of a small rise (map point A) (elevation 80 feet).

BUS: Route C Country Express or Route 40 to the intersection of Farrington Hwy. and Kaukama Rd. Walk 0.2 mile along Kaukama Rd. to the trailhead.

ROUTE DESCRIPTION

Walk *makai* (seaward) past a tree and turn left on an indistinct path upslope.

Presently, cross a concrete drainage ditch. Watch for the thorny introduced shrub klu and the native shrubs 'ilima and 'uhaloa.

Work right and then left around a small rock face. Keep to the left of a prominent boulder and a second rock face.

Go up a third rock face to reach the ridgeline and the first of many viewpoints.

Climb steadily along the ridge to another rock face.

Scramble straight up the rock face. Make sure you have secure hand- and footholds.

Reach a second, taller rock face and bear left around its base.

Angle right, up a rock dike to regain the ridgeline.

Turn left up the ridge and climb steadily along it. The trail briefly leaves the ridgeline twice to the left.

Pass a flat concrete roof below on the left and a small shed.

Reach a junction (map point B) (UTM 04 0585919E, 2366767N). For now, keep right, up the ridge past a concrete fire control station. (The switchback trail to the left is the return route.)

Pass a rusted cableway engine and reel on the left and more bunkers along the ridgeline.

Reach the summit of Pu'u o Hulu Kai by a split-level fire control station with the remains of a 1929 surveying station nearby (elevation 860 feet). Watch for whales in season.

Continue briefly along the level ridgeline (map point C). Do not descend to the water tank, which is on private property. Look for native a'ali'i shrubs.

Retrace your steps to the junction and continue straight, down the switchback trail.

Descend the cliff on three switchbacks.

On the left, pass a small banyan tree with its roots clinging to the cliff.

After passing a second one, turn right, straight downhill, following the rusted cable from the upper station. Watch your footing on the uneven rocks hidden by grass.

Reach several large concrete blocks, all that remains of the lower cableway station. Turn left onto an old army road with a crushed coral base.

Descend gradually along the hillside. The route detours left around some fallen trees. Watch for wire in the treadway.

Turn right and descend straight toward Kaukama Rd.

Cross the drainage ditch by two metal poles.

Angle left to reach the paved road between the tenth and eleventh light poles.

Turn left and walk back to your car (map point A).

NOTES

This rough-cut gem of a hike is short but well worth the long drive from town. The loop offers good climbing, grand views, and a glimpse into the island's military past. After the hike, drive a few miles farther along the coast to Pōka'i Bay for a swim and shaved ice.

Watch your footing constantly on this rough, rocky loop. The unimproved trail going up is mostly uneven and sometimes narrow. Make sure you have secure hand- and footholds on the rock faces. If you don't like scrambling, take the switchback trail both ways. Even that graded path has lots of loose rock, sometimes hidden by vegetation.

Watch closely for two weedy shrubs along the route. Klu has very sharp thorns and yellow, fragrant flowers resembling puffballs. Native to tropical America, the shrub was introduced to Hawai'i in the 1800s, perhaps to produce perfume from the aromatic blossoms.

The other scraggly shrub is native 'uhaloa with toothed, hairy, gray-green leaves. Its tiny yellow flowers emerge between the stem and the leaf stalk. Hawaiians pounded the stems, leaves, or bark to make a gargle to relieve sore throats.

From the bunkers, take in the expansive ocean and mountain views. *Makai* is the leeward coast from Kahe (flow) Point to Mākaha (fierce). Farther along the ridgeline is a second hill, Pu'u o Hulu Uka. Lualualei Valley stretches *mauka* (inland) to the Wai'anae (mullet water) Range. See if you can pick out the major peaks along the summit ridge: flat-topped Ka'ala (the fragrance), Kalena (the lazy one), Hāpapa (rock stratum), and Kaua (war hill), from left to right. Separating the peaks are Kolekole (raw) and Pōhākea (white stone) passes.

An old Hawaiian story links Pu'u o Hulu with Pu'u Mā'ili'ili (pebbly), the next hill along the coast. Hulu, a chief, fell in love with Mā'ili'ili, who had a twin sister. Hulu, however, could never tell the two apart. After several embarrassing instances of mistaken identity, a mo'o (lizard) turned all three into pu'u. To this day, Hulu gazes up the coast trying to recognize his lover.

The abandoned concrete bunkers along the ridgeline were once fire control stations for coastal artillery batteries clustered around Pearl Harbor and along the leeward coast. In 1923, the army began construction at the site, called Station U. Mules hauled materials and supplies, including disassembled concrete mixers, up the newly graded switchback trail. The first station became operational in 1924 and served the twin 16-inch guns of Battery Williston at Fort Weaver. Over the years, the army built additional stations, each controlling a specific coastal battery. All the bunkers were equipped with depression position finders, precision telescopes that could pick up surface targets over 70 miles away.

While at the fire control stations, scan the ocean for humpback whales. They migrate from the North Pacific to the Hawaiian Islands, arriving in October and leaving in May. The whales congregate off the leeward coast of Maui and occupy themselves calving, nursing, breeding, and generally horsing around.

After the last bunker, watch for the native shrub 'a'ali'i. It has shiny, narrow leaves and red seed capsules. Early Hawaiians used the leaves and capsules in making lei. When crushed or boiled, the capsules produced a red dye for decorating *kapa* (bark cloth).

49

Wai'anae Ka'ala

TYPE:	Ungraded ridge
LENGTH:	8-mile round-trip
ELEVATION GAIN:	3,500 feet
DANGER:	Medium
SUITABLE FOR:	Intermediate, Expert
LOCATION:	Wai'anae Kai Forest Reserve and Mt. Ka'ala Natural Area Reserve above Wai'anae town
TOPO MAP:	Wai'anae, Ka'ena, Hale'iwa
ACCESS:	Open for groups of ten or less; for larger groups, obtain a special-use permit. See the appendix for more information.

HIGHLIGHTS

The highest mountain on O'ahu is flat-topped Ka'ala. This rugged hike climbs to its misty summit from the hot leeward side. En route and in the bog at the top is an amazing assemblage of native forest plants.

TRAILHEAD DIRECTIONS

At Punchbowl St. get on Lunalilo Fwy. (H-1) heading 'Ewa (west).

Near Middle St., keep left on Moanalua Fwy. (H-201) to 'Aiea.

By Aloha Stadium, bear right to rejoin H-1 to Pearl City and on toward Wai'anae.

As the freeway ends near Campbell Industrial Park, continue along the leeward coast on Farrington Hwy. (Rte. 93).

Pass Ko Olina resort on the left and Kahe Point power plant on the right.

Drive through Nānākuli and Māʻili to Waiʻanae town.

Pass Waiʻanae Mall on the right.

Turn right on Waiʻanae Valley Rd.

Turn left on a one-lane paved road (still Waiʻanae Valley Rd.) by a bus turnaround marked with white curbs.

Pass several houses.

A locked gate blocks the road at the forest reserve boundary (elevation 580 feet) (map point A). Park in the dirt lot on the left across from a house.

BUS: Route 401 to the turnaround. Walk 1.1 miles along Waiʻanae Valley Rd. to the forest reserve boundary.

ROUTE DESCRIPTION

Register at the hunter/hiker check-in mailbox at the far end of the lot on the left.

Go around the locked gate and continue up the one-lane paved road on foot through scrub koa haole trees.

Pass a water tank on the left.

In a wooded area, the road levels off momentarily and passes Waiʻanae Well I surrounded by a chain-link fence (map point B).

Ascend steeply through a mixed forest of kukui, silk oak, and coffee. Listen for the Japanese bush warbler.

The pavement ends by Waiʻanae Well II (map point C). Continue up a dirt road through Formosa koa trees.

Reach the end of the road by a covered picnic table. Take the trail on the right, marked by several boulders. Nearby are some macadamia nut trees.

Ascend gradually along a broad ridge, keeping to its right

edge. On the left are several *lo'i* (terraces) once used for growing *kalo* (taro).

Bear right around a large rock outcrop and pass a utility pole on the left.

After the ridge narrows, turn left down into a gully.

Cross the streambed and turn left downstream past some kukui trees.

Climb out of the gully and traverse a side ridge through strawberry guava and Christmas berry trees.

Work right, up a partially open ridge. Ignore obscure side trails on the left.

Bear left off the ridgeline into a broad gully.

Cross a very small streambed and reach an obscure junction (map point D). Take the right fork up the gully past some kī (ti) plants. (The trail to the left is the return leg of the Wai'anae Kai loop.)

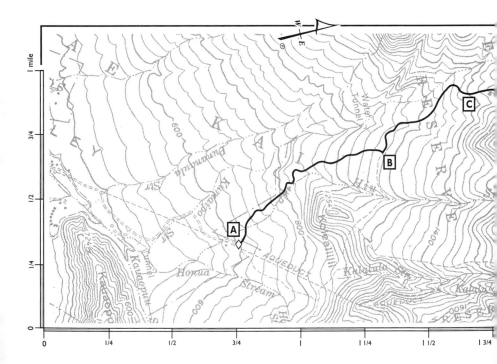

Work left out of the gully onto a side ridge and climb steeply up its left side.

The trail switchbacks once and then resumes going straight up.

Switch to the right edge of the ridge through native koa and 'ōhi'a trees and uluhe ferns. Look for maile, a native twining shrub.

As the ridgeline nears, ascend very steeply, perhaps with the aid of a rope or cable.

Reach the top of Kamaile'unu Ridge, a fence line, and a trail junction (map point E). Turn right, up the ridge along the fence. (The trail down the ridge to the left is the return leg of the Wai'anae Kai loop.)

Almost immediately, reach an overlook of Wai'anae Valley by some metal utility poles (elevation 2,720 feet). In front of the overlook are native 'a'ali'i shrubs.

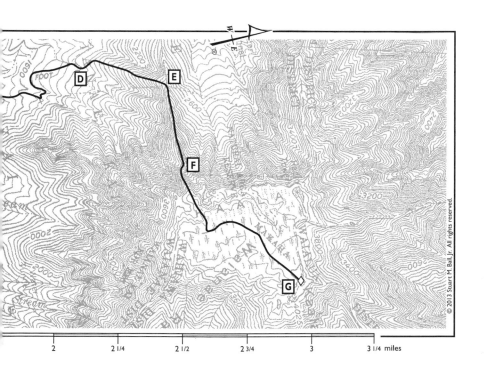

Climb steadily up the ridge through open native vegetation. Look for the native shrub pilo.

The ridge broadens and levels through a stand of ʻōhiʻa ʻāhihi.

Negotiate a series of large boulders on a steep and narrow section of the ridge. The last boulder is notorious. Scramble up to the right initially and then back to the left. A cable may provide some security.

Climb very steeply on the now-broad ridge through native forest. Between cables, look for olomea trees with their red-veined leaves.

Cut right, across the face of the ridge, and then resume steep scrambling. Several more cables may ease the climb.

Enter Mt. Kaʻala Natural Area Reserve, marked by a sign.

The ridge narrows and the angle of ascent decreases as the top nears. Watch for koliʻi, a native *Lobelia*.

Reach the Kaʻala plateau and bog (map point F).

Cross the bog on a narrow boardwalk through diverse native vegetation. Common are lapalapa trees and kūkaemoa (alani) and pūʻahanui (kanawao) shrubs.

Go through an unlocked gate, close it, and cross a helipad.

Reach paved Mt. Kaʻala Rd. and the summit (elevation 4,025 feet) (map point G) (UTM 04 0588804E, 2378582N), near an FAA radar installation.

For the best views, turn right on the road. Just before reaching the main gate of the installation, turn left along the outside of the perimeter fence. Circle halfway around the fence to a grassy lookout. Do not enter the FAA installation, which is a secured area off-limits to the public, and do not go down the road.

NOTES

The Waiʻanae Kaʻala hike climbs to the summit of the highest mountain on Oʻahu from the leeward side. The route starts in a hot, dry valley and ends in a cool, wet bog. The misty walk through the native forest in the bog is one of the great hiking experiences on the island. After that, the summit, with its road, radar, and fleeting views, is an anticlimax.

This rugged hike requires a number of cautions. The section through the boulders to the summit plateau is very steep and usually slippery. Watch your balance and footing constantly, especially on the descent. Test all cables before using them. If you feel uneasy about the exposure, turn around. On the final climb, blackberry bushes may overgrow the trail. Wear gloves and long pants for protection against the thorns. While crossing the bog, stay on the boardwalk to avoid damaging the vegetation. Finally, don't enter the FAA radar installation even though the main gate is sometimes open. The staff there does not welcome tourists!

On the ascent to the Waiʻanae Valley overlook, watch for the native shrubs ʻaʻaliʻi and maile. ʻAʻaliʻi has shiny, narrow leaves and red seed capsules. Maile has glossy, pointed leaves, tangled branches, and fruit resembling a small olive. Its fragrant leaves and bark have been used to make distinctive open-ended lei in both ancient and modern Hawaiʻi.

From the overlook, you can see Waiʻanae (mullet water) and Lualualei Valleys to the right. On the left is Mākaha (fierce) Valley backed by ʻŌhikilolo (scooped out brains) Ridge. Ahead, along Kamaileʻunu (the stripped maile) Ridge, are the imposing ramparts of Kaʻala (the fragrance).

On the final climb, take a break between cables and look for the small native trees, ʻōhiʻa ʻāhihi, pilo, and olomea. ʻŌhiʻa ʻāhihi have narrow, pointed leaves with red stems and midribs. Their delicate red flowers grow in clusters and are similar to those of the more common ʻōhiʻa, which you saw on the way up. Pilo has reddish orange berries and narrow leaves in a cluster at the branch tips. Olomea has shiny leaves with serrated edges and red veins and stems.

Olomea is a favorite habitat of endangered Hawaiian land snails. Look carefully for them on both sides of the leaves.

One variety has a white, spiral shell, and another has a brown, rounded shell. Do not disturb the snails or allow them to fall to the ground. Years ago, many valleys on Oʻahu had their own species of snail. Now most are gone because of shell collecting, habitat loss, and predation from introduced snails and rats.

On the flat top of the mountain is the Mt. Kaʻala Natural Area Reserve. Established in 1981, the reserve protects native plants and animals on 1,100 acres at the summit and along windward slopes of Kaʻala. For more information about the reserve, check the Division of Forestry and Wildlife Web site, whose address is listed in the appendix.

After entering the reserve, keep your eye out for koliʻi, an unusual native *Trematolobelia*. It has a single woody stem with triangular leaf scars. Its long, slender leaves are arranged in a rosette resembling a dry mop head. A circle of horizontal stalks from the rosette bears the lovely scarlet tubular flowers. After flowering, the entire plant dies, leaving a ring of seed capsules.

The one-lane boardwalk makes for easy and reasonably dry walking through the misty bog. Take time to enjoy the incredible variety of native plants there. See if you can identify these three common ones: lapalapa, pūʻahanui (kanawao), and kūkaemoa (alani). Lapalapa trees have roundish leaves that are arranged in groups of three and flutter in the slightest wind. Pūʻahanui, a relative of hydrangea, has large, serrated, deeply creased leaves and clusters of delicate pink flowers. Kūkaemoa (chicken dung) shrubs have curled, dark green leaves, which give off a slight anise odor. The fruits resemble miniature cauliflowers or chicken droppings.

From the lookouts along the perimeter fence at the summit, you can see the beautiful north shore, the Wahiawā (place of noise) plain, and, in back, the Koʻolau (windward) Range. In the distance are Pearl Harbor (Puʻuloa), Honolulu, and Diamond Head (Lēʻahi). Along the Waiʻanae summit ridge are the peaks of Kalena (the lazy one), Hāpapa (rock stratum), and Puʻu Kaua (war hill). If the view is obscured, wait a while, as the mist may lift suddenly.

The ridge and bog sections of the hike follow an old Hawaiian route from Wai'anae and Mākaha Valleys across Ka'ala to Waialua. The Wai'anae Kai loop, which starts from the same trailhead, incorporates the lower portion of the Hawaiian route, called the Kūmaipō Trail. To early Hawaiians, Ka'ala may have meant lofty and removed, even forbidding, an apt description of the mountain and this hike.

50

Wai'anae Kai

TYPE:	Foothill
LENGTH:	6-mile loop
ELEVATION GAIN:	2,200 feet
DANGER:	Low
SUITABLE FOR:	Intermediate
LOCATION:	Wai'anae Kai Forest Reserve above Wai'anae town
TOPO MAP:	Wai'anae, Ka'ena
ACCESS:	Open

HIGHLIGHTS

This hot, dry hike climbs around the back of Wai'anae Valley in the shadow of Ka'ala, the tallest peak on the island. Along the loop portion are a variety of native plants and good views of the Wai'anae Range and coast. The return route follows an old Hawaiian trail.

TRAILHEAD DIRECTIONS

At Punchbowl St. get on Lunalilo Fwy. (H-1) heading 'Ewa (west).

Near Middle St., keep left on Moanalua Fwy. (H-201) to 'Aiea.

By Aloha Stadium, bear right to rejoin H-1 to Pearl City and on toward Wai'anae.

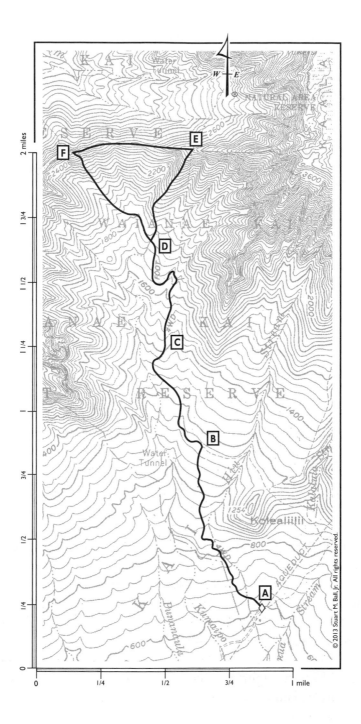

As the freeway ends near Campbell Industrial Park, continue along the leeward coast on Farrington Hwy. (Rte. 93).

Pass Ko Olina resort on the left and Kahe Point power plant on the right.

Drive through Nānākuli and Mā'ili to Wai'anae town.

Pass Wai'anae Mall on the right.

Turn right on Wai'anae Valley Rd.

Turn left on a one-lane paved road (still Wai'anae Valley Rd.) by a bus turnaround marked with white curbs.

Pass several houses.

A locked gate blocks the road at the forest reserve boundary (elevation 580 feet) (map point A). Park in the dirt lot on the left across from a house.

BUS: Route 401 to the turnaround. Walk 1.1 miles along Wai'anae Valley Rd. to the forest reserve boundary.

ROUTE DESCRIPTION

Register at the hunter/hiker check-in mailbox at the far end of the lot on the left.

Go around the locked gate and continue up the one-lane paved road on foot through scrub koa haole trees.

Pass a water tank on the left. Ahead, Kamaile'unu Ridge climbs to massive Ka'ala. Along the ridge to the left is the prominent peak of Kawiwi.

In a wooded area, the road levels off momentarily and passes Wai'anae Well I surrounded by a chain-link fence (map point B).

Ascend steeply through a mixed forest of kukui, silk oak, and coffee. Listen for the Japanese bush warbler.

The pavement ends by Wai'anae Well II (map point C). Continue up a dirt road through Formosa koa trees.

Reach the end of the road by a covered picnic table. Take the trail on the right, marked by several boulders. Nearby are some macadamia nut trees.

Ascend gradually along a broad ridge, keeping to its right edge. On the left are several *loʻi* (terraces) once used for growing *kalo* (taro).

Bear right around a large rock outcrop and pass a utility pole on the left.

After the ridge narrows, turn left down into a gully.

Cross the streambed and turn left downstream past some kukui trees.

Climb out of the gully and traverse a side ridge through strawberry guava and Christmas berry trees.

Work right, up a partially open ridge. Ignore side trails on the left.

Bear left off the ridgeline into a broad gully.

Cross a very small streambed and reach an obscure junction (map point D). Take the right fork up the gully past some kī (ti) plants. (The trail to the left is the return leg of the loop.)

Work left out of the gully on to a side ridge and climb steeply up its left side.

The trail switchbacks once and then resumes going straight up.

Switch to the right edge of the ridge through native koa and ʻōhiʻa trees and uluhe ferns. Look for maile, a native twining shrub.

As the ridgeline nears, ascend very steeply, perhaps with the aid of a rope or cable.

Reach the top of Kamaileʻunu Ridge, a fence line, and a trail junction (map point E) (UTM 04 0587412E, 2377990N). For now, turn right, up the ridge toward Kaʻala. (The trail down the ridge to the left is the return leg of the loop.)

Almost immediately, reach an overlook of Waiʻanae Valley by some metal utility poles (elevation 2,720 feet). Near the overlook are native ʻōhiʻa ʻāhihi trees and ʻaʻaliʻi shrubs.

Backtrack briefly down the ridge and continue straight at the junction. (The trail on the left was the route up.)

Descend, steeply at first, and then more gradually along Kamaileʻunu Ridge. Keep the fence on your right. Look for native alani trees and koʻokoʻolau herbs.

Cross a relatively flat section of the ridge. A cleared area used as a helipad provides good views into Wai'anae and Mākaha Valleys.

Climb gradually along the ridge toward Kawiwi peak.

Reach a junction in a small, flat clearing marked by a large silk oak tree on the left (map point F) (UTM 04 0586647E, 2377973N). On the ground is a concrete base, all that remains of a covered picnic table that once stood on the site. Turn left and down into Wai'anae Valley on Kūmaipō, an ancient Hawaiian trail. (The ridge trail continues straight.)

Descend steeply along a side ridge. Look for native alahe'e trees among the strawberry guava.

Reach the end of the side ridge where two streambeds converge by several mango trees. The gully is lined with huge kukui trees.

Walk down the right side of the gully very briefly and cross the rocky streambed to the left.

Angle up out of the gully and climb around a small side ridge.

Contour to the right around the next side ridge.

Swing left and down into a gully.

Reach the familiar junction with the route going up (map point D). Turn right and retrace your steps back to the road and your car.

NOTES

Wai'anae Kai is a short loop hike with a long tail. The route initially follows a hot, dry road to the back of Wai'anae Valley. The loop portion then climbs steeply to a breezy overlook, enters a lovely native forest along Kamaile'unu Ridge, and returns along an old Hawaiian trail.

Richard (Dick) Booth of the Hawaiian Trail and Mountain Club first scouted this meandering hike in 1976. Although modified several times since then, the loop portion remains steep, rough, and unimproved. The route is poorly defined in spots, and the junctions may be obscure. Follow the narrative closely and watch your step. Start early to avoid the intense sun on the access road.

From the road, look up at Kamaile'unu (the stripped maile) Ridge. Slightly to the left is a prominent peak, known as Kawiwi. According to legend, a lonely and bitter woman lived alone at the summit. When hungry, she cried out to the birds, which gave her scraps to eat. In later times, the *kahuna* (priests) heard about the legend and designated Kawiwi as a *pu'uhonua* or place of refuge during war.

From the overlook, you can see Wai'anae (mullet water) and Lualualei valleys to the right. On the left is Mākaha (fierce) Valley backed by 'Ōhikilolo (scooped out brains) Ridge. Ahead, Kamaile'unu Ridge rises toward the imposing ramparts of Ka'ala (the fragrance).

At the overlook are native 'a'ali'i shrubs and 'ōhi'a 'āhihi trees. 'A'ali'i has shiny, narrow leaves and red seed capsules. Early Hawaiians used the leaves and capsules in making lei (garlands). When crushed or boiled, the capsules produced a red dye for decorating *kapa* (bark cloth). Found only on O'ahu, 'ōhi'a 'āhihi trees have narrow, pointed leaves with red stems and midribs. Their delicate red flowers grow in clusters and are similar to those of the more common 'ōhi'a. Queen Lili'uokalani mentioned the 'āhihi lehua (blossom) in her haunting love song, "Aloha 'Oe."

Along Kamaile'unu Ridge, look for native ko'oko'olau herbs and alani trees. Related to the daisy and sunflower families, ko'oko'olau has pointed, serrated leaves and flower heads with yellow petals. Early Hawaiians steeped the leaves to make a tea used as a tonic. Alani has oval, opposite leaves, which give off a strong anise odor. Its yellow-green flowers turn into four-lobed seed capsules.

The route down roughly follows an old Hawaiian trail called Kūmaipō. The footpath started at the back of Wai'anae Valley, crossed over Kamaile'unu Ridge, and descended into upper Mākaha Valley. A spur trail climbed the ridge to Ka'ala and then went down to Waialua.

Among the strawberry guava on the way down is the small native tree alahe'e. Its oblong leaves are shiny and dark green. Alahe'e has fragrant white flowers that grow in clusters at the branch tips. Early Hawaiians fashioned the hard wood into farming tools and hooks and spears for fishing.

For more open views, continue along Kamaile'unu Ridge from the site of the picnic table to an unnamed peak short of Kawiwi. That extension quickly becomes an expert hike because of several narrow spots. For more climbing and more native plants, try the Wai'anae Ka'ala hike that starts from the same trailhead.

51

Kuaokalā

TYPE:	Foothill
LENGTH:	6-mile loop
ELEVATION GAIN:	1,200 feet
DANGER:	Low
SUITABLE FOR:	Novice, Intermediate
LOCATION:	Kuaokalā Forest Reserve above Kaʻena Point
TOPO MAP:	Kaʻena
ACCESS:	Conditional; open to individuals and outdoor organizations with a permit from the State Forestry and Wildlife Division. See the appendix for more information. Maximum group size is twenty persons in five cars.

HIGHLIGHTS

This loop hike initially tracks the crest of the Waiʻanae summit ridge above Kaʻena Point. Along the trail are lofty views of the rugged leeward coast, Mākua Valley, and Kaʻala, the highest peak on the island. The return portion follows a dirt road through the foothills on the Mokulēʻia side of the ridge.

TRAILHEAD DIRECTIONS

At Punchbowl St. get on Lunalilo Fwy. (H-1) heading ʻEwa (west).

Near Middle St., keep left on Moanalua Fwy. (H-201) to ʻAiea.

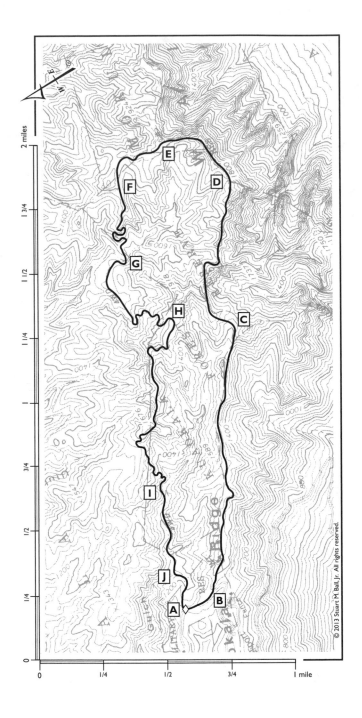

By Aloha Stadium, bear right to rejoin H-1 to Pearl City and on toward Waiʻanae.

As the freeway ends near Campbell Industrial Park, continue along the leeward coast on Farrington Hwy. (Rte. 93).

Pass Kahe Point power plant on the right.

Drive through Nānākuli, Māʻili, and Waiʻanae towns.

The road narrows to two lanes.

Drive through Mākaha and pass Keaʻau Beach Park on the left.

On the right, pass ʻŌhikilolo Mākua Ranch and then Mākua Military Reservation with its observation post.

Reach an intersection at Keawaʻula (Yokohama) Bay. Turn right on the paved access road to Kaʻena Point Satellite Tracking Station. (Straight ahead on the right are restrooms and drinking water at Kaʻena Point State Park.)

Show your permit to the guard at the station and get a visitor pass.

Switchback up Kuaokalā Ridge.

At its top, go through a gate and then turn right at the T-intersection onto Road B.

Curve left past the main administration building.

Go through a second gate and pass a paved one-lane road coming in on the right through some ironwood trees.

After a short descent, look for a dirt lot on the right. It's just after another paved side road that comes in on the right.

Park in the lot (elevation 1,300 feet) (map point A).

BUS: None within reasonable walking distance of the trailhead.

ROUTE DESCRIPTION

From the lot, walk across the side road to the signed trailhead.

The Kuaokalā Trail initially contours around a hill topped by ironwood trees. Look for native ʻiliahialoʻe shrubs (coast sandalwood).

Reach a junction at the crest of Kuaokalā Ridge (map point B). Turn left on a dirt firebreak road along the ridge. (To the right, the road leads down to the main administration building.)

Stroll through ironwoods and introduced pines.

Pass a covered picnic table on the right.

Contour on the right side of the ridge below its top. Scan the ocean for humpback whales during the winter and listen for the cackling cry of the Erkel's francolin.

The road descends briefly through kukui trees, switchbacks once, and then climbs along the left side of a shallow ravine.

At the head of the ravine, turn left along the edge of the ridge (map point C).

At the road's end, ascend along a rocky, eroded outcrop and then swing right.

Ignore two side trails coming in on the left. (The second one leads to another covered picnic table.)

Traverse a narrow, bare section. Watch your step if the trail is wet.

Climb briefly to a copse of ironwood trees.

Ascend a small knob in the ridge. Look for native pūkiawe shrubs and dwarf 'ōhi'a trees in the bare patches.

Climb a second knob to an awesome overlook of Mākua Valley (map point D). On the way up, watch for native ko'oko'olau herbs with their yellow flowers.

Bear left along the rim of the valley through black wattle trees.

Cross an open, scenic stretch recovering from a fire.

Pass another overlook with rock slabs. From here you can look over the main ridge to see the north shore. Farther along the crest of the Wai'anae Range is an abandoned Nike missile site.

Descend briefly and then climb steeply to reach another overlook and a junction (elevation 1,960 feet) (map point E) (UTM 04 0581528E, 2383274N). Turn left, away from the rim, on a dirt road. (The obscure trail straight ahead leads to Kuaokalā Access Rd. and the Mākua Rim Trail.)

Reach a junction with the well-traveled Kuaokalā Access Rd. Bear left on it.

On the left, pass a small water catchment tank for wildlife.

Reach a junction with the Keālia Trail (map point F). Keep left and down on the main road. (To the right, the Keālia Trail, which is actually a road, leads down to Dillingham Airfield on the Mokulēʻia side.)

At the next fork, turn sharp left on a section of the old road.

Descend steeply into Keʻekeʻe Gulch.

At the bottom of the gulch, bear left to rejoin the through road (map point G).

As the road splits again, keep left uphill on the through road.

After the old road comes in on the right, pass an overlook of the north shore.

Reach the top of a ridge (map point H). (On the left, a short trail leads along a barbed-wire fence to a bare overlook marked by a cut-off utility pole. On the left are several native naupaka kuahiwi shrubs.)

Descend initially and then contour on the left and right side of the ridge.

The road forks again by a wooden gatepost in an ironwood grove. Bear left and down on a section of the old road.

Descend steeply into Manini Gulch on the rough, rocky road (map point I).

Reach a junction with the through road and bear left on it, paralleling the streambed.

The road becomes paved by a water pump on the right (map point J).

Climb steadily out of the gulch to the parking lot (map point A).

NOTES

The Kuaokalā (back of the sun) hike loops around the cliffs, ridges, and gulches of the Waiʻanae (mullet water) Range in back of Kaʻena (the heat) Point. Outbound are impressive views of the leeward coast and Mākua (parents) Valley. On the return, you can watch the fixed-wing gliders soaring above the beautiful north shore of Oʻahu.

The best time of year to take this hike is February through April. The weather is cooler then, and you avoid the bird hunting season. Whenever you go, drink plenty of water and use lots of sunscreen.

The footing on the hike varies from solid to slippery. Much of the trail and road making up the loop is wide and graded. Watch your step, however, on the narrow, bare trail sections, which can be slick when wet. Also, do not descend into Mākua Valley, as it is a military range once used for live-fire exercises.

Along the initial contour section, look for ʻiliahialoʻe (coast sandalwood), a native shrub. It has oval, gray-green leaves about 1 to 2 inches long and tiny white star-shaped flowers. ʻIliahialoʻe is partially parasitic, with outgrowths on its roots that steal nutrients from nearby plants. Early Hawaiians ground the fragrant heartwood into a powder to perfume their *kapa*.

The outbound route passes through stands of ironwood, pine, and black wattle trees planted for erosion control and reforestation. Interspersed among the introduced vegetation are the native dryland shrubs pūkiawe and ʻilima. Pūkiawe has tiny, rigid leaves and small white, pink, or red berries. ʻIlima has oblong, serrated leaves, about 1 inch long. The yellow-orange flowers strung together have been used to make regal lei in both ancient and modern Hawaiʻi.

Listen for a cackling cry in the gulches below. The sound is made by the Erckel's francolin, a game bird originally from Africa. Although you probably won't see it, the francolin is brown with white spots on its breast and belly.

Before reaching the first overlook of Mākua Valley, watch for the native herb koʻokoʻolau, related to the daisy and sunflower families. It has pointed, serrated leaves and flower heads with yellow petals. Early Hawaiians steeped the leaves to make a tea used as a tonic.

The Mākua overlook is an awesome spot. A thousand feet below lie the green slopes of the valley leading to the beach and the Pacific Ocean. In back are the dark, sheer walls of 'Ōhikilolo (scooped out brains) Ridge. On the left, the spine of the Wai'anae Range rises to the flat summit of Ka'ala (the fragrance), the tallest peak on the island at 4,025 feet.

On the return portion of the loop, the narrative refers to the main or through road and the old road. The main road is the well-graded and traveled route. The old road consists of rough, eroded sections, which leave and then rejoin the main road. The route description sometimes follows the old sections because they are shorter and have less traffic. You can, of course, take the main road all the way back. Whichever way you go, watch out for occasional four-wheel-drive vehicles and mountain bikes.

The initial road section on the return is also the final stretch of the Keālia (salt encrustation) hike. It climbs to the overlook at map point E from the Mokulē'ia side. Unlike Kuaokalā, Keālia does not require a permit.

At the overlook with the utility pole, look for the less common dryland variety of the native shrub naupaka kuahiwi. It has clusters of spatula-shaped leaves and half-flowers with slim brownish yellow petals. The unusual appearance of the flowers has given rise to several unhappy legends. According to one, a Hawaiian maiden believed her lover unfaithful. In anger, she tore all the naupaka flowers in half. She then asked him to find a whole flower to prove his love. He was, of course, unsuccessful and died of a broken heart.

The Kuaokalā route is described as a counterclockwise loop. You can, of course, do the hike in reverse. If you don't like road walking, return the way you came, along the trail. For a longer hike, take the Kuaokalā Access Rd. from map point E toward an abandoned Nike missile site. As the road swings left around the site, turn right on an overgrown dirt road that climbs to a lookout near the start of the Mākua Rim Trail. Total distance is about 10 miles round-trip.

52

Ka'ena Point

TYPE:	Shoreline
LENGTH:	6-mile round-trip
ELEVATION GAIN:	100 feet
DANGER:	Low
SUITABLE FOR:	Novice, Intermediate
LOCATION:	Ka'ena Point Natural Area Reserve beyond Mākua
TOPO MAP:	Ka'ena
ACCESS:	Open for groups of ten or less; for larger groups, obtain a special-use permit. See the appendix for more information.

HIGHLIGHTS

Ka'ena is the westernmost point on O'ahu and a legendary entrance to the underworld. Along the hot, dry route are steep cliffs, pounding surf, and coastal native plants. You may also see humpback whales, nesting seabirds, and Hawaiian monk seals.

TRAILHEAD DIRECTIONS

At Punchbowl St. get on Lunalilo Fwy. (H-1) heading 'Ewa (west).

Near Middle St., keep left on Moanalua Fwy. (H-201) to 'Aiea.

By Aloha Stadium, bear right to rejoin H-1 to Pearl City and on toward Wai'anae.

As the freeway ends near Campbell Industrial Park, continue along the leeward coast on Farrington Hwy. (Rte. 93).

Pass Kahe Point power plant on the right.

Drive through Nānākuli, Mā'ili, and Wai'anae towns.

The road narrows to two lanes.

Drive through Mākaha and pass Kea'au Beach Park on the left.

On the right, pass 'Ōhikilolo Mākua Ranch and then Mākua Military Reservation with its observation post.

Enter Ka'ena Point State Park by Keawa'ula (Yokohama) Bay. In the first building on the right are restrooms and drinking water.

Park in the lot on the right at the end of the paved road (map point A). For safer parking, leave your car near the satellite tracking station guardhouse on the right or by the lifeguard stand on the left. Those options add 1 to 2 miles to the hike.

ROUTE DESCRIPTION

Continue along the coast on a dirt road through scattered kiawe trees. The route roughly follows an old railbed of the O'ahu Railway and Land Company. Watch for native 'iliahialo'e shrubs (coast sandalwood) on the cliff side of the road.

Take the short, periodic trails on the left for a better view of the coves and tide pools along the shoreline and humpback whales in the ocean. Native pā'ū o Hi'iaka vines and low-lying 'ilima papa shrubs carpet the ground.

Just past a large boulder and before several railroad ties are two blowholes. One produces a jet of water, and the other sounds like a whale spouting.

Pass two sea arches.

Occasionally, walk on old wooden railroad ties. Note the alternating layers of rough *'a'ā* and smooth *pāhoehoe* lava in the road embankment. On the right, look for a lone Ka'ena 'akoko, an endangered shrub found only in the Ka'ena area.

Pass an old utility pole on the right.

After passing a second pole, bear right and up on a make-shift trail to bypass a section where the road has washed out.

Go through a predator-proof fence and enter Ka'ena Point Natural Area Reserve (map point B).

Reach a junction. Keep left on the trail to the point. (To the right is the railbed, which is the return portion of hike.)

Walk through sand dunes covered with coastal native plants, including naupaka kahakai, naio, hinahina, and pōhinahina. Look for nesting mōli (Laysan albatross) in the winter and 'ua 'u kani (wedge-tailed shearwater) in the summer. Stay on the marked trail to avoid trampling the plants and disturbing the birds.

Reach a junction. Continue straight to a small beacon with an interpretive sign (map point C) (UTM 04 0574603E, 2385885N). Offshore is the legendary rock, Pōhaku o Kaua'i. *Mauka* (inland) is Pu'u Pueo. Explore the inlets and tide pools

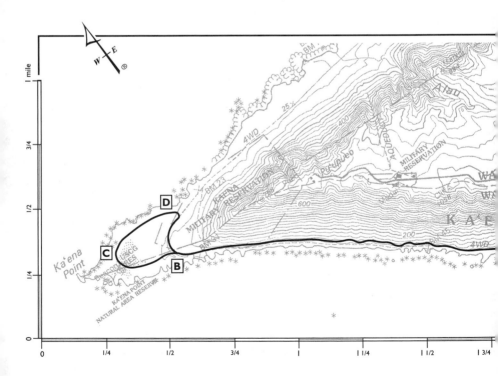

along the shoreline. Watch for monk seals on the rocks or in the ocean, but do not approach or disturb them.

Return to the beacon and then turn left on the wide path heading along the other side of the point. Look for the native shrubs 'ohai and naio.

Reach a junction with the railbed (map point D). For now, turn left.

Follow the railbed to a large, flat rock, marking Leina-a-ka-'Uhane, a legendary entrance to the underworld.

To see more endangered akoko, walk through a nearby opening in the fence and meander along the upper road.

From the flat rock, backtrack to the junction with the trail from the beacon. This time, continue straight along the railbed through a small cut in the rock.

Reach the familiar junction with the path to the beacon and retrace your steps back to the state park.

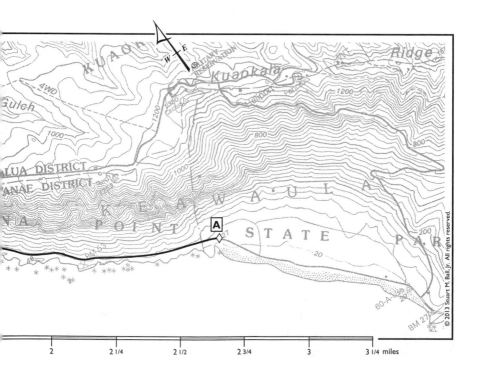

NOTES

Ka'ena means the heat, an apt description of the usually hot, dry, and windy western tip of O'ahu. Despite the heat, the hike along the coast to the point is richly rewarding. On view are wildlife, native plants, legendary sites, and the rugged beauty of an unspoiled shoreline. If the ocean is calm, go for a cooling swim at Keawa'ula Bay after the hike.

Take this hike during winter (November–April) to see migrating humpback whales and nesting mōlī (Laysan albatross). The temperature is also cooler then, and the sun is less intense. Don't forget the essentials for this walk: water, sunscreen, sunglasses, and binoculars. On the road, watch out for the occasional four-wheel-drive vehicle and mountain bike. Along the shore, never turn your back to the ocean.

The route follows the abandoned rail line of the Oahu Railway and Land Company (OR&L), founded by businessman Benjamin F. Dillingham. In 1898, the company completed its main line from Honolulu to Hale'iwa and Kahuku, via the Wai'anae coast and Ka'ena Point. Pulled by steam locomotives, the narrow-gauge trains carried sugarcane, general freight, and passengers. The company shut down in 1947, a victim of upgraded roads, a sugar strike, and a maintenance backlog from World War II. Along the railroad right-of-way are remnant wooden ties and lava rock embankments.

Carpeting the ground and cliffs along the road are two low-lying native plants. Pā'ū o Hi'iaka is a vine with thick, elliptic leaves and pale blue, bell-shaped flowers. The name means skirt of Hi'iaka and derives from a legend about the fire goddess Pele and her baby sister, Hi'iaka. One day Pele went out to fish, leaving the baby asleep on the beach. When the goddess returned to shore, she found Hi'iaka draped with a vine, protecting her from the hot sun. 'Ilima papa is a prostrate shrub with oblong, serrated leaves about 1 inch long. The yellow-orange flowers strung together have been used to make regal lei in both ancient and modern Hawai'i.

A predator-proof fence marks the boundary of the Ka'ena Point Natural Area Reserve. Established in 1983, the reserve protects the sand dune and boulder slope habitats of native coastal plants and provides a refuge for nesting seabirds. For more information about the reserve, check the Division of Forestry and Wildlife Web site, whose address is listed in the appendix. In the reserve, stay on the marked paths to avoid trampling vegetation and disturbing seabirds and their chicks. Leave your dogs at home, as they may attack and kill the chicks.

While walking in the reserve, look for three lovely native beach shrubs: hinahina and pōhinahina on the Wai'anae side of the point and ohai on the Mokulē'ia side. Hinahina has small white flowers and long, thick leaves arranged in rosettes. Shiny hairs on the leaf surface give it a silvery appearance and protect the plant from the strong sunlight. Pōhinahina has oval, gray-green leaves about 1.5 inches long and often forms extensive mats over the sand dunes. The lovely purplish blue blossoms are clustered at the stem tips and are a favorite of lei makers. 'Ohai has low-lying silver-green leaflets and scarlet winged and clawed flowers.

During winter, watch for a nesting colony of mōlī among the native shrubs on the dunes. Adult albatrosses are white with black upper wings and tail; chicks are fluffy brown. Courting pairs arrive in late fall and begin an elaborate mating ritual. The female lays a single egg in a makeshift nest scraped in the sand. By early summer, most mōlī have left Ka'ena to range widely over the North and Central Pacific Ocean.

From the beacon, look for monk seals lying on the rocks below or swimming in the ocean, but do not approach or disturb them. A sign near the beacon provides information about the seals' distribution, habits, and endangered status.

Ka'ena Point is the location of two significant Hawaiian legends. According to the first, the demigod and trickster Māui wanted to join all the islands together. From Ka'ena Point, he threw a great hook toward Kaua'i, hoping to snare the island. Initially the hook held fast, and Māui gave a mighty tug on the line. A huge boulder, known as Pōhaku o Kaua'i, dropped at his feet. The hook sailed over his head and fell in Pālolo Valley, forming Ka'au Crater, which is visible from the Lanipō hike.

Among old Hawaiians was a belief that when a person died, the soul left the body and traveled westward. Walk along the marked path on the Mokulē'ia side of the point to a large flat rock along the railbed. The rock marks the area known as Leina-a-ka-'Uhane, the soul's leap. As spirits of the recently dead reached this westernmost point of the island, they were met by the souls of their ancestors, who guided them to Leina-a-ka-'Uhane for the final plunge into the sea on their way to eternity.

After visiting the entrance to the underworld, walk through a nearby opening in the perimeter fence, turn right, and stroll briefly along the upper road. Watch for the endangered Ka'ena 'akoko on the left. It is a low-lying shrub with rounded, gray-green leaves opposite each other and about 2 inches long. The slightly reddish branches have light-colored rings and a milky sap. This species of 'akoko is found only on the boulder-strewn slopes above the point.

You can also get to Ka'ena Point from the Mokulē'ia side. Follow the directions for the Keālia hike. Instead of turning into the airfield, continue along Farrington Hwy. to the end of the paved road and park in the lot on the right.

APPENDIX
Hiking and Camping Information Sources

Division of Forestry and Wildlife, Na Ala Hele (State Trail and Access Program)
1151 Punchbowl St., Rm. 325
Honolulu, HI 96813
Phone: (808) 587-0166
Web sites: http://hawaii.gov/dlnr/dofaw, http://www.hawaiitrails.org

For a hiking safely pamphlet, individual trail maps, hiking and backcountry camping permits, including Kuaokalā, and special-use permits for and information about the Natural Area Reserves.

Division of Forestry and Wildlife–O'ahu
2135 Makiki Heights Dr.
Honolulu, HI 96822
Phone: (808) 973-9778
Web site: http://hawaii.gov/dlnr/dofaw

For Poamoho permits.

Division of State Parks
1151 Punchbowl St., Rm. 310
Honolulu, HI 96809
Phone: (808) 587-0300
Web site: http://www.hawaiistateparks.org

For state parks brochure and park camping permits.

Hawaiian Trail and Mountain Club
P.O. Box 2238
Honolulu, HI 96804
Web site: http://htmclub.org

For guided hikes on O'ahu.

Sierra Club, Hawai'i Chapter
P.O. Box 2577
Honolulu, HI 96803
Phone: (808) 538-6616
Web site: http://www.sierraclubhawaii.com
For guided hikes on O'ahu.

The Hawai'i Nature Center
2131 Makiki Heights Dr.
Honolulu, HI 96822
Phone: (808) 955-0100
Web site: http://www.hawaiinaturecenter.org

For interpretive hikes for children on O'ahu and the plant
pamphlet for Mānoa Cliff Trail.

Moanalua Gardens Foundation
1352 Pineapple Pl.
Honolulu, HI 96819
Phone: (808) 839-5334
Web site: http://www.mgf-hawaii.org

For pamphlets on Kamananui (Moanalua) Valley
and 'Aiea and Hau'ula Loop Trails.

⌘ FOR FURTHER REFERENCE ⌘

Ball, Stuart M., Jr. *The Backpackers Guide to Hawai'i.* Honolulu: University of Hawai'i Press, 1996.

———. *The Hikers Guide to the Hawaiian Islands.* Honolulu: University of Hawai'i Press, 2000.

———. *Native Paths to Volunteer Trails: Hiking and Trail Building on O'ahu.* Honolulu: University of Hawai'i Press, 2012.

Berger, Andrew J. *Hawaiian Birdlife.* 2d ed. Honolulu: University of Hawai'i Press, 1988.

Bier, James A. *Reference Maps of the Islands of Hawai'i: O'ahu.* 7th ed. Honolulu: University of Hawai'i Press, 2011.

Bryan's Sectional Maps of O'ahu. 2012 ed. Honolulu: EMIC Graphics, 2011.

Carlquist, Sherman. *Hawaii: A Natural History.* 2d ed. Lāwai, HI: Pacific Tropical Botanical Garden, 1980.

City and County of Honolulu. *Hiking on O'ahu.* Pamphlet. Honolulu.

Clark, John R. K. *The Beaches of O'ahu.* Honolulu: University of Hawai'i Press, 1977.

Dean, Love. *The Lighthouses of Hawai'i.* Honolulu: University of Hawai'i Press, 1991.

Gutmanis, June. *Pohaku: Hawaiian Stones.* Lā'ie, HI: Brigham Young University, 1986.

Hall, John B. *A Hiker's Guide to Trailside Plants in Hawai'i.* Honolulu: Mutual Publishing, 2004.

Hawaii Audubon Society. *Hawaii's Birds.* 6th ed. Honolulu: Island Heritage Publishing, 2005.

Hawai'i Nature Center. *Mānoa Cliff Trail Plant Guide.* Pamphlet, rev. ed. Honolulu, 1996.

Hazlett, Richard W., and Donald W. Hyndman. *Roadside Geology of Hawai'i.* Missoula, MT: Mountain Press Publishing Company, 1996.

James, Van. *Ancient Sites of O'ahu.* Honolulu: Bishop Museum Press, 1991.

Juvik, Sonia P., and James O. Juvik. *Atlas of Hawai'i.* 3d ed. Honolulu: University of Hawai'i Press, 1998.

Krauss, Beatrice H. *Plants in Hawaiian Culture.* Honolulu: University of Hawai'i Press, 1993.

Little, Elbert L., Jr., and Roger G. Skolmen. *Common Forest Trees of Hawaii.* Washington, DC: U.S. Department of Agriculture, 1989.

MacDonald, Gordon A., Agatin T. Abbott, and Frank L. Peterson. *Volcanoes in the Sea: The Geology of Hawai'i.* 2d ed. Honolulu: University of Hawai'i Press, 1990.

McMahon, Richard. *Camping Hawai'i.* Honolulu: University of Hawai'i Press, 1994.

Merlin, Mark. *Hawaiian Forest Plants.* Honolulu: Pacific Guide Books, 1995.

Miller, Carey D., Katherine Bazore, and Mary Bartow. *Fruits of Hawaii.* Honolulu: University of Hawai'i Press, 1991.

The O'ahu Mapbook. 2012 ed. Honolulu: Phears Mapbooks, 2012.

O'Connor, Maura. *A Walk into the Past*. Pamphlet. Honolulu: Moanalua Gardens Foundation, 1992.

Pukui, Mary Kawena, and Samuel H. Elbert. *Hawaiian Dictionary*. Revised and enlarged ed. Honolulu: University of Hawai'i Press, 1986.

Pukui, Mary Kawena, Samuel H. Elbert, and Esther T. Mookini. *Place Names of Hawaii*. Revised and enlarged ed. Honolulu: University of Hawai'i Press, 1981.

Roelofs, Faith. *'Aiea Loop Trail and Keaīwa Heiau: Field Site Guide*. Pamphlet. Honolulu: Moanalua Gardens Foundation, 1996.

———. *Hau'ula Loop Trail: Field Site Guide*. Pamphlet. Honolulu: Moanalua Gardens Foundation, 1996.

Scott, Edward B. *The Saga of the Sandwich Islands*. Crystal Bay, Lake Tahoe, NV: Sierra-Tahoe Publishing Co., 1968.

Sohmer, S. H., and R. Gustafson. *Plants and Flowers of Hawai'i*. Honolulu: University of Hawai'i Press, 1987.

State of Hawai'i, Department of Health. *What Is Leptospirosis?* Pamphlet. Honolulu, 1992.

State of Hawai'i, Department of Land and Natural Resources. *Hawai'i State Parks*. Pamphlet. Honolulu, 2010.

———. *Hiking Safely in Hawai'i*. Pamphlet. Honolulu, 2001.

———. *Hiking Safely with Your Dog*. Pamphlet. Honolulu.

———. *Ka'ena Point Natural Area Reserve*. Pamphlet. Honolulu, 2005.

———. *Mt. Ka'ala Natural Area Reserve*. Pamphlet. Honolulu, 1992.

———. *O'ahu Hiking Trails*. Individual trail maps. Honolulu.

———. *Pahole Natural Area Reserve*. Pamphlet. Honolulu, 1994.

Sterling, Elspeth P., and Catherine C. Summers. *Sites of Oahu*. Honolulu: Bishop Museum Press, 1978.

Wagner, Warren L., Derral R. Herbst, and S. H. Sohmer. *Manual of the Flowering Plants of Hawai'i*. 2 vols. Honolulu: University of Hawai'i Press and Bishop Museum Press, 1990.

❖ INDEX ❖